THE REAL DEAL

THE
REAL DEAL
My Story From Brick Lane to Dragons' Den

James Caan

Published by Virgin Books 2009

10 9

Copyright © James Caan 2008

James Caan has asserted his right under the Copyright, Designs and Patents Act 1988 to be identified as the author of this work.

First published in Great Britain in 2008 by
Virgin Books
Random House, 20 Vauxhall Bridge Road,
London SW1V 2SA

www.virginbooks.com
www.randomhouse.co.uk

Addresses for companies within The Random House Group Limited can be found at:
www.randomhouse.co.uk/offices.htm

The Random House Group Limited Reg. No. 954009

A CIP catalogue record for this book is available from the British Library.

ISBN 9780753515099

The Random House Group Limited supports The Forest Stewardship Council® (FSC®), the leading international forest certification organisation. All our titles that are printed on Greenpeace approved FSC® certified paper carry the FSC® logo. Our paper procurement policy can be found at www.randomhouse.co.uk/environment

Typeset by TW Typesetting, Plymouth, Devon
Printed and bound in Great Britain by CPI Bookmarque Ltd, Croydon CR0 4TD

I dedicate this book to my Father.
My destiny has been shaped by events connected with him
and without his influence life could have taken a completely
different direction.
He was a true inspiration, a guiding light and someone
I will always have the utmost respect for.

Acknowledgements

Success is not always about one's materialistic achievements but should also be measured by the relationships that one builds. For me, the amazing support, love and laughter I have shared with my wife Aisha and our two lovely daughters has been a wonderful foundation, enabling me to fulfil my drive towards success.

Aisha thank you for sharing this incredible journey with me.

I'd also like to take this opportunity to thank my family, friends and the people I have both worked with and who have all contributed greatly to the events in my life. My achievements have most definitely not focused on one person but have been about being part of a team – to all those who have played their part I thank you.

Special thanks to the team at Alexander Mann, my first business, to the team at Hamilton Bradshaw, the team at Curtis Brown, most recently the team at *Dragons' Den*, as well as the team at Virgin. You've all been amazing – each and every one of you.

I'd also like to thank Stephen Leveridge and Marilyn Tobias who are part of the team at home.

Finally to Jo Monroe who has worked tirelessly with me and shown utter dedication to this book, I thank you too.

CONTENTS

Preface

'Observe the masses and do the opposite.'

That may sound like a strange piece of advice, but it's something my dad used to say, and I believe it's been instrumental in my success. He told me that when the masses are all charging in one direction after The Next Big Thing, it's often the path in the opposite direction that leads to profit. As a kid I found this quite confusing, but as I got older I realised just how smart my dad was.

Doing the unexpected has taken my career on some very interesting journeys. I've never really planned all that much and, surprisingly, never actually made too many decisions either. The thing I've noticed over the years is that if you study the world around you and ask the right questions, the decisions make themselves: you just go on the journey and see what happens.

Increasingly in the past few years more and more people have started out on journeys into the world of business, as interest in companies, economics and entrepreneurs has boomed. *Dragons' Den* is one of the shows that has made it cool to be an entrepreneur, and every day I get asked about the best way to start a business. Whether I'm in a restaurant, or in a departure lounge, or at Stamford Bridge watching Chelsea, someone always comes up to me to tell me about their brilliant idea for a new business.

A few months after I first appeared on *Dragons' Den*, I went to give a talk on entrepreneurship at a conference. I nipped to the bathroom before I went on stage and this guy recognised me.

'Hi. James, isn't it? I've got this great idea for a business. Perhaps you could give me some advice? How do I make sure it succeeds?'

I was tempted to tell him it was all about timing but I didn't think he'd get the joke. The truth is there's no quick answer: success takes time, but there are techniques I've developed that limit my chances of failure and vastly increase my chances of success, so I started to think that writing a book would be the best way to tell people about my career.

I'm surprised – shocked, even – how often fans of *Dragons' Den* come up to me and say that it must have been easy for me. It seems that if you're successful people assume you've always been successful, and when I tell them I started my first business with no money and no support in a broom cupboard with only the Yellow Pages for company they are genuinely surprised. Anyone can start a business the way I did. All it takes is a good idea and the determination to tell people about it. It just requires you to be willing to start out on a journey even though you don't know the destination.

Since my days in the broom cupboard, I have started more than fifteen companies and invested in as many again, in industries as diverse as recruitment, financial services, property and publishing. I have started companies with small amounts of capital that have gone on to deliver £100 million turnovers and then sold them for substantial sums. Did I sit there in my broom cupboard and know how it would turn out? Of course not. I just wanted to see what would happen if I set out on a journey. Let me tell you, it's been quite a ride.

James Caan
London, June 2008

Chapter 1

Brick Lane (1960–1971)

'*My father taught me that successful business is not about good transactions, it's about good relationships. There are few things anyone has ever said to me that have had more of an impact than that.*'

I WAS BORN NAZIM KHAN in Lahore in Pakistan. I came to Britain in 1962, when I was two years old, and my earliest memories are of our home just off Brick Lane, in the East End of London. It was a pretty, big Victorian terraced house with four storeys: on the top floor was my dad's workshop; then me and my parents and my brother and sister took up the next two floors, and a friend of my dad's lived on the ground floor to help out with the rent. There was always something going on, and whether it was my dad's customers visiting or one of our friends asking if we could go out and play, the front door was in constant use.

Outside was pretty noisy, too. In those days the area was dominated by the rag trade, and the noise of the machines in the garment factories was constant. However, it was nothing compared to the sounds of the Sunday market. Once a week, the streets all around our house were swamped by traders selling everything from vegetables and linen to brassware and radios. It was an exciting place to live, and a terrific place to be a kid.

My dad had come to Britain in 1960, the year I was born. Like so many of his generation, his life had been shaped by the Partition of Pakistan and India at the end of British rule in 1947. As a Muslim living in Lahore he was spared the migration that millions of others endured when they were forced to relocate according to their religion. Nevertheless, the turmoil that followed Partition affected my dad greatly. The economy was a mess, there were hardly any jobs and the entire country was blighted by the upheaval. He had previously run a successful fabrics shop in Lahore, but when his customers could no longer afford his wares he had to look elsewhere for money. That meant working abroad, and he travelled to Iran, Iraq and Saudi Arabia and took work where he found it. For a few years he did quite well travelling to India buying silks and fabrics, which he then sold on in Iran.

Millions of young men left Pakistan in the 1950s, emigrating to the USA, Canada, Australia and Britain, and my dad would get postcards and letters from old friends telling him about their new lives. Of course, these letters only told the good parts: to my dad it seemed that everyone who came to Britain earned fabulous amounts of money and lived in big houses.

By the late fifties, he was married with two young children, my elder sister Nahid and my brother Azam. When I came along in 1960, he realised he needed to provide his family with security and decided he would travel to Britain, despite the fact that he couldn't speak a word of English.

We were living with his mother in Lahore when he boarded a boat for Southampton. He took hardly any money with him, and by the time the boat docked he was practically broke. The most valuable thing he had on him was a piece of paper with an address on it, and, through a combination of smiling and pointing, he boarded a train to London. From Victoria station he took a bus to east London and eventually arrived on the doorstep of a friend's house in Brick Lane.

He didn't have to pay rent until he found a job, but of course the work available for immigrants was hard and poorly paid. He started work in a leather garments factory and took all the overtime he could get. I think he earned £7 or £8 a week and lived on about £1.50. For him, working in London was no different from working in Saudi or Iran: the aim was to make as much money as possible and then go back home to Lahore. It must have been very lonely for him, and he didn't want to be apart from his family for any longer than he had to. So he saved for the air fares to fly us to London so we could be together. Although he had started to think he might spend longer in Britain than he had stayed anywhere else, there was still no doubt in his mind that the move was temporary.

I am still amazed at what my father achieved in those years. Not only did he save enough money by 1962 for our tickets and the deposit for a house, but he also started his own business. He had spotted that the market for leather was changing: thanks to rock'n'roll and movie stars, leather jackets were hot property, and he started making them directly for the West End boutiques. What makes this all the more remarkable is that he still didn't speak much English and couldn't read or write English either. To this day, I don't understand how you can run a successful business if you can't fill out an invoice, read the letter from the bank or write a cheque. It was an incredible achievement.

At home in Brick Lane, my parents spoke Punjabi to each other and mostly Urdu to the other Asians they met. I grew up understanding both languages, but my parents always told us to speak to them in English. With the three of us at school and nursery, English quickly became the dominant language in our house. These days, the Brick Lane area of the East End is known for its sari shops and curry houses, but in the 1960s it was still a predominantly Jewish neighbourhood (the mosque that's there now was a synagogue then), and integrating was so natural that none of us even realised that was what we were doing. I don't even remember there being an issue when I started attending the local Church of England primary school.

We only went to a mosque for the major religious festivals, as my father wasn't a particularly religious man. He believed, but he didn't practise, and so it must have been my mother who arranged for us to get the little bit of Islamic schooling that I remember. We were sent to a house nearby where we were taught a bit of Arabic and the most important prayers and key teachings from the Koran.

In our house, my father was the disciplinarian, and his word was law. If we gave him any trouble, or answered back, we'd get a telling off. He was also very protective of my sister, and while my brother and I could do pretty much what we wanted as long as we were home by a certain time, my sister had less freedom. He was in control of everything in the house because he saw that as part of his role as the head of the household. So it was my father who did the shopping because he saw it as his job to make sure that we were getting good cuts of meat, and it would have been his decision to buy a new fridge or redecorate a room if he thought we needed it and could afford it.

My memories of him from those years are of a slim, smartly dressed man who had always washed and shaved by the time he got us out of bed in the morning. He wasn't a very demonstrative man, but even though he wasn't tactile with us we were in no doubt that he loved us. He would have done anything for us: nothing was more important to him than his family, and every decision he made was intended to guarantee our security and opportunities. The problem with my dad's decisions was that they were almost always final. Once he had made up his mind, that was it, and there was no pleading with him to change his decision.

My mother was much softer and very caring. She was the one we would run to if we were hurt and needed a cuddle, and she was always the one who checked that we'd done our homework, or brushed our teeth or packed our bags. She helped Dad out with the business, but she was always there for us. I suppose she was a typical Asian mum in her salwar kameez, making curries and chapattis for our dinner, but she was also a strong woman. She was the only person who could ever make my dad change a 'no' into a 'yes'. In front of us, she would always back him up, but in private she could sometimes persuade him to soften his stance.

There is only a year between me and my brother, and only three years between me and Nahid, so the three of us were very close, despite the fact that we were all quite different. I was definitely the one who wanted to be outside exploring or playing, while my brother and sister were happier with books or playing indoors. Although my father worked seven days a week, because his workshop was upstairs he was always around, and he would occasionally join in for a game of Ludo or Monopoly or watch a bit of TV with us.

Over the years, several of my parents' friends also made the journey from Pakistan, and of course it was important for my mum and dad to see their friends and maintain that connection with the country they missed so much. We used to go round to their houses, but for us kids those family trips out were formal and awkward. We wouldn't speak unless we were spoken to and had to listen to conversations about people we didn't know and places we'd never seen.

The highlight of my week as a young kid was Sunday, when the whole area became part of Petticoat Lane market. Whether it was people selling junk from their back gardens, the latest watches, bathroom taps, fruit and veg, diamond rings or leather jackets, you would find it in Petticoat Lane. It's one of the biggest street markets in Europe, and it was incredibly exciting.

On Sunday mornings I'd meet up with friends and we'd go to watch the traders setting up and see what new products they'd found. When digital watches first appeared we thought they were amazing, and I found the constant activity exhilarating.

I was always really interested in how a trader pitched his product, how he would interact with his customers, and when he had a crowd round his stall I was always in that crowd. They were often very funny, making sales by making people laugh. 'It's not £10, it's not even £9 or £8. Today, ladies and gentlemen, I'm going to make it £5 because you're such a good-looking crowd!' There was usually a price at which people would start getting their wallets out. I don't think there's any doubt that the spirit of Petticoat Lane has stayed with me.

Just as influential to me were the headquarters of the banks and brokerages that stood just the other side of Bishopsgate, about half a mile away. In those days you could buy a ticket – it was called a Red Rover, I think – that meant you could ride the buses all day, and I would often board a bus just to go and look at the sleek, new offices and the Bank of England. Back then, the NatWest Tower was brand new, and it seemed like something from the future. And whether I was looking at skyscrapers or the old private banks with liveried doormen outside, I thought it was all equally impressive. From the top deck I would try and peer through the windows, trying to get glimpses of the dealing-room atmosphere that I found so appealing.

I was just as impressed by the guys in their pinstripe suits and braces. They made a real impression on me because they looked like people who were making things happen, and I looked up to them in the way other people viewed pop stars and movie stars. There was no doubt that these were the people I aspired to be like.

There was never really any chance that I wouldn't go into business when I was older, and in my father's mind that always meant *his* business. As a kid I didn't give it a second thought because it seemed so natural to follow in his footsteps. The problem with that was that school didn't seem as exciting, and so I never really bothered in lessons. I was bright, and if I applied myself I got good marks, but because I knew what I would do when I left school I never had the motivation to work all that hard.

After a couple years in Britain, our family started to grow. In 1964 my younger brother Ayub was born, and so my father started working even harder to support us all. That meant that the best way to spend any time with him was to help him out with the business, which I was always happy to do. He did a lot of bespoke work, and sometimes customers would come to the house to describe exactly what they wanted. This was the 1960s, and people had some pretty whacky ideas about leather jackets – my father wouldn't always understand what they wanted, so I was asked to explain and translate. Although his English was good enough for most situations, he still couldn't read and write, and so I helped him fill out cheques, invoices and forms.

Looking back, I can see that my father was grooming me to take over the business even then. My elder brother was more obviously and naturally academic, probably more of an introvert than me, and I think my father saw something in me that was suited to business. From an early age I absorbed lessons and information that others would go to university to acquire. He was always giving me tips and explaining how things worked, and one of the lessons that has really stayed with me was my father's appreciation of a 'win-win' formula.

Typically, when you're in business you're seen as ruthless and aggressive, and winning means that someone else loses. My father was adamant that you could only operate successfully in the long term if you could put yourself in the other person's position – whether your supplier or your customer – because to him the art of success was making the other person feel as if he'd won. If you could do that it meant he would come back to you time and time again, and it's always easier to do business with people you've worked with before. He told me not to squeeze the last drop of the lemon but always to leave something on the table for them, too.

I used to go with him to the tanneries where he bought his leather. We didn't have many days out or holidays in our family, so trips out with my dad were a real treat. To this day, if you blindfolded me and gave me a piece of leather to feel, I could tell you if it was calf's leather, sheepskin, lambskin, pigskin or suede, thanks to those trips out with my dad. When you buy leather it comes in rolls of ten skins, and my father would always inspect each skin. As they are a natural product, sometimes they would be an awkward shape, or have a hole in them and the pattern wouldn't work. He could visually calculate how many pieces he could get out of each skin, and if he couldn't make the right patterns he rejected the skin because otherwise the wastage was huge.

As we'd be leaving, I'd asked him why he'd agreed to pay more for the leather than the trader had initially asked for. The dealer had been prepared to sell at £10, but my father had asked him if that was enough.

'You could have got it for less!' I told him.

'Sure I could, but if he had sold it to me for the lowest price, he wouldn't have made any money on the deal himself.'

I didn't understand, so he explained that everyone was entitled to make a living, and if dealing with him allowed the trader to stay in business rather than go under, then he was building a relationship with the trader that benefited everyone. The trader got to expand his business and find better deals, and he could then pass those deals on to his best customers.

'Successful business', he taught me, 'is not about good transactions, it's about good relationships.'

There are few things anyone has ever said to me that have had more of an impact than that.

My father's business did well, and as kids we always had nice clothes and toys and food on the table. However, I knew my dad could have afforded a much nicer house, a far better car and that we could have had holidays like the other kids at school, but he was still saving his money so that he could go back to Pakistan.

As we got a bit older, the idea of going back became more unappealing, and then it simply became illogical: why would we want to go to a country where we didn't know anyone and where we barely spoke the language? Nevertheless, this was my dad's dream, and so he kept saving his money. Looking back, I can see this has influenced me, too, because I've never been much of a saver: he worked so hard and never really saw the benefit. I knew that if I ever had money I would have no problem spending it.

The smell of leather went right through the house in Brick Lane. The walls of my father's workshop had hundreds of paper patterns hanging up, and there were rolls and rolls of skins, fabric, lining materials and all sorts of machinery. Hindsight makes this easy to realise, but it was clearly always a fire risk.

The inevitable happened one night in 1971. My father was woken by one of the heavy irons falling over in his workshop, and at first he thought we were being burgled. He went upstairs to see who was there, and as he went to open the door, the handle was red-hot and the paint was peeling with the heat. He burned his hand quite badly before he saw the smoke coming out under the door.

The first I knew about it was when he came into the room I shared with Azam. He was screaming at us to get up and got us out of bed. My mum fetched my sister and Ayub, and as my dad carried us out of the room – just as we were getting to the door – the ceiling caved in. A few more seconds and there is no doubt we would have died. I remember being absolutely terrified, trembling and shaking, in part because I had never seen my father so panic-stricken. I still wasn't quite sure what was going on because I was half asleep, but when that ceiling fell in the noise was incredible. There was no way we would have survived.

We ran down the stairs and stood in the street in our pyjamas just looking at the flames leaping out of the top-floor windows. I don't remember who called the Fire Brigade, but a fire engine turned up, and all we could do was watch as they got their ladders out and turned their hoses on. I have a very clear memory of standing on the pavement, looking up at the firemen on ladders putting their hoses through our windows. By the time the flames were out, the whole roof had disappeared, and what hadn't been burned had been ruined by the blackened water.

We had nothing except our pyjamas. Not only had we lost all our clothes, all our possessions and my mother's jewellery, but we had lost my father's business. From the stock to his order book and his list of clients and their telephone numbers, absolutely everything had gone. We had no home and no business. And, it turned out, no insurance.

Chapter 2

Growing Up Fast
(1971–1977)

'Watching my father taught me two very important lessons: firstly, that nothing is achieved without dedication and effort; and secondly, that there is little point in hard work if you can't take the time to enjoy the rewards.'

I DON'T KNOW WHERE WE STAYED that night – possibly with neighbours – but the council quickly gave us emergency shelter and we were moved into temporary accommodation. I had never understood why my father had saved his money, but we were now all very thankful that he had. The next day we had clothes to wear and bedding to sleep on, and within a month we also had a new house.

My father used his savings to buy – in cash, as far as I recall – a detached house in Forest Gate, a suburb of north-east London. In many ways it made no sense, as his business was centred around the Brick Lane area: he was well known there and he had lots of customers and suppliers there. On the other hand, the family was still growing – my parents would soon have a fifth child, my younger brother Nadeem – and we needed more space.

In Forest Gate we had a garden and a garage and I got my own room for the first time, which meant my brother and I no longer had to fight over who got to put their posters up: he liked Bruce Lee, I had Farah Fawcett-Majors, although she had to share the walls with pictures of Chelsea FC. In 1970 they'd won the FA Cup, and in 1971 they won the European Cup Winners' Cup, and they completely captured my imagination. No one else in the family cared for football, so I never got taken to any matches, but I became a lifelong fan in the early seventies.

Not long after we'd moved, my parents announced that we were going on holiday. This was incredibly exciting news, but when they said we would be going to Pakistan my heart sank. They now had children their families had never met and they wanted to see old friends and relations. Kids at school were going to cool places like Florida and Spain: Pakistan seemed incredibly boring in comparison.

I don't think my parents realised just how little I felt about the country I'd been born in. I couldn't remember it and I didn't feel any particular connection to the place. When my father talked of home he meant Lahore, but for me home was London. After we came back from our holiday, it would be another twenty years before I'd find a reason to go back to Pakistan, and in time I would come to understand my father's love for the place.

There was a secondary school at the end of our road in Forest Gate where I enrolled at the start of the new term. On my first day I remember feeling completely lost. My school in Brick Lane had had about 200 pupils, and by the time I left I knew everyone in the building. Suddenly I was one of more than 1000 pupils in this vast building with science blocks and playing fields: after the upheaval of the move and the trauma of the fire, I felt quite isolated for a while.

However, I quickly found a group of friends and started to settle in. My best friend was a guy called Phillip, and we hung around with Sunil, Kirk and Mustafa. We were quite a tight group and we pretty much all stayed friends until we finished school. We'd go to the pictures together, play a bit of football, hang out at the Wimpy bar and go to the odd West Ham match. Of course, I really wanted to go to Stamford Bridge, but Upton Park was our nearest ground.

I'm sure hanging around with such a mixed bunch of friends insulated me from any racism. Even though there were only a handful of other Asian kids at school, I never felt different and never knowingly experienced any prejudice. I look at some of the communities that exist now that are almost entirely Asian, and I'm very grateful that our family lived in such mixed neighbourhoods. Looking back, I think it was probably easier to integrate then, precisely because the neighbourhood was so mixed. If you don't mix with other communities, the chances of you breaking out on your own are pretty slim. I think if you separate yourself, if you don't adapt your way of life, then you stand out, and that's when you tend to experience prejudice.

I believe everyone prospers from integration. If I had grown up in a neighbourhood where every face I saw was Asian, I think I would have found it harder to express my identity as an individual, not just as part of a community. And if a child doesn't express himself, then he lacks confidence and opportunities fade away. If I'd grown up in that kind of environment, I'm not sure if I would have had the confidence to break the mould and go on to have the career I've had.

Having a strong group of friends meant that I started to spend more time away from home, but as long as my homework was done and I was in by a certain time my parents let me go. My parents were still quite strict with my sister Nahid, and, as Azam was far more studious than me and happy to stay at home with his books, I was the one who pushed the boundaries and got into trouble. I just wanted to be out, to be with other people and to have a bit of fun.

I did OK at school, and if I had been motivated I might have done quite well. The school was streamed, with the name of each stream starting with one of the letters in FOREST, with F being the top and T being the bottom. I was put into F stream in the First Year (now called Year 7, I think), which made my parents happy, and I basically did whatever I needed to do to stay in F stream, but no more than the minimum. I also played in the school football and cricket teams, which I enjoyed.

In the early 1970s there was only one bike you wanted to be seen riding, and that was a Chopper, the sort with outsized handlebars. All my friends had one, and naturally I wanted one, too, but when I asked my parents if I could have one they said no. My dad was still saving up for his return to Pakistan, and that was the kind of expense he didn't see the sense in.

'If you really want it,' he told me, 'you'll find a way of getting it yourself.'

'How?'

'Save your pocket money.'

'But that'll take for ever.'

I think it was my mum who suggested getting a paper round. One of my friends had one, so I asked him how much he got for it. I seem to remember it was almost exactly what I was getting in pocket money – which wasn't very much, maybe £2 or something like that – but with the paper round I figured I could have the bike twice as fast.

I would get up at 5.30 a.m., go to the newsagent, deliver the papers and then go home for breakfast. By the time I'd finished school I was exhausted, so as soon as I had enough money to buy the bike I packed it in. It helped that I'd found a much better way of making a bit of extra cash.

My dad still had a workshop at home where he made bespoke clothes for some of his clients. The bulk of his business had now changed from manufacturing garments himself to supplying clients with stock he'd outsourced to other factories. This meant that the pieces he worked on himself were all one-offs, and of course they were finished to a very high standard. There were often several in the house at once, and so I started wearing the jackets to school.

The other kids would ask me where I'd got them from, and so I started telling them that they could have one made if they liked them that much. I asked my dad how much he would make a jacket for, and he said £20. Now, I knew that they retailed at £35, so if I told the guys at school that they could have one for £30, they would think they were getting a very good price.

My dad told me that he would need a deposit to cover the materials, so I got £10 from one mate who wanted a jacket and handed it over. Then, when my friend came over to collect it, he handed me another £20, of which I gave a tenner to my dad. I think Dad must have cottoned on to the fact that I was taking a cut because he asked me what I'd sold it for. I was a bit nervous that I'd done something wrong, so I just laughed.

'Why are you laughing?'

'No reason.'

'Then why won't you tell me what you sold it for?'

Eventually I cracked and told the truth. It was his turn to laugh.

'So why didn't you tell me? If you sold it for thirty quid you should have given me the thirty quid.'

Now I thought that was unfair.

'But you told me you would make one for £20 so you should be happy with £20.'

He was still laughing, and I realise now that it was with pride. He was absolutely delighted that I was showing a bit of initiative and demonstrating some talent for business.

'Right,' he said, 'I'm going to get you a price list!'

After that I probably sold one or two jackets a month, which meant I was making a lot more than I had delivering papers, and I didn't have to get up at 5.30 every morning.

As I got a bit older, my dad became increasingly keen on educating me about the business, and I was equally keen to learn everything he could tell me. It was just accepted that I would join him, and he often talked of opening a boutique selling leather goods that I could run. Business was a lot more interesting to me than school, so I was happy to be involved, and now my father started to ask my opinion on whether he should change suppliers, or find new clients.

My father worked extremely hard to replace the savings he'd spent after the fire. I couldn't understand why he still wanted to return to Pakistan, but that was his mindset. So Monday to Friday he'd be in his workshop, or overseeing orders he outsourced to factories. On Saturdays he would visit clients, going to their boutiques and meeting their customers so that he could see what they were buying and pick up ideas; and Sundays were spent seeking out new clients in new neighbourhoods and finding out what they needed.

Watching him taught me two very important lessons: firstly, that nothing is achieved without dedication and effort; and secondly, that there is little point in hard work if you can't take the time to enjoy the rewards of that effort. I loved and respected my father, but I was slowly realising that I would never be able to dedicate myself to a job that involved working seven days a week with no time for fun.

Because of my elder brother Azam's academic bent, he was encouraged in his studies and everyone expected him to go to university and become a banker or an accountant. I had always shown more interest in the business, and so I was the natural successor. For my dad, the business was never just about earning money: it was about building something for the future, something that would be passed down through the generations to support the entire family. My interest in the business was therefore a great source of satisfaction for him, and he was nearly as keen for me to finish school as I was.

The problem was that I was finding business *too* interesting, and I started to wonder if being handed a company to run on a plate was just a bit too easy. Although I wasn't really articulating it to myself yet, I was definitely starting to think that I would prefer to start a business of my own. I hadn't given any thought to what that business might be; I just knew I wanted something that would be *mine*.

Our family kept on growing, and while I was at secondary school my sisters Nazima and Irem were born. There is a seventeen-year gap between Nahid and Irem, and for us older kids that meant doing homework to the accompaniment of crying babies, or little ones playing, not to mention countless other distractions. I find it pretty easy these days to work anywhere, and I wonder if this is because I grew up in a house with so much going on.

I got on extremely well with all my brothers and sisters – we always looked out for each other – but my friends were becoming increasingly important to me. I was starting to get invitations to parties and discos, but there was no way my father would let me go. As one of seven kids, I understood that if I was allowed to go out all the time my father would find it impossible to discipline the younger ones. So, of course, I started sneaking out.

I would have to wait until my parents had gone to bed, and then I'd go to places like the Palais in Ilford. At fourteen and fifteen I never had any problem getting in, and I'd stay out until the early hours of the morning. When I got home, the door was locked, and as I'd never been given a key because my mum was home to let us in, I would throw stones at Azam's window and he would open the door for me. My brothers and sisters all knew what I was doing, and to them it was a bit of fun because we all knew that I would get a colossal telling-off if I was caught. After a while, I realised that they would also be punished if they were caught helping me. That wasn't fair, so I got a bit smart. Before I left I would unbolt the back door and leave the latchkey under the doormat.

I didn't drink or smoke, and there weren't any girls involved, so going out was just about me and my mates having a laugh and enjoying the music. We probably thought we were very cool, like John Travolta in *Saturday Night Fever*. As far as I knew, my parents didn't have a clue about my social life, and so I kept on sneaking out whenever I could. Looking back, it's clear to me that I just wanted to break free. The expectation that I would join the family business was starting to feel like real pressure, and I felt the need to rebel before I started my years of service.

Occasionally I would try to say to my father that 'I might like to do my own thing', but as soon as I started that kind of conversation he would end it. My father was a very strong character and he was absolutely adamant that I would join his business. When he had made up his mind that was it. You weren't going to talk him out of it.

He would often say things like, 'I came to this country, and I built this for you.' Every sentence was loaded with the words 'I'm doing this for you, I'm doing this for your wellbeing and your education.' Culturally, among many, if not most, Asian entrepreneurs it's all about handing the business on to your kids. You establish something for your sons, and they carry it on; that's just the way it is, and so that was always his mindset. It's a bit like arranged marriages: if you're brought up in an environment where arranged marriages are standard, it's just accepted, there's no debate because it's just what happens. It's the same with businesses: they are built to be taken over by the sons, and that's just the way it works.

The couple of times I remember actually tackling him about this, the conversation was over within seconds. After a few attempts, there was no point mentioning that I wanted to try to build something on my own, as it would only start a row. He would tell me of his plans to start a biker range or to open our own factory, but to me it was just more of the same. It was still *his* business, not mine. It wasn't *my* dream, it was his, and deep down I was starting to understand that I would never feel the same way about it as he did. It's no coincidence that now, when I invest in a business, I actually invest in the person leading that business. If they don't have that dream, if I don't feel their passion, then it doesn't matter to me how good their financial forecast is.

I had always looked up to my father and admired him as much as I loved him, but his insistence about the business made my need to rebel even stronger. I just wanted to escape, and for the time being that meant spending as much time with my mates as possible.

In the spring of 1977 I was becoming desperate for independence, and like most teenagers I just didn't want to be told what to do. Sneaking out was like getting one over on my dad, and so I started to go out even more. Even on school nights. One night I went out to a club called Room at the Top in Ilford with a friend I had met called Bernie. He was a year or two older than my other friends and had already left school, so he was up for going out any night of the week. He was quickly becoming my best friend, and we'd had such a good night that we didn't want to go home right away. We stopped off for a takeaway, and that meant I didn't get home until 3.30 a.m. I crept up the drive, opened the side gate and stole up to the back door to get the key from under the mat. Only the door wouldn't open. It was bolted from the inside.

At that moment I knew instantly what had happened: my father must have got up, maybe for a glass of water, seen that the door was unbolted and realised that one of us had gone out. I also knew that my bedroom was the first place he would have checked for an empty bed. Not only was I locked out, but there was no doubt that it had been my father who had deliberately locked me out. I was pretty scared.

I tried the downstairs windows, but this was early spring and they were all closed. I couldn't think of a way to get in without breaking in, and there was no way I was going to do that. So I went to go and sleep in the car, which was unlocked because this was the 1970s, and, remarkable as it sounds now, you really could leave your car unlocked all night back then.

Needless to say, I didn't sleep all that well. At 6.30, the car door opened. It was my dad. He looked at me, and I was petrified. But he just handed me a blanket and went back to the house! I couldn't understand why he hadn't just given me a lecture. Now I was really scared.

I had school to get to, so at around 7.30 I knocked on the front door so that I could get my things and have breakfast. I was standing there not knowing what to expect: the silent treatment or a row. When my father opened the door, I didn't have to wait long to find out which one.

'What do you think you are doing? Where have you been? Who have you been with?'

I didn't get a chance to answer, and nothing I could say would have made any difference anyway.

'What's wrong with you? Why are behaving like that?'

I had rarely seen him so angry and all I could do was stand there and take it. He gave me a lecture about going to clubs, told me he hadn't brought me up to behave like that: I got the whole 'You've let me down' speech.

'What kind of example are you setting to the younger ones? You're supposed to be better than that. What will people say?'

Not only was I letting him down, but I was showing him up. My dad was very much a law-abiding figure; he was respected in the community, and there was always this issue of what other people would think.

Eventually the tirade subsided and I was allowed to get ready for school. I think it was probably that morning that made me realise that I couldn't stay. The tension between us was too great. I was going to have to leave home.

Chapter 3

Breaking Free (1977)

'I had to prove to my dad that I could make it without him. That was the only thing that would make sense of what I had done. I had to prove him wrong.'

I HONESTLY FELT I HAD NO CHOICE but to go. If I stayed and joined my dad's business, I knew I was going to be miserable. Without the option of talking to my parents about my feelings, I felt the only thing I could do was make plans to leave home. At sixteen, I was so confused and desperate to break free that I wasn't thinking rationally. And that meant I was on a collision course with my father.

It didn't help that there was pressure at school, too. This was my O-level year, and as the end of the spring term approached I had to revise for my mocks. The desire to break free was overwhelming.

I talked to my friends about my need to move out, and of course they thought it was the coolest thing in the world. At first I thought I could stay with one of them so that I would be able to remain at school, but I was so restless that I wanted to leave school, too. I had already decided that I was going to run my own business some day, so what good would a handful of O levels do me anyway?

I went to talk to one of my teachers and asked if it was possible to quit. He told me that, legally, you could leave school at the end of the spring term as long as you were old enough. Hearing that was like having a huge weight lifted: suddenly I felt that escape really was possible.

'You're not serious though, are you, Nazim?'

No one from F stream had ever left school early.

'Actually, I am completely serious.'

'But your studies are going well. You'll do OK this summer. It's only natural to be scared of sitting exams. We can get you extra help if that's what you need.'

I wasn't listening.

'So you can't stop me from leaving then?' That was all I could focus on.

'No, no one can stop you, but you should think seriously . . .'

I had already given it very serious thought, and my mind was made up. In a couple of weeks' time, as soon as term was over, I would be leaving school. And leaving home.

I told Azam what I planned to do, but I don't think he believed me. No one did. It was unthinkable that I would leave home at sixteen. In my parents' culture the boys never leave home, even when they marry, as it's traditional for their wives to move in. The girls are taught to cook and clean and take care of a house, but the boys are indulged because they will never need those skills. So it wasn't just that I was thinking of leaving home at sixteen that was so radical: it was the fact that I was leaving home at all.

When I talked to my friends about it, they treated it as if it was some kind of adventure. 'You could get your own place and we could stay up all night. It'll be great.' Although no one else took the idea seriously, I did. I knew I was suffocating under the weight of my father's expectations, and since the night I'd slept in the car things had been so tense at home that the idea of working with him had become oppressive.

My friends' enthusiasm for my escape helped me turn a vague idea into a concrete plan. I was as scared as I was excited, but the problem was that, once I had told them I would do it, my pride wouldn't let me back out. Even though I doubt any of them believed I would actually leave, for some reason I felt I couldn't change my mind. And although they egged me on, their encouragement was probably only offered because they didn't really believe I would do it.

I started making plans to leave, and the big question was where I would live. I had absolutely no idea, but one of my friends said that flats to rent were advertised in the *Evening Standard*. So I picked up a copy and saw one advertised in Kensington, an area I knew because there was a club on Kensington High Street that we sometimes went to. Living in Kensington sounded exciting and unbelievably glamorous, so I went to take a look at the flat.

It was pretty small – the kitchen was little more than a counter with a Baby Belling camping stove on top, and the phone was a payphone in the communal hallway – but the rent was only £11 a week, which was less than I was earning from my Saturday job at Mr Buyrite in Stratford shopping centre. I decided it would be my new home. The landlord didn't ask for references, just a month's deposit and a month's rent in advance, so I handed over the money.

I got so caught up in the practicalities that I didn't really stop to think about what I was doing. I was sixteen, I had no qualifications, only a Saturday job for money and I was about to walk away from my family.

I talked to my eldest brother about it a lot, and he finally took me seriously when I told him that I had paid the deposit on a flat. He was shocked, because he realised that not only was I serious, but that I was going to do it imminently. By now, most of my brothers and sisters also knew what I was planning, and that meant I wouldn't be able to keep it from my parents for much longer. My hand was being forced: it was time to tell my father.

We were all scared about how he would react. In the history of our family no one had ever stood up to him. This was new territory for all of us. I think my brother spoke to him first and said I was talking about moving out, but my dad wouldn't believe it unless he heard it from me. I remember just pacing up and down, not sleeping, not knowing how I was going to explain it to him. All I could think about for days was him and what his reaction would be, trying to anticipate what he would say and if I would be able to respond.

The following Saturday, before he went out to see his clients, I plucked up the courage and went to talk to him. My brothers and sisters all knew what I was going to tell him and so they stayed upstairs. My dad was in our drawing room and as I stood at the doorway I had a lump in my throat so big I wasn't sure if I'd be able to speak.

'Can I have a word?' I managed.

He nodded.

My heart was beating so hard that I had trouble getting the words out, but eventually I told him that I didn't want to go to school any more. At first he perhaps thought that this was because I wanted to start working with him, but then I dropped my bombshell.

'I don't want to join the family business. I want to do my own thing. And I am moving out.'

There was silence for a moment. His first words were: 'Well, where are you going to go?'

I think he thought I would crash at a friend's.

'I've found a place.'

He was calmer than I had expected.

'And where have you found a place? How have you found a place?'

'It was advertised . . .'

'Whose place is it?'

From his behaviour I was pretty sure he was thinking that I would be back in a week, but I made it clear that I was going for good. He was livid and visibly upset and started saying things like: 'I brought you up better than this! After everything I've done for you this is how you repay me!' And, of course, 'You're letting me down.'

He told me how he had all these plans for me and how we were going to build up the business together. I knew this was his main concern and so I told him that if I carried on at school and went to university I wouldn't be joining the business until I was twenty-one anyway.

'I don't need qualifications for what I'm going to do, I need experience. Please let me do this, and then I can come and work for you when I'm twenty-one. For you it's no different, but for me it's a chance to learn in the real world.'

To my amazement he accepted that this was probably true, but he was still furious. 'What are your brothers going to think? What kind of example are you setting?'

Our conversation went on for maybe forty minutes, and I knew that I had to stop myself from rising to the bait. I couldn't give in; I told myself, 'Whatever he says, however he tries to persuade me that I'm stupid or selfish or thankless, I know I can't say anything that will give him any hope that I will change my mind.'

'I understand,' I said when he told me what a good job working with him would be, 'but it's not for me.'

Throughout the discussion I didn't say much, but I was quite clear. I knew that I couldn't let him draw me into a debate because it would have escalated into a row, and, as our conversation went on, his anger and incomprehension grew.

'You're wrong, you're not going!'

'I'm sorry, but I am.'

I kept my sentences short and answered with lots of 'yeses' and 'nos' in an attempt to keep a lid on his anger. Finally, his temper subsided and he just became upset, and obviously hurt.

'You'll never make it. You don't know what you're doing.'

I said nothing.

'You'll last a week, you'll be back, just you see.'

Again, I knew I just had to try and keep my cool.

'You'll never make it. You've got no money, you're too young, you're clueless. I've given you everything, you don't even know where to get food from.'

As he was saying that I realised that he was 100 per cent right: I didn't have a clue about anything. But I was also thinking, 'I'll find a way.'

After I'd spoken to him, I went and talked to my mum. My brother had already told her that I was leaving and so as soon as she saw me she burst into tears and hugged me.

'What are you doing?' she asked. 'What's wrong with you?' She didn't care that I wasn't going to join the business; she just wanted to know where I would sleep. The worst moment was when she said, 'I have let you down.' I had to tell her that she hadn't.

'Mum, it's not your fault, it's nothing to do with you, you've done nothing wrong.' Back then, I couldn't understand why she would think that, but now I'm a parent I understand that you always blame yourself. 'There's nothing you could have done differently.'

I was really upset by this point and we were both crying. I had never seen her that distraught and I couldn't believe that I was causing her so much pain. I then went upstairs, and as I was clearly so upset my brothers and sisters all gave me a hug. They were scared about what was going to happen next, not just for me but because they were going to have to live with my father for the next few weeks. It was the biggest thing to happen in our family by far.

I had actually packed three weeks beforehand – just a holdall with the essentials because I'd agreed with my brother that I couldn't walk out with a huge amount. That mental image of walking out with lots of suitcases felt wrong. So my brother and I agreed that I'd just take a handful of stuff so that I could avoid a big exit. He agreed to take one bag of my things out of the house at a time a bit later and give them to a friend of mine with a car who would then drop them off in Kensington.

By the time I was ready to leave it was mid-afternoon. My mother was in the kitchen, my father in the front room. Neither of them would say goodbye, so I just walked out of the front door with my bag as my brothers and sisters watched from an upstairs window.

The walk from the house to the railway station had never seemed so long. I was so tense that it was all I could do just to keep looking forward and put one foot in front of the other. I was just a skinny kid – I wasn't even fully grown yet – and yet there I was, walking out on my family towards uncertainty. I only knew that I couldn't look back: one tiny moment of weakness and I might not have been able to carry on.

I half expected – and maybe half wanted – someone to come after me. If my dad or my brother or my sister had followed me out on to the street and asked me to go home, I absolutely would have, not just because they'd asked but because by this stage I was broken. It took everything I had to hold it together. I had spent all my time thinking about the practicalities – I'd worked out what to say and where I would go – but I had never really considered how I would feel. I'd always known it was going to be bad, and because of that I hadn't wanted to go there and had just blanked it out.

As long as I was still in Forest Gate there was a chance someone would run after me, so I had to keep up the appearance that I was OK with what had happened. I walked along the street as casually as I could, but as soon as the train came in and the chances of someone I knew finding me had gone, I let go. As the doors closed, I started crying. Those closing doors meant there was no going back. It wasn't theory any more, it was real, and I was off to start a new life about which, frankly, I didn't have a clue.

I started reliving the things my parents had said. 'My mum thinks it's her fault and that she's let me down.' How could I have done this to her? I had underestimated how much it would hurt her because I had been so preoccupied with what my dad would say. Of course, my dad's words were ringing louder in my ears, and even though I had expected him to say everything he'd said, when your father says those things to you in anger it still hurts. I realised that I had let him down massively.

It was now clear that I couldn't go back. I had to prove to my dad that I could make it without him. That was the only thing that would make sense of what I had done. I had to prove him wrong.

Chapter 4

Teenage Kicks
(1977–1978)

'I got paid every Friday, and there were many weeks when I'd get to a Thursday – or even a Wednesday – and I would have nothing but cornflakes until pay day.'

I HAD ARRANGED TO MEET my mates at the flat in Kensington that evening. Everybody knew what had been going on, and I think they were all excited because I was doing something none of them had ever done. They thought it was cool to have a mate with his own place; it made them feel grown up.

I had been so caught up in the celebrations – which club we would go to, where we would eat – that I never stopped to consider if I would actually be in the mood to party. Needless to say I wasn't, and they realised I was too upset to go out. I don't think they had really thought of what I was doing as anything more than a game, and it hit them quite hard to realise that I had really hurt my family, and in so doing had hurt myself.

We hung round the flat for a few hours, but most of them drifted off. Only Bernie stayed all night, and it helped to be able to talk things through with someone. It was after 2 a.m. when I finally went to bed. Being sixteen, I hadn't packed any bed linen, but the landlord had some blankets in a cupboard.

In the morning, we went for a walk just to get a change of scenery and ended up aimlessly strolling round Queensway while we continued the 'What am I going to do?' conversation. I wondered if I should go back, but I realised that I didn't have that option: I had hurt my father so badly that I didn't think I would have been welcome.

While we were out we bought things like pizza and Coke, but I don't remember buying anything sensible such as a pint of milk, and when Bernie went home I returned to my tiny, empty flat. I was pretty low, but also pretty determined: I was going to have to find some work.

On the Monday I picked up the early edition of the *Evening Standard* and started looking at the job ads. I had never really given all that much thought to what I wanted to do, or what I would be good at, or what I had to offer an employer. There were hundreds of ads, but they were all asking for qualifications or experience. So I called a recruitment agency from the payphone in the hallway as they had lots of jobs available and I thought that I must be able to do one of them.

'Hi, I saw your ad in the paper.'

'Which position are you interested in?'

'I don't really know.'

'What line of work are you in?'

'I just left school.'

'And what qualifications have you got?'

'None.'

'Hold on one moment.'

I was put through to a recruitment consultant who said she might be able to help me. I took down their address – which was in Earls Court, so not too far away – and went straight round there. The consultant had one of those boxes of file cards and flicked through it looking for something that didn't require any qualifications or experience. She set up three interviews for me for that week, and by the Friday I had landed a job as a sales rep. The basic pay was tiny, but if I sold well I could earn a decent commission. I didn't really care what it was, as long as it meant it paid enough to cover my rent and meant I didn't have to return home saying I'd failed. Just in case, I kept my Saturday job at Mr Buyrite, although I switched to the Oxford Street branch, which was much nearer.

My job was selling shop fittings and supplies to independent grocers. I was given the merchandise and an A–Z, and told to work my patch. I basically had to go door to door, and I learned the true meaning of the expression 'cold-calling'. I was frozen most of the time – I got soaked and never dried out – and it was absolutely miserable.

I'd always known I could sell because of the leather jackets, and I knew I was good at communicating, so I suppose I'd thought being a door-to-door salesman was a pretty natural fit. But I hadn't realised it would be so lonely, that I would be on my own all day long, wandering from street to street. It shattered my illusions a bit because I'd always assumed I'd be a great salesman, but the truth was I was just average.

Work was a thousand times harder than I'd expected. I'd never been in the situation where I *had* to do something before. Previously, work had been about a bit of fun or a bit of extra cash. Now I needed a job to stay afloat because I couldn't ask my dad for a tenner any more. Not being able to pay the rent scared me.

At the end of the month I got my first pay packet; it was fairly pathetic for such a difficult job and I decided I had to quit. If I was going to keep my flat, I had to find a job that I could stick for longer than a month. However, the door-to-door work had taught be something valuable about the kind of work I wanted to do, and

I went back to the recruitment agencies and told them that I wanted to work in an office. I couldn't be too fussy because I absolutely had to earn enough to pay the rent, but as long as it was in an office, not only would I be warm but I would be working with people.

Working and living on my own would have been pretty lonely if it hadn't been for my mates. The first three months in the flat were absolutely amazing: I could have whoever I wanted round, go out when I liked, come back when I liked, have five people crashing on the floor. You couldn't take the grin off my face. Everyone else still lived at home in suburbia, so my pad in Kensington became the place to hang out, and it was just fantastic.

Bernie didn't have a regular job – he was the kind of guy that did a little bit of this and then a bit of that and would suddenly turn up in a suit because he'd got some flash new job. He had the gift of the gab and was always talking himself into – and out of – jobs. We became incredibly close in those days, and he would often stay on my sofa after a night out. It was only when I saw him a couple of days later in a really familiar jacket and pair of trousers that I'd realise he had got up and helped himself to my wardrobe before leaving for work!

One day he told me he had a great new way of making money – selling clothes in Ireland. The fashions in London were more adventurous, he said, and all we had to do was take some samples over there and get some orders. And that's exactly what we did. We persuaded some manufacturers to let us have some samples, then we went to Dublin on the ferry and sold the samples door to door. We took orders and deposits, placed the orders in London and then went back a month or so later to deliver the goods. It was a bit of extra money, but just as soon Bernie was on to his next project, so we never did it again.

After about three months, the novelty of being a constant party host had definitely worn off. It was a bit of a shock to realise that

I had to go out and buy Jif and bleach and that the cola that had spilled on the table wouldn't wipe itself up. As a son in an Asian community I had been smothered: I had never cooked, or cleaned, or done my own laundry. When I had to spend a couple of hours at the launderette on Sunday watching the spin dryer go round, the shine started to wear off my new life.

I was also missing my mum's cooking. At first the idea of eating junk food was exciting because I'd always got a lecture about it at home. Being able to eat takeaways and Pot Noodles was cool, but I was useless at shopping for myself and often I'd get in to find my cupboard bare.

My next job was definitely a step in the right direction. I had always been quite good at maths at school, and so the recruitment agency put me forward for a position in the accounts department of Grand Metropolitan, a conglomerate that owned Forte Hotels at the time.

As soon as the agency mentioned it to me, I knew I wanted it, but because I didn't have any relevant experience they took some convincing to put me forward for the interview. 'I was always good at maths at school,' I told the consultant.

The moment I walked into Grand Met's offices I was desperate to work there. They were based in a gorgeous cream-painted terrace overlooking Regent's Park. Not only did it remind me of the plush buildings I'd admired from the bus when I was a kid, but when I walked into the reception it was full of people in nice suits – and it was warm. I didn't care that I didn't even know what an accounts department did. I had helped my dad fill in invoices and make his VAT returns. I'd be able to work it out.

The job involved processing expenses – taking the receipts from the senior employees, writing them up, adding them up and passing them on to someone else in the department for payment – and I was determined to show the woman interviewing me that I was up to the job. She kept coming back to my lack of my experience, so I said, 'I'm really good at maths, ask me anything. Go on, give me a sum.'

She quite liked my cheek and my determination, so she asked me something simple like seventeen times three, which I did instantly. Then she reached for her calculator and asked me something harder, which I also got right.

'Give me another one.'

But she didn't need to, I had got the job and so she showed me round the offices and introduced me to my new colleagues. The best bit was being shown the staff canteen, which was more like a restaurant. I didn't even know that companies had canteens and I was stunned to find out that the food was subsidised. I could get a really good meal in a really nice, warm place for 30p! It was a godsend, because all the partying was taking its toll on my finances. I got paid every Friday, and there were many weeks when I'd get to a Thursday – or even a Wednesday – and I would have nothing but cornflakes until pay day. Eventually I had to write myself out a budget – so much on rent, so much on bills, this much for my Tube pass, and then live off what was left.

It had been several months since I'd spoken to my parents. I was still in contact with my brothers and sisters, so they knew I was all right, but there was no way I was going home until I could prove to my dad he was wrong and that I could stand on my own two feet.

Then one day my brother called me and said, 'Nazim, there's a family wedding and you've got to come. Mum and Dad will be very embarrassed if you don't show up. You've got to be there.'

I knew what these weddings were like, and if I didn't show up I knew the focus would be on my absence and not on the bride and groom. So I had to go. I borrowed some money from a friend and went and bought a new suit so that I could turn up looking smart and, crucially, looking as if I'd made it. I also bought a beautiful shirt and tie and I thought I looked really smart. I thought I looked successful.

At the wedding, when people asked how I was doing I told them how wonderful everything was, how I was making a good life for myself, and I let them think I was enjoying a fabulous lifestyle. It was important to me that no one knew things were just about OK.

When I saw my dad, I walked straight up to him in my new suit and let him know I was fine, if not better than fine. By approaching him I knew I was making a statement. If I had let him come to me, it would have signalled that maybe things hadn't worked out as well as I was letting on.

After the wedding, there was a meal back at the family home in Forest Gate but for some reason I wouldn't eat my mum's food.

'Aren't you hungry?' she asked.

The truth was I was starving, but somehow eating her cooking was like admitting defeat, that I wasn't taking care of myself as well as I claimed. I couldn't give the impression that I needed anything they had to offer, so I just watched them all eat even though my mouth was watering!

I swear that all the way home I could still smell that food. By the time I got to the flat I was kicking myself. I should have had the meal, but it wasn't just that I couldn't admit that I needed them. There was another reason why I should have eaten with them: the more I said how everything was fine, the colder the atmosphere became because it wasn't what they wanted to hear. Looking back, it was a clearly the wrong thing to have done. I had three brothers and three sisters, and as a parent you wanted to demonstrate to the rest of your kids that your errant son's behaviour was wrong. And there was I glamorising leaving home at sixteen, making it out to be a cool thing, which it wasn't. The more I said how good things were, the harder it became for my dad to be warm. If I'd said, 'Actually, Dad, I'm really struggling and I've not had a proper meal for months and I'm working seven days a week,' I think the whole atmosphere would have changed. Seeing them again hadn't repaired any of the damage.

Chapter 5

Finding My Way
(1978–1979)

'*I was making a very strong connection between work and fun: the harder I worked, the more I earned, the more fun I had.*'

A FTER THREE MONTHS AT Grand Met, I was starting to get bored. Writing out expenses claims was extremely tedious, but I liked the office, and the canteen, and so I hung around for nine months until I couldn't take the boredom any longer. Going out was the only priority in my life, so I still hadn't given any thought to what I might like to do for work. I was only concerned that it paid well.

I answered an ad in the paper for a 'trainee interviewer'. I had no idea what one was or what one did, but I thought it was an interesting job title so I went along to the interview. As I walked into the offices of Premier Personnel in Holborn, I couldn't have known that I was actually taking the first steps towards a career that would make me a fortune. Premier was a small recruitment agency, and I was told the job was basically interviewing candidates for jobs. I then met the guy who owned the company and, after a third interview, I was amazed that he offered me the job. I didn't have any experience, but I suppose I was quite an easy person to talk to, and that's one of the qualities you need in recruitment. It might sound a bit obvious to say it, but it is a people business, after all.

There were two things I remember thinking about Premier: firstly, I thought the work might actually be interesting; secondly – and far more importantly – the salary was £38 a week. Not only was that a couple of quid more than I was earning at Grand Met, but every time I placed somebody in a job I would get paid commission. 'If it doesn't work,' I told myself, 'I'm still earning what I'm earning now. But if I place a few people in jobs, I'll more than double my money.' I couldn't see a downside.

I really liked the idea that my pay was incentivised: it made sense to me that the better I was and the harder I worked, the more I'd get paid. I can't remember the exact figures, but I think the agency charged 15 per cent of the first year's salary, which on a £6k a year job was £900, of which I'd get 5 per cent. That £45 was a real motivator – I might even be able to afford a car if I did well enough. What I wasn't old enough to realise, though, was that if I didn't place any candidates I'd get sacked. I hadn't worked out yet that the downside of sales is that if you don't perform you're out. You're only as good as your last month.

The concept of interviewing somebody was a lot more interesting to me than looking at a batch of expense sheets, but on my first day I found out that, before I got to the interesting bit, there was some hard work to be done. Clive, the owner, showed me my desk and then gave me my very own copy of the Yellow Pages.

'So the first thing you do is canvass for vacancies.'

He may as well have been speaking another language, so he had to take me through the whole process.

'You ring up a company . . .'

'Yes.'

'Ask to speak to HR, personnel, the store manager, anyone who is responsible for hiring . . .'

'I understand.'

'Ask them if they've got any vacancies . . .'

'Yes.'

'Then you take a job description from them. Got it?'

'I think so.'

'Look, I'll do the first couple of calls, then I'll watch you make a couple, and then you'll be away.'

He didn't mind what sector I found the vacancies in as long as I wasn't competing with anyone else on the team. So I chose fashion, presumably because I thought my background in the leather trade might give me some affinity for the field.

Needless to say, I got a lot of rejections, and it was pretty clear that if I didn't find a way of swimming I would quickly sink with the demoralisation. So I started saying what I thought they wanted to hear, and, sure enough, my calls started lasting a bit longer.

'We're a specialist fashion agency. We've just placed candidates with Yves St Laurent and Gucci . . .' and with each line I sounded more credible. I was learning that every time someone said 'no' or put the phone down, I had to work out a way to make sure the next call didn't end the same way. It certainly made the work more fun, and I was able to pick up tips from the others in the office – there were four or five of us, with one of them doing banking, another secretarial and so on – and I started to think that I might have found something I was good at.

At the end of each week, Clive would look at each of the vacancies we'd picked up, and if there was a reasonably good job that sounded interesting he'd write an ad to place in the *Standard* the following week. The entire business was speculative: we sought out the vacancies and then drummed up the candidates. In effect, Clive was creating a business out of nothing. When the candidates turned up for the initial interviews, that's when the job got interesting for me. If they were good enough, we would put them forward to the client for consideration, so it was my job to find out all I could about their suitability.

Dealing with the candidates was definitely the best part of the job. Interviewing someone you've never met before is fascinating, and, being quite cheeky, I'd always ask questions that the person sitting next to me wouldn't have bothered with. I would really try to get into the candidates and understand a bit more about them. Where my colleagues might write down: Secretary, forty words a minute, shorthand, lives in Clapham, I'd want to get a bit more detail. I'd want to know what she had done before. What she had liked about the job. And what hadn't she liked? What did she really want to get out of the new role? There was definitely something about that interaction that played to my strengths. Finding out that I was good at talking to people and could get away with stuff other people couldn't was great for my confidence. Once I'd placed a few candidates and earned a bit of commission, I could afford nicer clothes and go to nicer restaurants. Things were starting to click.

I decided to use some of my money to buy my first car, a second-hand MG Midget. Like a lot of teenage boys, I had miraculously acquired the ability to drive without needing to take lessons, so I started driving on my provisional licence before I'd technically passed my test. The car impressed my mates, and it impressed girls, too. One of the unexpected benefits of choosing the fashion sector was that a lot of the applicants were female. And being upfront and growing in confidence, if I liked a girl I asked her out. I found it easy to get dates and that in turn also boosted my confidence.

For a seventeen-year-old, life was pretty near perfect – money, clothes, cars, girls, clubs – whatever I wanted, I could pretty much have. It certainly beat studying for A levels I would never use. I was also making a very strong connection between work and fun: the harder I worked, the more I earned, the more fun I had. It wasn't unusual for me to earn £200 a week, and my rent was still only £11.

That December, Bernie asked me what I was doing for Christmas, because I obviously wasn't going to be spending it with my family. Then as now, Britain shut down over Christmas, so it had always been a time that we'd spent as a family, having a big meal and watching TV like the rest of the country.

'I don't know. Haven't thought about it.'

'Fancy going away? Getting some sun?'

Of course I did, but where?

'Italy's hot all year round and the flights are pretty cheap.'

'Book it,' I told him.

A couple of days later, he called me up and told me it was booked. I'd never heard of the resort, but as long as I could ride round on a Vespa and wear shades, I didn't mind. I packed my coolest clothes – we were going to the most stylish country in Europe, after all – and headed for the airport.

When we landed, we noticed that everyone was getting off the plane with these big bags, and they were all wearing boots and jackets. The coach came to transfer us to the resort, and while we were on the bus I started a conversation with one of the other travellers.

'So have you been here before?'

'We come every year.'

'What's there to do here?'

He looked at me as if to say: *are you that stupid?* 'We ski.'

I didn't want to sound like too much of an idiot so I asked: 'And once you've skied, what do you do then?'

'We ski again.'

I turned to Bernie. 'Excuse me, but *what* exactly are we doing here?'

Neither of us had skied before, but seeing as we were there we thought we might as well give it a go, so we hired the gear and had a laugh. It was a good story to tell the guys when we got home.

Not long after we got back, I went to the cinema with some people from work and it turned out to be quite a significant night. As the opening credits came up, I saw the name James Caan, and it struck me for the first time that the name I was born with – Khan – could be spelled in a different way. In fact, I actually thought that Khan was misspelled. There is no 'kh' sound in English, and I thought Caan was spelled as it's pronounced. While my friends followed the plot, I went on my own mental journey thinking about how Caan made more sense than Khan, and how it also happened to be the name of a really cool actor, and when we came out and were standing around in Leicester Square working out where to go next, I told my colleagues that I thought I would change the spelling of my name.

'You can't do that' was the initial response.

'Why not?'

'No one changes their name. Don't be daft.'

'Actually,' said another, 'I think it's pretty cool. Why don't you change your first name, too?'

Anyway, for the rest of the evening they decided to call me James Caan, which I quite liked. After all, who wouldn't want to have the same name as the coolest guy in Hollywood?

The next day at work they kept calling me James, and as a bit of a joke I asked Clive if he would get me some business cards printed with the name James Caan on them.

'Don't be stupid.'

'Seriously, Clive, it would be such a laugh, just for a week to let them think I've changed my name.'

'No.'

'You can deduct it from my wages.'

Anyway, I think just to amuse me he got the cards printed and I quickly discovered that every time I handed out a card it was a great ice-breaker. 'Oh, like the actor?' At the time James Caan was really popular because of *The Godfather*, so as soon as I handed my card over it got the conversation going. And as soon as I got people talking, I was halfway to getting my commission and so the name just kind of stuck.

In a way, the name thing was just part of my new lifestyle, an accessory like my membership card to the Playboy Club or the MG. Everyone assumed I was older than I was. I think when someone is interviewing you for a job there is an assumption that they have a fair bit of work experience. And because I was wearing a suit and asking intelligent questions, I probably passed for twenty-four or twenty-five when I was still only eighteen.

Chapter 6

A Career in Recruitment (1978–1979)

'If you've got nothing to lose, it's amazing what you can get away with.'

ONE NIGHT WHILE I WAS OUT I met a guy who was working for another recruitment agency, and he suggested I should meet his boss. His firm was City Centre Staff Bureau, which was a lot bigger than Premier – it had five or six branches – and although I wasn't looking for another job, or even really a career in recruitment at this stage, I went for an interview out of curiosity. I got a second interview, and, as I was by now pretty confident, I said to the guy, 'Look, I would be interested in joining your firm but not unless it's for a branch manager's job, because I'm not really looking to move at this stage.' I couldn't see what I had to lose. I thought I might as well ask, because if he said 'no' I was happy to stay put. If you've got nothing to lose, it's amazing what you can get away with. He offered me the job.

I liked the idea of running my own branch, of having the keys and opening up; it was a bit like the business was yours, so I saw it as a step towards my ultimate goal. Psychologically, it felt like a step up. It also meant more money, and I was hoping that being at a bigger company would give me a bit more structure and might even provide some training. Clive had given me a start, but now I realised I was ready for the next step. All of a sudden, I didn't have a job: I had a career.

My branch of City Centre Staff Bureau was in Victoria, and one of the first jobs I had was to recruit my own staff as it was a brand-new branch. I was quite lonely those first couple of weeks, so I asked Bernie to meet me for lunch. He was obviously impressed by my office, by my job title and maybe even by my suit.

'Hire me. Why don't I come and work for you?'

Big mistake.

With just the two of us in the office not a lot of work was going to get done, but in Bernie's first week in the office just about the worst thing that could have happened, happened: he picked up a vacancy for a fashion model. Even less work was going to get done now.

Fashion buyers often need regular-shaped women to model the clothes, as there's no point having a size-8, six-foot-tall woman wearing street fashions: they needed to try them on women who looked like their average customers. So, as you can imagine, when we placed an ad in the *Standard* for a 'Size-12 model, no experience necessary', we were inundated. The phone didn't stop ringing! We must have interviewed hundreds of women: they were booked in every hour for weeks, and there was only one vacancy.

As young guys we saw it as a great way to meet girls, and so we decided to specialise in fashion models. Needless to say we didn't do very well that year and only just made enough placements to cover our costs, which just about kept my boss at bay. Eventually the morning came when I woke up and thought: *what am I doing?* I wasn't making any money and I hadn't developed. I'd had an absolutely fantastic time working with Bernie and dating models, but I'd forgotten the golden rule of working in sales: you're only as good as your last month. I realised that I couldn't carry on like this because I was going to go broke, and get sacked. The novelty had worn off and something had to change.

I was also starting to get quite a bit of pressure from my boss – we had quarterly reviews and management meetings – and my branch had always been bottom of the table. In the first three quarters that hadn't bothered me because the fun had compensated for whatever embarrassment I experienced at those meetings, but by the last quarter that pressure had started to mean more to me than the fun. I'm not sure I know why that was, but something kicked in and the part of me that wanted to amount to something took over. Maybe I knew I was in danger of letting it all slide away, and that meant giving my dad the chance to say 'I told you so.' Somehow, I was going to have to sack my best mate. It wasn't an easy conversation.

'Hi, Bernie.'

'Hi, James, how did you get on with the blonde?'

'I didn't take her out.'

'I had a wild time with that girl from Croydon, let me tell you . . .'

'Bernie, we need to talk.'

'What's up?'

'Bern, this just isn't working. I've got to ask you to leave.'

'Good one, James.'

'No, I'm serious.'

'You're firing me?'

'It's just not working. Two best mates . . . we're just playing.'

He was shocked and angry, and he pitched quite hard to keep his job. But even though he promised things would be different, I had to let him go. Looking back, I see that day as the real start of my career: firing my best mate was when I started taking work seriously.

We didn't speak for about three months after that, which meant that my social life calmed down a bit. I was still going out most nights, but without Bernie around things were quieter, and I could really concentrate on work.

I replaced him with somebody else, really knuckled down and started to focus on actually placing people rather than dating them! The results in terms of placements and commission were pretty much instant, and getting that immediate return on my efforts was very satisfying.

By now I was seeing a bit more of my parents. Things were still fairly formal between me and my dad, but I started going home once or twice a month for a meal, and it was fantastic to spend time there. My brothers thought it was cool that I had changed my name and had started calling me James. After a few months they decided to change their names, too: Azam decided he wanted to be known as Adam, Ayub chose Andrew and Nadeem told us we should call him Stephen. It wasn't all that uncommon for Asians at the time to Anglicise their names, but going from Nadeem to Stephen – or Nazim to James for that matter – was quite a leap! My parents had taken my name change as a childish phase I was going through, like obsessing about a pop star, and hadn't said much about it. It was only when my brothers also started changing their names that they became upset, but even then they thought it was something we would grow out of.

By this point it was dawning on my dad that I probably wouldn't join the business at twenty-one, as I'd said I would. As far as I was concerned it was out of the question because in my mind I hadn't achieved anything yet. I still thought that I would start my own business one day, and proving I could do it on my own continued to be important to me.

In the meantime, the Victoria branch had really started to take off, and when the manager of the Oxford Street branch resigned I was moved across to manage it. This was City Centre Staff Bureau's flagship branch, so it was definitely a promotion. After a couple of months in the West End I was approached by Alfred Marks, probably the biggest employment agency in the UK at the time, to see if I would be interested in joining them.

In comparison to City Centre Staff Bureau, Alfred Marks seemed very sophisticated. Their staff didn't have boxes of file cards – they had computer systems and printouts on green computer paper (I don't know why it was always green, but that was cutting-edge in 1980). I was very impressed, and when they offered me a basic salary of £8k I really started to take notice. I'd been on £6k at City Centre.

Alfred Marks offered me a job as manager at their Edgware Road branch, which was one of their biggest, so I thought that they must have rated me. When they offered £8k I thought I had an opportunity to negotiate a bit harder. After all, they had approached me and I had only just moved to the Oxford Street branch and was making pretty good money. They upped their offer to £10k, so I said to them:

'Make it £11k and I'm interested.'

'But that would make you the highest-paid branch manager.'

Not to mention the youngest.

Anyway, they offered me the £11k I wanted, and so I said yes. I suppose it was at this point that my dad started to think I must have been doing OK for myself. He could see Alfred Marks on every high street, so he knew I was working for a big company, and being a branch manager had a certain status. It was the only job I ever remember going home and telling him about because it was a big deal, but the first thing he said was:

'Not again!'

He couldn't believe how often I changed jobs, and I'm convinced he thought I was flaky.

'You've only been at the other place five minutes!'

However, coincidentally, the following week he *just happened* to be in the West End midweek and called to suggest we had lunch together. He came into the branch and was impressed. He definitely saw it as quite a prestigious job, and it was around this time that he seemed to understand why I hadn't wanted to join his business and started to accept that I probably never would. After that, I sensed we would be able to rebuild our relationship.

I guess I thought I was doing pretty well for myself, too: I was maybe nineteen by this stage, I managed quite a few staff, most of whom were older than me, and had good clothes, some money in my pocket and I drove a nice car. It was a completely different life from the one my mates from school were living, and I rarely saw them now: some of them were resitting exams, others had signed on after their A levels or had jobs in retail earning less than half what I was taking home. It's sad, but I suppose it was inevitable that we would drift apart.

As my career progressed, my relationship with my dad continued to thaw, though it was still too much of a touchy subject for me to say something casual like 'How's business?' It was an area we just didn't touch on, and as long as we skirted round that topic of conversation I could really enjoy going home for lunch and watching my younger brothers and sisters grow up. When it was announced that my elder sister Nahid was getting married, much of our conversation for the next few months was about the wedding.

Nahid had an arranged marriage, which was something my parents never suggested for me. My sisters were all quite comfortable with the concept of arranged marriage; they had been brought up to accept it, so when my parents selected somebody for Nahid it was the natural thing to marry him. As it was the first wedding in the family it was a big event, and whenever I went home there were preparations going on. My dad was in charge of the arrangements, and we were all given our tasks to carry out. I was very proud of my sister, and it was important that the family appeared united at the wedding, so I was included in all the plans.

Being involved brought me closer to my family than I had been since I left home, which made the wedding itself even more of a celebration.

Of course, an even bigger event was the arrival of Nahid's first child, my parents' first grandchild. As a family we love kids, and whenever Nahid and her son came over he was passed round between us all evening, being tickled and talked to and played with until he fell asleep.

By this stage I felt that the trauma of leaving home was behind me. I had gone a long way to showing my father that I wasn't a complete waste of space, and even though I had stumbled on a career in recruitment by chance, I had found something I was good at. I had started to knuckle down and was beginning to earn good money, and as the new decade approached I felt I was ready for anything.

Chapter 7

The Job That Changed My Life
(1980)

'*Most people instinctively knew that that their lives were pretty boring, and the interviews became really interesting when I was able to tell them that they could get rid of that predictability.*'

I N MY FIRST MONTH AT Alfred Marks I was feeling very confident, important even, but it quickly became clear that it wasn't quite me. Alfred Marks was a big plc, and that meant it had a corporate structure, which as branch manager I was expected to fit into. A major part of my job was monitoring targets, making sure staff were getting their reviews, and checking the financials. At first I felt quite sophisticated looking at reams and reams of computer printouts, but I knew it wasn't making the best use of my skills.

I had worked in an accounts department, so I knew how to read the figures, and I knew where to look on a spreadsheet to see if my branch was meeting head office's targets, but I was never going to enjoy a detailed analysis of the numbers. Thankfully, there was a woman called Penny working with me who loved that kind of detail, and so I made it her job to work out the margins or the commission. It has been one of my strengths always to recognise my weaknesses, and another of my strengths is being able to find people like Penny.

Alfred Marks was very strategic, very theoretical. Previously I'd been in an environment where I had a lot of freedom to select clients and candidates; now I got memos saying we were targeting the pharmaceutical industry in April in the W1 area, or that I had to focus on my temp margin. It just wasn't me. The meetings were very boring, so I didn't learn anything, which in turn meant I stopped paying attention. Deep down I'd always been a bit of a maverick, I'd never really conformed, and by this point I'd learned that I needed to be given some space. So when those memos from head office started to fill every hour of the week with a new directive or monitoring mechanism, I knew I wouldn't be sticking around for long. This worried me: why wasn't I enjoying it? Hadn't I always wanted to be one of the corporate guys in a suit? What was missing?

I didn't have time to find out, because I was quickly offered yet another job. And although I didn't know it at the time, my next job would change my life. I had just placed a lot of candidates with a financial services company called Reid Trevena, and one day I got a call from the MD.

'You're doing a great job, James.'

'Thank you very much. Always nice to get some feedback from clients.'

'Do you think you could find any more candidates for us?'

'Sure.'

'Then why don't you come and work for us directly?'

I would have been tempted by any offer that took me away from Alfred Marks at the time, so I went to meet the two guys who ran the company, Tom O'Dwyer and Len Gearing. They wore fantastic suits, handmade shoes, drove amazing cars and they both had a great sense of humour. They reminded me of the men I'd admired from the bus when I was a kid. Reid Trevena employees went to conferences in Barbados, and the top guys were all driving sports cars. Tom was like Bobby Ewing from *Dallas* in his red Mercedes with the roof down. He had a big mansion in Surrey and was married to a beautiful Swedish girl – he had it all, really, and when he walked into a room he was 'the guy'. Everyone wanted to talk to him, and I wanted what he was offering.

Reid Trevena was expanding so quickly that they couldn't get enough staff, and that meant they were spending a fortune on recruitment agencies. With me in-house, they hoped to be able to save themselves a lot of money. Tom then made me an offer I couldn't resist: he would split the savings with me.

Tom offered me £12k basic and a range of bonuses depending on how I recruited. If I used an agency, I'd get a small bonus; if I hired them direct, I got a third of the fee he normally paid an agency, and this could be up to a grand. The more senior the appointment, the bigger my fee. I thought Tom was smart, and I was already getting caught up in the Reid Trevena atmosphere. Let me tell you, it was an electric place to work. The staff were all fairly young, they were earning a lot of money, and the place was growing fast – I had never experienced such a dynamic environment.

Reid Trevena made its money selling savings and investment plans to the public, and every time they signed up a new customer the company got the first two years' contributions as their fee. The fee was so generous that they could afford to pay the individual sales consultants around £200 of it. The commissions were so high that consultants were earning £50–60,000 a year – the equivalent of over £150k a year today. And with commission that good, Reid Trevena didn't need to pay any basic, which is why Tom was keen to expand as quickly as possible: I could hire as many people as I could find, as the only cost to the company was the extra office space.

Reid Trevena was in the process of moving offices when I joined, and they didn't have space for me, so Tom said he'd stick a desk for me in his office and I could share with him. Recruiting for the company was considered quite an important role, and for the first couple of months he said he'd like to see me in action. At the time I was a bit annoyed as I really wanted my own office, but within two weeks I'd begun to think that I'd do the job for free just so I could observe Tom work.

Sitting and watching him sell and recruit I was learning from the master. The guy was phenomenal. I used to watch him interview someone who was earning £30,000 or £40,000 a year – which was a very good salary for the time – and by the end of the interview the candidate was thrilled to be giving up a great salary with terrific benefits, like BUPA cover and a pension, to take a job that paid absolutely no base. He showed candidates how working at Reid Trevena would lift them out of the ordinary and give them the kind of income they had only been able to dream about. To me, Tom's skill was similar to that of an artist or a writer or a musician: it's an art to be able to inspire someone to do that, and Tom became something of an idol to me. I watched everything he did, the suits he wore, the way he sat, the way he spoke, and I started to copy him, almost down to the way he picked up the phone, or how he would stand, or the way he pronounced his words, or the way he used his hands. What he did clearly worked, so when I was interviewing somebody I literally mimicked him.

After a few months in the job, I had perfected my version of Tom's technique. Let's just say I'd placed an ad for sales consultants in the *Evening Standard*, and a rep from Rank Xerox had applied and had come in for an interview. I would know from his CV that he was on £13k a year, that he was twenty-two and that he'd been there for two years. The secret in getting him to give up his security was to understand what he really wanted out of life.

'So, Brian, tell me about yourself, what do you do?'

The first fifteen minutes would usually be taken up with me asking fairly standard questions like, how long have you been in this job? What did you do before? Where are you going? What's your career plan?

'I see you're on £13k at the moment, Brian. What do you think your salary will be after your next review?'

'I'm expecting £15k.'

'£15k, that's fantastic. Tell me, have you given much thought as to where you will be when you reach retirement, salarywise?'

This kind of question opened up the interviewee to talk about his aspirations: was he thinking of getting married, or having kids?

'So you like the idea of a big family then. Is private education important to you? What do you think of the state system?'

I was steadily building up a picture of Brian's life, asking questions that mapped out his future. The amazing thing I discovered at Reid Trevena was that for most people their journey is fairly predictable. Most people instinctively knew that their lives were pretty boring, and the interviews became really interesting when I was able to tell them that they could get rid of that predictability.

'You know most people who work here don't send their kids to a state school. They've had the opportunity to earn so much here and they've realised they can do so much more with their lives. If you had a chance to earn a lot more money what difference would that make for you?'

I'd then tell them a bit about our company. 'We're in the business of financial planning. We're an independent brokerage, which means we're not tied to any company, and that allows us to work with the best-of-breed products with Lloyd's, Abbey and Hambro. Let me tell you a bit about Lloyd's of London . . .' I'd tell them it was one of the biggest financial institutions in the world, and how we had hundreds of millions under management with them. The big number made us sound very credible, very professional.

'One of the things we strongly believe in here is independent financial planning, we think that people should have security for the future . . .' I started to talk about how important it is to save, and of course most people won't disagree with you when you say something so sensible. The amazing thing I had learned from Tom was that if you start a conversation with a series of statements that you both agree on, it sets the tone for the rest of the conversation: I was building up a rapport that meant the candidate was more likely to agree with the things I would go on to say. I moved on to tell them how contributions were invested, and how their money grew faster through careful fund management and gave them the figures for past growth. By the time I'd given them a twenty-minute introduction to the concept of saving, they were thinking what a great idea it was to put something away for the future. This was absolutely key to enabling them to believe that they wouldn't have any problems selling investment plans: who wouldn't want to invest?

'So, Brian, if we went along and got someone to invest £20 a month for the next ten years, what do you think that would be worth in terms of commission to the guy who sells the policy?'

Remarkably enough, most people had the same answer. They weren't going to say £20 because, logically, if you sign somebody up for £20 and you get £20 in commission for it, it sounds like you don't make a margin. So pretty much everyone I asked said: 'About ten quid?'

Throughout the conversation, I continued talking about the idea of somebody building security for his family, for his children, putting something aside, an amount he wouldn't miss but that would be there if he got married or needed it for any reason at all. I was justifying in Brian's mind why Reid Trevena was so important.

'So how many saving policies do you think you could sell in a week?'

'I don't know, maybe ten?'

'So what's that? Two a day?'

We're agreeing between us how achievable that sounded.

'What if I told you our commission was more like £100?'

Now he would be really impressed, and I'd get out a pad and pen and do some sums with him.

'So if you sell ten a week . . . you make about a grand a week . . . you could make four grand a month.'

'Wow.'

'What are you earning at the moment?'

'£13k.'

'Which is about . . . £1100 a month.'

For the rest of the interview, I was pretty much guaranteed Brian's attention. Watching Tom had enabled me to steer the conversation so that candidates believed in what was achievable. I had made them see that saving was desirable and therefore easy to sell, and I had made the number of sales they would need to make a week seem plausible. If I had just said to them 'Come here and earn a fortune,' the chances are that they wouldn't have believed me, and, crucially, they wouldn't have believed that they could do it, which is why Tom's techniques were so good.

'Obviously, you've not done financial sales before, Brian, so I think we should be conservative about your targets, because I don't want you to take a big risk that you might regret. So let's just go back. Is there anything about the concept of saving that you're unclear about?'

'No, I understand that.'

'OK, so let's halve your estimate, let's say instead of two sales a day, you only made one a day. Does that sound doable? Would that scare you?'

'I've got to be able to do that. It's still double what I'm on now.'

'Let me ask you a really ridiculous question, Brian. What if I said that if you don't sell one a day, you wouldn't earn anything. Do those five sales a week still seem realistic?'

'I must be able to do one a day, because it's only £20 a month I'm asking people for.'

'I'm glad you said that, Brian, because what we do here is about breaking the mould, this is about breaking out of being mediocre. If you want to make big money there has to be an element of risk and reward. Would you describe yourself as safe? Are you OK with taking a risk?'

Of course, in the right candidates this kind of question provokes their fighting spirit and allowed me to be sure that they had what was needed. It was my job to make sure that candidates were confident that they could achieve what I was telling them they could achieve, and one of the ways I did this was to introduce them to a member of the sales team. After a few months in the job, I had placed a lot of candidates, so I usually knew someone with a similar background to the candidate I was interviewing.

'Let me introduce you to Steve.' I'd pick up the phone, and call Steve. 'Can you pop into my office for five minutes, Steve?'

What happened next was very powerful and was really important in making the candidates believe in what working at Reid Trevena could do for them.

'Hi, Steve, come in. Steve used to work in sales at Canon. You won't mind me saying this, will you, Steve, but before you came here your earnings were pretty ordinary, weren't they? What were you on?'

'Just over £10k.'

'And how long have you been here now, Steve?'

'Just over a year.'

'What did you earn in your first year here?'

'£27k.'

'And how's it going now, Steve?'

'I think I should clear £40k this year.'

'And tell us, how do you feel about the fact that if you don't perform, you don't earn?'

At no point did I tell Brian there wasn't a basic salary. I never actually said those words because if I took Brian on the right journey, he would overlook the lack of a basic salary. Tom had shown me that if there's enough gain, people are willing to risk a little pain.

'I thought it would be difficult at first,' Steve would say, 'but initially it wasn't so bad because I signed up all the people I knew. The first couple of months I did OK and then I started picking up referrals and now I've got into a routine.'

'Thanks for that, Steve. So, Brian, what do you think?'

'God, he's on double what I'm earning.'

'Can I tell you what he actually had to do to earn that, Brian? He didn't sell ten a week. He didn't even sell five a week. Most weeks he only needs to sell two.'

Brian would now be looking very confused.

'We actually pay £200 for each sale.'

So now Brian was sitting there thinking, 'Two a week, double my salary . . .' With most people I had a pretty good chance of getting them to come and join us and exchange the security they had elsewhere for the opportunity to earn a life-changing salary. The drive I had to close each deal was immense, and with every new recruit I grew in confidence. Knowing that I could lead people on that journey and get the result I wanted was unbelievably satisfying, and, of course, it was lucrative for me, too, and my earnings snowballed.

It was incredible to see these fairly ordinary guys come to work at Reid Trevena and grow in stature. First they'd start wearing better suits, then they'd take better holidays, then they'd buy a sports car, and then maybe a penthouse. And when you've got 500 people living that kind of life, it's impossible not to get high on the atmosphere.

Reid Trevena was an early example of the brokerages and financial services firms that came to epitomise the 1980s, and everything the company did was designed to make the employees sell more policies. Tom and Len arranged for motivational speakers to come and address the team; there were sales charts on the walls so that consultants could compare their performance against their colleagues', and every time they made a sale they had to ring the sales bell. And when the bell rang, everyone had to applaud, even if we were in the middle of a call ourselves. The atmosphere in this place was awesome, the place was always buzzing, and the noise was incredible. Every day someone would walk in with a new suit, a new car, a new gadget or a tan from a long-haul holiday: these were dynamic, hungry and confident people, and that environment spurred the team on to greater sales figures and bigger incomes.

I learned so much in those days about the dynamics of business and about how people perform, how they respond to encouragement and how they succeed. It was fascinating to see how people performed when they didn't have the safety net of a basic salary. From watching the motivational speakers and observing my colleagues, I quickly realised that I could use all of their sales techniques in recruitment, and the skills I learned in the early eighties were, without doubt, the foundation of the companies I would go on to create in the years to come.

I remember some of those motivational speakers very clearly. One told us how important appearances are when you work in sales. 'Everything about you is like a shop window – how you look, how you sound, how you present, how you walk, how you speak, your hair, your briefcase, your watch – everything about you becomes the window display. If you don't invest in yourself why would you expect to be successful? If you don't train yourself, if you don't dress yourself appropriately, what makes you think that your product is going to sell very well?' I must have heard this twenty-eight years ago, but that thirty-minute speech is still stuck in my head. It made perfect sense to me: after all, I had a budget for holidays, for my car, so why wouldn't I have a budget for myself? Ask yourself what you're going to invest in you this year. Should you go on a few more courses? Should you buy a few more clothes, buy a new pair of shoes? I stopped seeing these things as purchases, but as part of the investment in 'me'.

We had sessions on anything that would boost performance, like reading other people's body language, or what we could tell from the way someone shook hands. And when I started to use the techniques, I was surprised to see that they worked. Things like sitting on the same side of the desk as someone is more collaborative and more likely to build consensus.

I also watched Tom closely to see how he ran the business: I had always known that I wanted to start my own business, and now I was starting to see what kind of a business I wanted it to be. I was intrigued by how he was able to motivate people to such an extent, and how you could turn fairly ordinary performers into dynamic sellers. To do that, Tom worked hard at charging up the team and keeping the energy levels high.

The days at Reid Trevena were so well planned to ensure the momentum was maintained. Every morning there was a team meeting that got everyone psyched up. Sometimes I would go to some of the sales meetings just to experience the phenomenal atmosphere. The team leaders would get their people ready for the day by boosting their confidence about how well they were going to do.

'John, who are you going to call this morning? How many names have you got? Talk me through the names, John. That's terrific, are you going to do better than yesterday?'

'You bet!'

By 9.30 a.m. everybody would be on the phone, and if the team leader noticed someone had started slouching in their chair because they'd been knocked back five times in a row, he'd come round, get them off their chair and make them stand up. If you stand when you talk on the phone, your posture changes, you become more animated, and your mood improves. If people were getting a lot of rejection, they tended to bounce back better if they stood up.

Everything was about keeping the motivation levels high, and when people had been with us for a couple of months, the team leaders would start to talk to them about Porsches and long-haul holidays just to get them dreaming and thinking big. If you could make a guy believe he could drive a Porsche, then he started working harder to earn the money to pay for a Porsche. All the techniques Reid Trevena used were designed to increase people's belief in themselves, and I realised that what I was witnessing was a group of people talking their way to a fortune. Every day I watched everything that went on, observing how this huge sales machine enabled Len to drive an Aston Martin and Tom to have a choice of Mercedes parked in his drive when he was only thirty-five. I was like a sponge soaking it all up.

Everything the company was achieving was by dint of its passion, its adrenalin, its corporate self-belief, and if you worked there you couldn't help but be inspired. The place was electric all day, and I knew how rare that kind of atmosphere was because I'd worked in places like Alfred Marks. Even though I wasn't on the sales team, my time at Reid Trevena changed my perception of what I could achieve. Taking ordinary people and putting them into an environment where they were made to feel they could do things they had never previously thought of doing was simply exhilarating.

You might think I'd have been sitting there wanting to join the sales team so that I could earn as much as them, but it never crossed my mind. I was just sitting, watching, learning, absorbing. I knew I was acquiring a level of expertise that the recruitment industry doesn't generally have, nor does it teach. I had started to see recruitment as part of my own journey, and I worked hard at evaluating the future.

All around me were sales guys reviewing every lost sale, and just like them I would constantly review my technique, my failures and my successes: after all, if I hadn't placed people I'd have had a very mediocre lifestyle. So after every candidate left my office I would ask myself what I could have done differently. Did I match that person right? Did I not ask the right questions? Did I fail to close it? I reviewed my performance clinically.

I compare the process to something top sports professionals do. Take Roger Federer. Why is he a better tennis player than anyone else? It's a combination of talent, practice and analysis. If you play tennis for an hour a week, maybe you hit the ball 250 times. But imagine you play eight hours a day: how many times are you hitting the ball now? When you play that much, you learn that if you hit the ball in a certain way, or to a certain part of the court, you get different results. The slightest change in technique can mean the difference between winning and losing, and if you analyse every stroke then you teach yourself what works for you. And that's all I did: each call, each interview, each pitch was thoroughly analysed.

If there was a thermometer for recruitment, then I was starting to hit the red zone in terms of ability. In normal recruitment, consultants just match candidates and vacancies. At Reid Trevena I was selling someone an opportunity. However, no matter how good I was at getting people to believe in what was possible, I found that when candidates got home and started talking to their husbands or their wives, they would hear the words: 'What happens if you don't sell? We won't eat!' I could have spent over an hour with a candidate, but sometimes I couldn't get them to join us after they'd spoken to their partner, so I started looking for ways that would help me find out if a candidate was likely to say yes or not.

Without the skills I was acquiring, 95 per cent of the people who came in for an interview would have said, 'It sounds interesting but it's not for me.' So the skills I was honing allowed me to dig deep into their inner sense of security, their aspirations and ambitions. I believe that deep down everybody has those; there's just something inside that says 'I want to be more successful, I want to make a lot of money,' either for their family, for their security, for a sense of wellbeing, a sense of satisfaction or self-esteem. But those emotions don't just appear at an interview, people don't share them with you; my skill was to draw them out, to make people realise those feelings existed within them, make them understand that those emotions are real, and then to show them the journey that could fulfil them.

Introducing them to members of staff they would relate to was one way, and another was not to rush them into a decision: it had to be theirs, not mine, and I discovered a way of finding out just how keen they really were. I started to keep the initial interviews a bit shorter – it just wasn't viable to spend an hour with people who weren't going to say yes – and at the end of an initial chat I would say:

'That's great. I've got a number of people to interview, so why don't you give me a call. Let's see, it's Thursday today . . .'

I'd pick up my diary and look at my appointments.

'Monday's quite difficult, I've got a meeting at 2.30, it should finish at 3 p.m. What would be useful would be if you could give me a call around 3.10 p.m. and I'll give you a quick update on where we are.'

I'd write 3.10 p.m. and the candidate's name in my diary. I knew that if I'd oversold the opportunity, they'd call at 2.30; if I'd done the job exactly right and I'd pitched it correctly, they wouldn't call me until the clock struck 3.10 p.m., because if they really wanted it they would sit there, watching the clock until it was exactly ten past three. If I'd not done a good enough job and they still had some doubts and reservations, they'd call at four o'clock.

Over hundreds of interviews that barometer never lied, and I believed in it wholeheartedly. If I'd said to somebody, 'Give me a call back next week,' it was too vague and I couldn't gauge anything by when they called. So I started to say, 'Give me a call on Monday,' but, again, I couldn't learn anything. Then, when I started giving people a specific time to call, it began to get interesting. If I'd said call at noon and someone called at 1.30, I realised that was telling me something. So when I booked them for a second interview, I made a note in the diary 'She still has reservations'. Then, when she came in, I'd really try to drill down and see what was bugging her, because otherwise there was no point in carrying on with the process. I wouldn't discuss anything about the job until I'd found out what was bugging her. Maybe her mother had told her that her mortgage was at risk; whatever it was, I wouldn't stop until I had uncovered the 'but' or the 'however' that was unsettling her.

'It's great, James; however, I'm not sure because I've got this promotion due at the moment and I've been there eight years. I'm not sure if this is really the right time.'

Bingo! That's what's bothering her, it's the promotion. If I wasn't able to glean those little nuggets, I could do another two interviews and at the eleventh hour she still wouldn't have joined.

Obviously I was motivated to get results because I was on a commission, but I was also genuinely concerned that candidates were happy to join the company. It goes back to my dad's philosophy, his 'win-win' formula. I couldn't build a relationship with candidates – who I'd be working with for the next few years – if they thought they were being misled or oversold the opportunity. If they weren't genuinely happy about the prospect of joining Reid Trevena, then neither was I.

Perhaps the most lucrative technique I borrowed from the sales team at Reid Trevena was the one that secured referrals for future sales. As soon as the sales force had signed up a new customer, they were told to ask if they knew anyone else who might also be interested in saving for their future. If the customer believed he'd just made a smart move, more often than not he would want his friends to know about it and give the sales rep the names and numbers of four or five people. Most of our sales team were making £20k to £30k a year, but those who got the most referrals could be making £60k a year.

Cold-calling is not only time-consuming but it's also soul-destroying, so having a name, a number and an introduction allows you to make many more sales in the same timeframe. I realised that if I used the same referrals techniques there was no limit to what I could earn.

There was one guy, Adrian, who always came back to the office with a fistful of referrals. After he'd rung the sales bell, he would sit down and get straight on the phone. He had clearly perfected the art of referrals, so I asked him if I could go on the road with him on the pretence of being able to tell new recruits more about the job. I was amazed at his skill. He would say things to his clients like: 'So are you married, have you got brothers, sisters? Yes? What does your sister do? She's a doctor. Wow, that must be fascinating, tell me about your sister . . .'

Without fail, the client would drop their sister's name into the conversation because Adrian would ask something seemingly innocuous like, 'Are you close?', and the client would say 'Annabel and I never got on as kids, but now . . .' and Adrian made a mental note of the name.

'Where did you say your sister worked?'

'The Royal London Hospital.'

'And how's Annabel getting on?'

Using the sister's name seemed friendly; it made clients relax and then they were even more likely to sign up. At the end of each sale, Adrian would turn to his client and, say: 'Samantha, are you pleased with what you've done with us today?'

'I'm really happy.'

'Do you think Annabel would find something like this useful in terms of building for her future?'

And so he left with Annabel's number as well as an endorsement from her sister. He was brilliant, so I started to use his techniques, too. Referrals would mean I could drive a Mercedes like Tom's.

'So tell me, Anthony, how long have you been with Rank Xerox?'

'Three years.'

'So you must know the place pretty well. How big's the sales team there?'

'Eight.'

'Is that just your team, or are there lots of teams?'

'There are five teams.'

'Out of interest, Anthony, where do you think you rank in your team?'

'Honestly, I'm probably the number four'.

By the time I'd finished with a candidate, I'd have the names of the three best sales people in the company. I would even say things like: 'You must have a league table at Xerox – have you got a copy of the league table?' and people would leave me a copy of their league table that had the entire sales team's names on it and told me how long they'd been there and all sorts of other pieces of information that helped me persuade them to join the company. With more success, I started to get a bit more confident, and by the time I left Reid Trevena I had developed another technique that helped me get people to join us.

'So, Jo, based on what we've discussed today, do you think there's anyone else in your office who might like to work here?'

'Well, there's Kate . . .'

'Tell me about Kate, how would she do here?'

'I think she'd love it . . .'

'Can you do me a favour, Jo?'

'Sure.'

At this point I'd hand Jo the phone.

'Would you call Kate for me?'

What was she going to say in front of me? She was going to say: 'Kate, I'm sitting with this guy James Caan who's just offered me an amazing job at this fantastic company and I've been telling him how great you are. I'm going to hand you over to him.'

'Kate, hi, Jo's told me you'd fit in brilliantly here. What are you doing on Tuesday morning? Can you make 10 a.m.?'

If this seems incredible, let me break it down into its basic component: all I ever did was ask questions. That's the only secret. I'd learned that whatever it was in the world that I wanted to know, it was already in someone else's head. I just had to ask them. Try it. You'll be surprised how readily people will give you the answer you're after. People like to help; they don't naturally lie, so when you say, 'What's the average pay in your office?' or 'Can you give me three names of someone who can start work tomorrow?', it is surprisingly easy to get surprisingly good results. Seriously, all you have to do is ask.

It got to the stage where the vast majority of people I hired came through referrals, which meant my income soared. I would usually take home £3–4k a month, and often that would be closer to £7k. My best ever month netted me £13k when I poached an entire sales team from another company.

Like any nineteen-year-old earning that kind of money – and with inflation I guess I was averaging £15k a month in today's money – I wasn't putting it into a pension. Despite the fact that I was selling the wisdom of savings plans to every new recruit, I was never tempted to take one out myself. I had long believed that my father had never benefited from his savings, and I wasn't about to repeat what I saw as his mistake. So I spent it.

Where previously I might have spent £500 on a watch, now I spent £5000; I spent £13k on a Mercedes; I went from spending £100 on a suit to £400; and in a restaurant the bill doubled as I discovered better and better places.

I moved out of the flat in Kensington because the commute to Reid Trevena's offices in Farringdon was a bit of a schlep. A friend was moving out of a two-bedroom flat nearer the office. Although it was more in rent – £18 a week, I seem to remember – I sublet the other room, which covered my share of the rent.

Although the new place was bigger and had a proper kitchen, I still didn't spend very much time there. After work I would go for a drink with colleagues – I had recruited most of them so I had a very good relationship with pretty much everyone in the company – and then we'd go on to dinner, and then maybe to a club. I think we were all earning so much money that we were naturally drifting away from our old friends and towards each other. Some of the people I met at Reid Trevena are still great friends today.

I said earlier that working at Reid Trevena changed my life, and I really mean it. Working in such a dynamic environment inspired and moulded me and gave me the confidence really to believe in myself. I now knew about recruitment from the agency side and the client side, and I was really laying the foundations for what would come next.

I continued to deal with outside agencies as I couldn't always meet our demand for new members of staff, and I maintained good relationships with them. When I went to visit their offices I couldn't help but be struck by the difference in atmosphere between Reid Trevena and pretty much everywhere else. Their offices were all so dull, with no buzz and no atmosphere, and it got me thinking that, by and large, the recruitment industry was seriously lacking in sales skills. If the team at Reid Trevena averaged a nine or a ten for sales skills, then most people in recruitment were a three or a four because they essentially just matched candidates with vacancies.

However, I also knew that recruitment agencies made a lot of money, even though the individual consultants didn't – even getting 10 per cent commission was rare. I suppose it was then that I had an idle thought: *I wonder what would happen if you took the atmosphere of Reid Trevena, the techniques for getting referrals, paid a generous commission that attracted the best people and took it into the recruitment industry?* I wasn't seriously considering going it alone just yet, but something was definitely brewing.

Before that 'something' could develop, though, there are two more reasons why Reid Trevena has had such a lasting impact on me. The first is that within a few years the company went bust. When the Financial Services Act of 1986 was introduced it changed the way financial products were sold and forced companies like Reid Trevena to reveal the commission they were getting. So when a rep went out, he had to show his client that Reid Trevena was getting paid the first two years' contributions as their fee. Unsurprisingly, pretty much everyone then turned round and said: 'So for the first two years, I'm not actually saving anything?' It became virtually impossible to sell any more policies.

It ruined Tom. He lost everything. The house, the business, it all went because he had expanded too quickly and had branches outside London that just couldn't pay for themselves. His fixed overheads – rent, rates, professional services – stayed the same when his income crashed and the company went under. This made a lasting impression on me: the Koran teaches us that there are several things in life that we are not in control of – things like when we are born and when we die – and one of them is also that we are not in control of our wealth. For years I couldn't see how this could be, but in recent years I have come to understand that it is true. I've now met many people who have lost fortunes and I know that whatever we have, we could all lose it. So much of what I have achieved in the years since Reid Trevena has been motivated by the fear of repeating their mistakes, and I tell myself that nothing lasts for ever. Next year it could all disappear. To this day my biggest drive is my fear of failure. I used to want to emulate everything Tom did, but that changed when his company went under.

The other reason why I still say that Reid Trevena changed my life is Aisha.

Chapter 8

Aisha (1981–1982)

'To Aisha I must have seemed like a respectable guy in a nice suit with a good job, and I wasn't about to shatter that illusion.'

WHEN YOU SIT DOWN to write your life story, you can see there are days and events that changed your life immediately, irrevocably, and sometimes it's only with hindsight that you can spot the moment things changed. One of those days when my life changed without me knowing it was 9 November 1981, the day my future wife came in for an interview. By this stage I was so good at judging whether or not someone would fit in at Reid Trevena that the preliminary interviews only lasted fifteen minutes. I knew instinctively if the candidate had what it took, and, if they didn't, I was good at closing the interview very quickly.

'Thanks for coming in, Tiffany. Great to meet you. Leave it with me, and if you give us a call next week, I'll let you know.' Bang, close, move on, next person. I had just done several hours of interviewing four candidates an hour, and the last person who was booked in that afternoon was a chic Asian woman who had responded to an ad I'd placed for a marketing trainee, which was really just a way of saying 'Insurance salespeople required'! It was the end of the day, I was a bit tired and I was far more interested in going out that night than talking to the final candidate, so I just went through the motions.

'Tell me a bit about yourself, what have you done before?'

As she started talking, I realised to my surprise that I was quite intrigued by her. She wasn't like most Asian girls I'd met. She had dressed fairly soberly for the interview – something I would soon find out was pretty unusual – but her personality was really feisty, and I was really quite taken aback by her confidence because most Asian girls I knew were more demure. I became quite intrigued by her, in part because I'd never been out with an Asian girl before. She was very attractive, slim, bright, well educated – I could see from her CV that she'd got a distinction from the London College of Fashion – but she'd taken a job as a designer that wasn't working out and now she was wondering if she should be doing something else.

It was a bit unfair on her because I got to ask all the questions, and because I did it for a living I was very good at fishing for information. I'd seen how my sisters had been raised, so I knew there were cultural protocols to be observed, but I didn't want to seem crass and come right out and say 'Are you allowed to date?' So I started asking fairly plausible questions that appeared to be about the job but that had a double meaning for me.

'One of the things I thought might be worth bearing in mind is a lot of the clients can't see us during the day, so sometimes we have to see clients in the evenings. Does that cause you any problems at all?'

'Absolutely not, I'm pretty relaxed about that.'

That was exactly what I wanted to hear.

'And sometimes we have conferences in other cities and we have to stay the night. Are you comfortable with those issues?'

'Very comfortable.'

She was giving as good as she got, and there was a bit of fire about her. I had never met a girl like her and I just wanted to know more. At twenty-two she was nearly two years older than me. Although I wouldn't be twenty-one until the end of December, people had assumed I was older than I was for so long that by this point I couldn't actually tell you the last time I had dated anyone younger than me. It took me a while to realise that the usual fifteen minutes I spent with candidates had become an hour, and I'd moved on to ask her about her family. 'How many sisters have you got?' 'Where do you hang out?' I had a licence to ask her anything I wanted. Her background was very different from mine: her parents were from Bombay and had professional careers – her dad was a civil servant and her mum worked for the Law Society – and she had been encouraged to study. It struck me how different our influences had been, and I found that difference really intriguing.

Towards the end of the interview, I'd definitely gone beyond 'Is she right for the job?' to 'I think she's right for me!' but I didn't quite know what to do about it: asking her straight out seemed inappropriate, even though I had done that with candidates before. All I knew was that I wanted to see her again.

'I think you'd really fit in here, so I'd like to see you again for a second interview.'

I gave her a training script we used with new recruits.

'Take a look at this, and when you come back we can go through it together and see how you get on. Let's talk on Monday and put a date in the diary.'

It just so happened that I was having lunch with my parents that weekend and found myself telling them that I'd met a girl. I never told them about my private life, so they knew instantly that something was going on.

'What's her name?'

'Aisha Patel.'

There was a moment's silence as they took in that it was an Asian name.

'You're wasting your time,' my father said. 'She's a Hindu.'

It's true that 99 per cent of Patels are Hindu, but I was sure she'd said something or other about a festival that had made me think she was definitely a Muslim.

'You probably weren't listening properly because you were too busy looking.'

Obviously, having never dated an Asian woman before I didn't really care about her religion and didn't understand the implications, but my dad was adamant that a Hindu girl wouldn't be allowed to date a Muslim boy.

My father might have completely dismissed her but I hadn't, and the following week I decided I was going to make it my mission to get Aisha to join the company.

'Hi, Aisha, it's James Caan from Reid Trevena. I just wanted to catch up with you, find out your thoughts about the position we discussed last week.'

'Hi, James.' Instantly there was something in her voice that made me think she wasn't interested.

'I thought we should put a date in the diary for your second interview.'

'Oh.'

'What? Are you busy this week?'

'It's not that. I talked it over with my father and showed him the script you gave me. He made me realise that the job you're offering isn't really marketing, it's selling insurance. We talked it over and we decided that I should stick with being a fashion designer. It's what I trained to do.'

What?! You can't do that! That wasn't part of the plan! So I immediately had to back-pedal: I realised that she wasn't going to be my colleague, but I still wanted to see her. So as casually as I could manage, I asked her to tell me more about fashion and the career she was hoping for.

'What aspect of fashion are you looking to pursue?'

I really didn't know that much about fashion – I certainly wasn't going to mention Mr Buyrite – but I just needed to keep her talking for a few minutes while I came up with a strategy.

'So are you thinking of manufacturing, or retailing?'

We talked for a few minutes but I wasn't really listening because I was collecting my own thoughts. *How do I get control of the situation again?*

'You know, that's very interesting; it's really strange because I've always been interested in fashion, my dad is a specialist in leather garment manufacture. In many ways it's the second love of my life. To think that's what you want to pursue, that's incredible!'

She started to tell me about her hopes and ambitions for her career.

'Ultimately, what I really want to do is have my own brand, my own boutique. I've always talked about having a boutique called the House of Aisha. It might be a bit far-fetched, but it's actually what I want to do.'

A boutique? A business! I was in.

'When you say setting up your own boutique, how would that work? Where would you have it?'

I can't remember her answers, but I said something like: 'I think this could be really interesting, I know some people who might be useful, so why don't we meet for lunch and we can talk about it.'

She seemed a little surprised. 'OK, well, I'm always in town, so why don't I give you a call when I'm next around?'

'I'd really like that.'

We met for lunch the following week, and it was clear there was a bit of chemistry between us, but I still wasn't quite sure where we stood because she was an Asian girl. I'd established by now that she definitely was a Muslim and, as dating Asian Muslim girls is traditionally a no-no, I wasn't quite sure where the boundaries were. I knew I couldn't just ask her out on a date, so the conversation was all about her dreams of opening a boutique. As she talked I realised that she didn't just have a dream, she had a plan, and I found that really impressive. I had never had a plan in my life, but she had real structure to back up her ambitions.

As she talked, I couldn't help but get swept up in her passion for the idea, her commitment to it, and I actually found her quite inspiring. At times, I was saying things without really thinking because the conversation was flowing so freely. She told me that her dad was going to back her, and I realised that this was my chance to get involved in her plans.

'You know, when you find this boutique I would love to back you, too, because I think it sounds pretty incredible. So if you want, you could have me as a business partner.'

Did I just say that? Oops, I think I really did. *Never mind, it's just talk. Most likely nothing will come of it.* The conversation moved on and I pretty much forgot that I'd said it, and I suppose I was hoping that she would forget, too, but towards the end of the week she called me up.

'I've spoken to my dad and told him that you're interested in backing me. He's a bit concerned because he doesn't know you. I've told him a bit about you and I've convinced him you're genuinely interested.'

'I am.'

'So he was suggesting that you put half the money in each. Is that OK?'

'Sounds great.'

'I thought you'd say that, so I've set up some viewings of premises with a couple of agents. There are three booked in for Saturday and I was wondering if you'd like to come along.'

'Sure.'

My first thought, if I'm honest, was 'What a great reason for us to hang out together', and if I really did somehow invest in her business then we'd have a reason to be together, and from her parents' point of view that would be acceptable. I was pretty confident at this point in my life, and I made the decision that I was going to continue to push the boundaries with her until somebody told me to stop.

The following Saturday, Aisha and I went to look at shops in South Molton Street and Camden Town but I wasn't really paying much attention, because I didn't really think for one second that I would invest in her. And there was a very good reason for that: I didn't have that kind of money!

To Aisha I must have seemed like a respectable guy in a nice suit with a good job, and I wasn't about to shatter that illusion with a confession that I didn't have whatever kind of money she would need. Besides, as we talked to the agents I was quickly realising that the chances of her being offered a lease were pretty slim. We were learning that retail was – and is – all about covenants, and every landlord wants to rent his shop to somebody who's got a track record. The chances of somebody in a prime location saying 'Let's take a flyer on a designer who's never run a business before' were pretty slim. I reasoned that I would never need to confess my lack of funds.

We stopped off for a bit of lunch and the conversation was really flowing. All of a sudden, Aisha looked serious.

'I need to ask you a question.'

'OK. Ask away.'

'I'm a bit confused about you. Who are you, where are you from?'

'How do you mean?'

'Let's start with the name. James Caan – you're an Asian guy but the name doesn't fit.'

'Why do you ask?' By this stage I was very well trained at interviews and I knew that you should never answer a question directly. You should always ask a question yourself until you understand what's really being asked. I was realising that she was checking me out, which was understandable: her father wouldn't let her go into business with just anyone.

'I suppose I'm just curious to see whether you're a Muslim or not.'

'Would you like me to be a Muslim?'

'No, I just want you to tell me!'

'Of course I am!' I'd said it quite flippantly and she obviously thought I was playing with her.

'You're not, are you?'

'Absolutely. And I'll prove it.' When I was growing up, my mum had sent me and my brothers and sisters for religious education to learn about the faith as well as a bit of Arabic so that we would be able recite the most important prayers.

'What's the most relevant prayer in Arabic that a Muslim would know?'

She thought about it for a second. 'Surat Al Fatiha.'

So I recited this prayer in Arabic, and her face just glowed! I could tell from the look on her face and her body language that it was quite important to her. I was now sure that there was more going on here than just shopping around for a boutique.

From then on we started to see a little more of each other, but always on the pretext of the business. So I would call and say that I wanted to get together to go over the numbers, or to talk about the pros and cons of a particular location. Over the next few months we saw several shops all over London, and then one day Aisha rang and said there was a unit available in a shopping centre in Wood Green.

'Do you want to come with me?'

'I'll pick you up at ten!'

It was a really nice shopping centre with all the big brands, so I instantly said to myself that they wouldn't take us seriously but that we'd have a nice lunch somewhere and make a day of it. Before we left, we met the centre manager and a couple of other executives and I was quite surprised that they were making encouraging noises.

'We're interested in your idea for a boutique, so if we were to consider your shop, what would you want to do here?'

To my amazement, Aisha came up with a brilliant pitch. I worked with the best salespeople in the country at the time, so I knew a good pitch when I heard one.

'All shopping centres and high streets today are dominated by the same brands and every high street is the same. What I think they need is individuality, individual designers. Customers need a choice. Let's face it, Miss Selfridge, BHS and Chelsea Girl all sell pretty much the same thing. I think what I can do is bring a new dimension, be different, be creative. Here's my portfolio . . .'

She also showed them excellent references from her college which went a long way to convincing them that she would be a good tenant. I just sat there without saying anything and watched how the manager was really engaging with everything she was saying, and I was very impressed. If I'd bothered to save any of my earnings and had accrued any money in the bank, I had no doubts that I would have invested in her like a shot. I liked her already, but I was really falling for her now.

'Well, Aisha, I think you're exactly what this place needs. A bit of individual design could really work for us. We'll have a think about it and get back to you.'

As we walked to lunch, Aisha was really positive. She couldn't stop talking but I was quiet. At the back of my mind I was thinking: they might just run with this. I'd still not really given any thought to what would happen if she asked me to come good on my offer.

So, of course, two weeks later Aisha rang me up and was absolutely ecstatic: they'd offered her the shop!

'Wow, that's incredible, amazing, well done!'

I don't know if my voice betrayed what I was really feeling, but when I put the phone down all I could think was *What am I going to do now?* All of a sudden, what had started out as a jokey comment had actually come down to one thing: where's the money? If I didn't come up with the money, I guessed I would probably never see Aisha again.

I had no idea what kind of money was involved. I knew how much the rent was on the shop, but nothing else. I decided not to panic too much until I knew what the other costs were. Over the next couple of days we totted up the costs of fixtures and fittings and buying the stock. The idea was that she would buy in 50 per cent of the stock and the other 50 per cent would be her own designs.

Aisha knew someone in the display department of Miss Selfridge who was getting rid of old fittings, so that saved us some money, but the other costs kept adding up. In the end, the figure we came to was £60,000. I had no idea where I was going to find my share. Sure, I was earning good money, but £30k represented about half my annual salary. Even if I poached an entire sales team I couldn't earn that kind of cash in the timeframe.

By now, it had definitely become more about dating than business, and we had started to go out socially. Aisha had been given the same level of freedom I had enjoyed growing up. Her parents were pretty liberal, which made her quite unusual for an Asian girl. I remember being with my brother in a nightclub when Aisha turned up in a metallic electric-blue jumpsuit. She really was the epitome of a fashion designer, wearing black lipstick and thick black eyeliner, and I can still see my brother's face as he took her in: *Where did she come from?*

When I took Aisha to meet my parents they had a similar reaction: they had never met anyone like her either. I hadn't taken a girl home before, so they knew I was serious. Everyone was very polite, but my dad – typically – wasted no time in getting to the point:

'So your name is Patel – where does that name come from?'

Aisha patiently explained that her grandmother was from Burma and her mum was from Bombay. The fact that her family was from India and mine from Pakistan had to be discussed. The

Asian community is very concerned about ticking boxes – your sect, your religion, background, country of origin, family – but even though those boxes were utterly irrelevant to me, my dad had really strong views on each one of them.

By this point, Aisha knew how important my father was to me, and she made a real effort with him. She is naturally a very tactile person, and in our house this was very unusual: I had never really seen anyone hug my father, but the remarkable thing was he didn't back off when she hugged him, which was weird to see. The family really took to her – I think they were all intrigued because she was so modern and well spoken – but because it was only the first time they'd met her no one was going to give me their opinion of her. Except, of course, my dad.

'It won't work out,' he told me afterwards.

He thought she was too strong, had too many opinions and knew what she wanted. My dad's perception was that I would need somebody domesticated, who would stay at home with the kids, very much the traditional wife – and that's just not Aisha. My dad's observations about Aisha were absolutely correct, but where he was wrong was in thinking that was what I would want in a wife. For me to marry a woman who wasn't strong was an absolute no-no: it just wouldn't have suited my character.

As the months went on, my dad started to change his opinion about Aisha, and it was clear he was really responding to her. She would sit in his lap – something not even my sisters did – and when she was around the whole family dynamic changed. She had completely charmed him, and his scepticism about our future began to subside.

When I had met Aisha's family, obviously we'd had the boutique to talk about, but the day came when Aisha told me that her dad wanted to talk to me, and it wasn't about the business.

I found her dad really quite charming, and it was nice that he wanted to look out for his daughter and check that I wasn't a bad influence. He wanted to know what my plans were, where I worked, what I was earning: basically, if I was good marriage material. He never asked me whether I had the funds to back Aisha, which was funny, because it was something I never mentioned to my parents either. But that was because I knew they were going to say 'Where will you get the money from?' and I still didn't have an answer. By now, the thought of letting Aisha down, of being found out, was just awful. I had to find the money.

In fact, there wasn't much I wouldn't have done for Aisha. At first, I wondered if I could borrow it from my dad, but I knew my dad was going to think 'Is he thinking with his heart or his head?' and be reluctant to get involved. Besides, having left home to prove I could do things on my own, I wasn't minded to ask him for money now. However, since making the flippant comment that I would back her, I'd become more and more convinced that Aisha was a good investment: she had passion, commitment, determination – all the qualities of a successful entrepreneur. Even if I wasn't dating her I would have invested in her, so I had to find the money from somewhere.

I was definitely starting to think that we had a long-term future, but I was still only twenty-one and didn't feel ready for marriage. For me, marriage meant having a family, and that meant having enough money to give the kids a good home and a good education. And while my income might have given me a great bachelor lifestyle, I didn't feel it was a good enough income for a family.

Ever since we had met, I had known that Aisha had assumed I was older than her, and I wasn't in any rush to shatter that illusion. We'd been seeing each other for about six months when we went to a party where, by chance, we bumped into a mutual friend. Aisha asked him how he knew me.

'He was in the same class as my brother.'

As soon as he said this, I could see Aisha's face change. She knew his brother, and she knew that he was no older than twenty-one. Her face was saying, *How could he have been at school with him? The maths don't add up.*

In the car driving her home she asked if I remembered the brother.

'You know what, I'm not sure.'

'Come on, you must remember!' She wasn't about to let it go.

'I don't know. He might have been at my school.'

The next time we saw each other, it soon became clear that she had done a bit of research. She'd called up the brother and found some reason to ask him about me, and, unfortunately for me, he had remembered me very well and confirmed that we'd been in the same class.

'It seems you were at school together,' she said.

'Really? I still don't think I remember him.'

'I don't care if you remember him, I care how old you are.'

I looked at her and couldn't stop myself from laughing.

I told her the truth and she was genuinely shocked. I was at least five years younger than she had expected, and nearly two years younger than her. My saving grace was that there was a similar age gap between her parents – her mum is a couple of years older than her dad – and if it hadn't been for that, I'm really not sure how we would have moved on from there.

I was starting to panic about my lack of funds for the boutique, although I somehow knew that I would find the money. I was calculating that it would take a lawyer a while to negotiate the lease, so that would take six weeks or so, then there would be another delay waiting for stock to come in. In reality, I reckoned I had a couple of months to find the cash.

The conventional source of funds is a bank, so that was where I looked first. My conversations with bank managers usually went like this:

'Have you got any experience?'

'No.'

'Have you got a business plan?'

'Not really'.

'Have you been in business before?'

'No.'

'Do you own your own property that you can offer as security?'

'No.'

'Then I'm afraid we can't help you, Mr Caan.'

I then got the idea that I should try a branch of a bank in Mayfair or Park Lane, somewhere where £30k wasn't very much in comparison to their other deals. There was no logic to that, but as I was sitting in reception in the Mayfair branch of Lloyds, I noticed a leaflet promoting a new credit card. 'Apply for an American Express Gold Card today.' If it came to it, I thought, I could get a credit card, so I put it in my pocket and headed for another pointless meeting with another unhelpful bank manager.

On the Tube back to Reid Trevena's Farringdon offices I started reading the leaflet. To apply for a gold card, you had to open an account, but if you had a gold card Lloyds would give you a £10,000 overdraft facility. It sounded too good to be true, so I rang up Amex to check the details. They told me that as long as I had an income of £20k a year I would get their gold card. I earned over £20k, so that wasn't a problem. And I checked with Lloyds that they would give me an overdraft. The key thing about the overdraft was that it was unsecured – I didn't need an asset to offer as security. So I opened a bank account and applied for the card. When I got my first statement is said the magic words: *Overdraft facility – £10,000.*

This was great, but I was still £20k short. However, it turned out that NatWest had teamed up with Access to offer the same deal, and Barclays was doing the same with Barclaycard. By the time the House of Aisha needed my contribution, I had the overdrafts in place.

The fact that I was so comfortable going into debt for Aisha was telling me something about how strong my feelings for her were.

She was clearly more significant than any girl I had dated before, and I thought that – even though I was only twenty-one – I wanted to spend the rest of my life with her: I just couldn't imagine not having her in my life.

When I was round at my parents my dad asked how things were going with Aisha and I told him that I was very serious about her.

'Do you want to marry her?'

'One day, I think that's exactly what I want.'

'One day? Why not now?'

I told him that I felt I didn't have much to offer. 'I can't afford a house, and I can't afford to give a family a good start. I think I should have those things before I can ask her to marry me.'

My dad then said something that made perfect sense to me. 'Why do you think it's your responsibility to provide those things? Marriage is about "we" not "I". Why don't you get those things together?'

He had met Aisha enough times by then to know she was never going to be a typical housewife who would expect her husband to provide for her. Marriage was a journey we could start out on together, and as he spoke I could hear the penny drop. Rather than leaving it for four or five years until I'd saved up, why didn't we get those things together?

I was due to go on holiday in a couple of days' time, and my dad suggested that while I was away I should think about it. Getting married was a big step for a twenty-one-year-old, but the more I thought about us starting out together as equals, the more confident I felt about our future. Looking back, I can see just how smart my father was: because Aisha and I have built everything together we've always been a partnership of equals, and I think that gave us the best possible chance of happiness right from the start. By the end of the holiday I had decided that I would propose, and one of the first things I did when I got home was drive over to her house and ask her to marry me. She said yes.

When Aisha told her parents, their response was that – in our culture – what really needed to happen was for my parents to visit them and make a formal proposal for their daughter. There were rituals that needed to be observed, gifts that needed to be exchanged: it was all new to me.

My parents were quite excited when I told them and were enthusiastic about going to Aisha's parents' house to give each other gifts, but I hadn't anticipated any of this, and suddenly a relationship that had been between just the pair of us was feeling a little crowded. It was all a bit . . . official.

However, after a few weeks I got completely caught up in the celebrations and preparations, and it started to dawn on me just what a commitment I was making. What surprised me was how much I liked that feeling, how much I realised I wanted to be married, and how ready I felt for that commitment.

I decided we needed a place of our own, so I looked around for a flat to buy and found one in a building in Highgate. It was the penthouse in a really nice block in North Hill, and the agent who was showing me around had another flat left in the block to sell.

I was young, I was cocky, so I asked the obvious question: 'What if I buy both? Would you give me a better deal?' I think I negotiated to pay £45k for both flats, but of course I only needed one, and could only get a mortgage for one. So I persuaded Bernie to buy the one on the ground floor and I moved into the penthouse. I asked Aisha to move in with me, but that was out of the question. We would have to be married first.

Chapter 9

Open for Business
(1982–1984)

'*I never would have imagined that there would be days when we took no money at all, or that there would be weeks when the takings didn't cover the rent.*'

NOW WANTED TO get married as soon as possible, and while our parents made arrangements for the wedding we concentrated on getting the shop open. Although I continued to work at Reid Trevena Monday to Friday, I spent every Saturday in the shop, and it was clear from the start that Aisha and I had completely opposite views on almost everything.

I was very driven by margin and profit: to me it was all about what a customer paid for a garment versus what we'd paid for it. For Aisha, it was about the designs and developing a customer base through attentive service. Sometimes I'd watch her put an outfit together for a customer and she had a choice of a silk blouse at £80 and a cotton blouse at £30 with a much smaller profit margin, but if the cotton blouse looked better that's the one Aisha would choose. And if I was with a customer who was umming and ahhing about the price, I'd be willing to negotiate, but for Aisha what it said on the ticket was what the customer ought to pay.

There were a couple of times when we just couldn't agree, so I took her out for dinner and said: 'Look, every time I say black you say white. This is never going to work. We need to have some parameters, so let's agree what we're both good at.'

We took out a piece of paper and made two columns – A and J. In Aisha's column were all the things she was good at, like design, knowledge of trends, merchandising, dressing the shop; and in my column was all the stuff I was going to deal with, like rent, overheads, cash flow, banking. We agreed that she could have an opinion about how I ran the finances but nothing would be her decision, and I could have an opinion on whether she bought a certain range or not, but those things would ultimately be her decision. We had quite a formal, serious debate about what each of us would do, and after that the business started to find its feet.

I had wanted to start a business all my life, and, although this was Aisha's boutique, it was our business. We learned so much in those early days; whether it was hiring an accountant or handling cash flow, I was building on the skills I had picked up at my dad's side. We hadn't written a business plan for the House of Aisha, and if we had it would have been utterly useless because there were so many things that we just couldn't have anticipated. I never would have imagined that there would be days when we took no money at all, or that there would be weeks when the takings didn't cover the rent. I was learning what a responsibility running a business is and that ultimately the buck stopped with me.

We were married on New Year's Day 1983 in Regent's Park mosque, just four days after my twenty-second birthday. It was a fairly traditional wedding, and a lot of the rituals were unfamiliar to me, so I basically did what my mum told me to do! For instance, I was told it's traditional for the groom to buy the bride's sisters' outfits for the wedding, so that's what I did. It was oddly daunting suddenly to be immersed in a culture I was a part of and yet distant from, but I found the actual wedding really exciting.

For the first time, I was doing something permanent. Since the age of sixteen, whether it had been a flat or a girlfriend or a job, I had always seen myself in transit from A to B. All of a sudden I was making this big statement, this solemn commitment, and it made a big impression on me. Mentally, I changed when I got married. I realised that I had to be a responsible adult, and the remarkable thing was that I wanted to be that responsible person. I was happy to say goodbye to the flippant past and I was ready for the commitments and responsibilities of marriage. I also couldn't wait to become a father.

We'd been married for about three months when three bank statements came through the post. I was opening the mail while we were having breakfast, and Aisha must have seen the statements over my shoulder.

'What's that for?' she asked.

'Oh, nothing much. I took a loan out.'

'You didn't tell me you had a loan.'

'It's not a big deal.' I was hoping the matter would go away, but Aisha wasn't going to be satisfied without a proper answer.

'What did you need the money for?'

I looked at her, not quite sure what I would say. I chose the truth.

'That thirty grand.'

Her face was a picture.

'What did you say?'

I explained what I had done, and she couldn't quite believe it.

'You mean you didn't have the money?'

I had to tell her that I didn't. 'What matters', I said in my defence, 'is that I said I would back you and I did. I could have borrowed from my dad, or somebody at work, I don't know; all I know is that I was supposed to come up with my share.'

There was a trace of anger in her voice, but on the other hand she was also quite impressed. I explained I was relaxed about the repayments – I could easily afford them – and the debt wasn't secured against anything anyway.

As I embarked on a family life of my own, my father announced that he was moving back to Pakistan. None of his children showed any interest in taking over his business, and without that as a possibility he didn't see the point in carrying on.

'What am I doing it for if it's not for you?'

He had saved enough money to keep him in retirement, and so the decision for him to move back was straightforward. For my mother and my youngest siblings it wasn't so easy. They didn't want to go – my mother didn't want to live in a different country from any of her children – and the kids were upset at having to change schools, lose friends and go to a country where they really didn't speak much of the language. Nevertheless, as ever it was virtually impossible to disobey my father, and so they went with him.

Instead of moving back to Lahore, they chose Karachi, which is more cosmopolitan, more developed, and my dad probably felt they were more likely to adjust to Karachi than Lahore. I didn't feel good about him going because I knew he felt that we had let him down by not wanting to take over the business. Him going to Pakistan was like when I'd left home, only in reverse: I'd said, 'I'll show you,' and now he was doing the same thing.

My younger brother Andrew was old enough at eighteen to defy my dad, and he stayed in London. I wanted to look out for him, and one of the ways I did this was by buying my parents' house in Forest Gate. I paid the market price for it, a) because my father wasn't about to sell it cheap, even to his son, and b) because the rent on it was nearly twice the mortgage. So I told Andrew that I would buy it and he could rent the other rooms out, and in exchange for managing it for me he could live there for free.

With the money from the house and my income from Reid Trevena, the boutique didn't need to make a profit for us to eat, but we were definitely not running the shop as some kind of hobby for Aisha. She had been asked to start lecturing two days a week at her old college, the London College of Fashion, which was quite a pat on the back for a former student, so we hired a manageress to work full time in the boutique. Lecturing allowed Aisha to immerse herself in the fashion world and keep up to date on trends, colours and seasons, which would ultimately be good for the business.

Inevitably, though, in the first few months we made our mistakes, the biggest of which was buying a range that just didn't sell. Out of 100 pieces we managed to sell ten, and for weeks we sat staring at these garments knowing that we were never going to shift them. Marking them down was actually quite hard emotionally, and when they got down to our cost price and we still couldn't shift them, we were really stumped. What were we supposed to do with them now? Offloading bad stock to market traders below cost price certainly wasn't something we'd anticipated. There were even ranges that we just had to bin. And then there was the weather to consider: if we had summer clothes on display and the temperature dipped, we would struggle. But then if a pop star wore something that we had in stock it would fly out of the shop.

We learned quickly and, after three or four months, the boutique had sales of a couple of grand a week. After a few more months, we realised that we had actually underestimated the market, underestimated the customer base and the opportunities in Wood Green, and we started talking about expansion.

I still spent every Saturday in the shop, and Sunday was taken up with trips to designers' studios, to factories, and to check out the competition. It was impossible not to be aware of history repeating itself as I was doing exactly what my father had done, and exactly what I said I would never do! However, I found the business fascinating, and it didn't feel like work.

By the end of our first year the business was pretty comfortable, and as we geared up for Christmas 1983 we were stunned by how much money the boutique was taking. I reckon we made £100k profit that first year, and with my commissions tailing off at Reid Trevena as the financial services market slumped, Aisha's income from the shop and from lecturing far exceeded mine. After overheads and the manageress's wages were paid, we'd had enough left over really to invest in the shop. We bought new shop fittings and new stock, and the following year was a good one. In September, sales really started to come through as people bought early presents and outfits for Christmas parties. October was also fantastic; November was brilliant; in December, the till was ringing all day long.

That Christmas we paid Aisha's dad back and paid off the overdrafts: from now on, all the money we made would be ours, and I was definitely starting to get a sense of purpose, of direction. I really felt that I wanted to create something in business, and that the boutique was just a start. I felt I was developing as an entrepreneur, and the more I realised that this was where my future lay, the more I found myself coming to the inevitable conclusion that I had to resign from Reid Trevena.

Although the legislation that would kill Reid Trevena wouldn't be introduced for a couple of years yet, business was already starting to tail off. It was harder to recruit, and that meant my earnings were falling, from around £50k or £60k a year down to £30k. It was time to leave. With the shop doing so well, I thought the time was right to work at it full time and do something about our plans to expand.

It was a huge decision to walk away from a job I loved and that still paid better than any other job I could get in recruitment. Walking away from recruitment itself was pretty momentous –

that's what I did, and in some respects it was also who I was. But by now there was something in me that was eager for a challenge, eager to fulfil that childhood ambition to run my own business. After a big discussion with Aisha, we decided it was the right time to open another shop and that I should quit.

When I handed in my resignation, Tom thought I had completely lost the plot. He thought it was all about young love and not profit and he tried quite hard to talk me out of it. But I could see that Reid Trevena had grown so big and the momentum was starting to falter as profits fell and overheads didn't. Maybe if Reid Trevena had been flying Tom might have been able to talk me round, but I was so motivated at the thought of making a success of the business that I doubt it.

We opened a second shop inside the Wood Green shopping centre, and this one specialised in leather. It was exactly the kind of shop my dad had talked about us opening together all those years before. When we spoke each week on the phone I never had the heart to tell him that it was more profitable than the first shop.

With the second shop, we were able to learn from all the mistakes we'd made with the first. For starters, we had the confidence to negotiate a better deal on the lease, and then we sought much better terms with our suppliers. With the first shop we had gone to the fashion shows, ordered ranges and paid upfront for them, but with the new shop we knew to buy stock on a 'sale or return' basis. We couldn't always buy on those terms, but when we could it was a huge help to our cash flow because in many cases we didn't have to pay for the goods until we had sold them.

It also helped that I really understood leather. I knew the material, I knew how to judge the quality and I was able to establish really good relationships with the manufacturers. If a celebrity was seen wearing a particular coat, I could get copies made and in the shop within a fortnight.

One of the best things about the leather boutique was that the mark-up was huge. You can't mass-produce leather – because each animal skin is a different size – and that means each piece is individual. With most clothing, shoppers can go and compare with similar products, but with leather that's not so easy, and there were some garments for which we could almost name our price. Anything a little out of the ordinary that wasn't available anywhere else might cost us £80, but we could sell it for anything between £195 and £295.

With the second shop flying, it made sense to open a third, and when a unit became available in the shopping centre we opened a boutique specialising in cotton clothing. For the next year, I immersed myself in the business, and as long as we were expanding, I was learning, and that meant I was pretty content.

On the home front, we moved from the flat in Highgate to a three-bedroom house in Mill Hill in anticipation of having kids. As I've said, I was keen to start a family, but Aisha was less so. With three boutiques and her lecturing commitments, she wasn't ready to take the time off to have a baby. I would have to be patient.

In fact we were so busy that certain tasks just never got attended to. Having previously lived in flats, I wasn't quite prepared for the amount of maintenance an entire house needed. For several weekends in a row, I remember Aisha asking me to mow the lawn, and eventually I found time to do it. I went out to the shed, got the mower out and started giving the lawn a much-needed haircut. When I was about a quarter of the way through, I had a bit of an epiphany.

'How much is this job worth?' I said to myself. 'About £5 an hour. How much am I worth? A lot more.'

So I stopped, put the mower away and went back to my paperwork. Of course, Aisha came home a few hours later and saw the lawn and wondered why I was sitting on my backside. I explained that, from now on, if something needed doing around the house I would pay for it.

'It will take me hours, I don't have all the right tools and I'll do a lousy job. Tomorrow I'll find a card in a newsagent's window for a gardener and I'll get an expert in.'

She couldn't argue with that, and from that day to this I haven't even hung a picture. My skill, I realised, is in knowing where to find a man who knows how to hang a picture much better than I do.

Much as I enjoyed running the business and working with Aisha, after a couple of years I started to realise that the boutiques weren't making the most use of my talents. I had been really good at recruitment and I'd enjoyed it, and now we'd got into such a routine with the boutiques that it was getting easier, and that meant I was starting to miss the challenges of recruitment. I realised I actually had the same problem with Aisha's business that I'd had with my dad's: it wasn't mine. It wasn't my dream, it wasn't my passion. I'd proven I could run a business; now I wanted the challenge of running my own.

Chapter 10

The Beginning (1985)

'I now understood the principles of running a business, and I knew that if you didn't have a unique selling point, a USP, then you were going to be dead in the water.'

ABOUT THREE MONTHS AFTER we moved to Mill Hill, a friend of mine told me about an auction for top-end cars. I thought car auctions were all about rusty Cortinas and Austin Metros – I had no idea you could buy Porsches and Ferraris at auction, too. So I went along with him, just to see what kinds of bargains were available, and, of course, when I got there I fell in love with this Rolls-Royce Silver Spirit. It was bottle-green with a cream interior and was probably the most beautiful car I'd ever seen. So, inevitably, I got caught up in the bidding, and then, of course, I ended up winning the auction.

By early 1985, the boutiques were making around £12k a month, and that gave us a very nice lifestyle, which meant there was enough money in the business account to pay for it. Aisha, naturally enough, went ballistic when I confessed that I had just spent the best part of £40k on a car, and the only way to get myself out of the doghouse was to say 'Why don't we buy you one, too?' She chose a Porsche.

A Rolls is not what you expect a twenty-four-year-old to buy, but, I tell you, driving it felt absolutely fantastic. People stopped to look at it, drivers let me out at junctions just so that they could check out the car, people even waved. I had seen enough businesses go bust over the years to know that entrepreneurs who had created a lot of wealth could be left with nothing. They ploughed everything back into the business and never enjoyed the fruits of their labours. Equally, I had seen several entrepreneurs take all the profits out of their businesses and squander the money on expensive toys to the detriment of their business. I've always thought that the wealth of the business owner should be in line with the wealth of the business, and the boutiques were more than capable of paying for two very nice cars at that stage.

On one level I really felt like I'd arrived, but on another I was eager for more. I suppose I could have devised ways of turning the House of Aisha into a national brand, but, as I've said before, it wasn't my dream or my passion, and I had a really strong desire to get back to working in the centre of town and making use of my recruitment skills.

In retail there are always times of the day that are quiet, and so I used to sit in the shop and daydream. If we weren't expanding there wasn't all that much for me to do: no lease to negotiate, no staff to hire, no costings to forecast. In short, I was getting bored, and so I started daydreaming about what else I could do.

After a few months of this I'd started to visualise a new business. For a couple of years I'd had a vague idea about taking the sales skills and energy levels of Reid Trevena into the recruitment industry, and as I daydreamed this idea really started to take shape. I had a book that I doodled in and wrote down the attributes my dream business would have. What I really wanted, I realised, was to start a recruitment business with a difference. I now understood the principles of running a business, and I knew that if you didn't have a unique selling point, a USP, then you were going to be dead in the water. Without a differential you are just a 'me too' business, and 'me too' businesses are notorious for failure. So, I tried to think about what I could do differently in the recruitment field, and remembered my time working in agencies where there hadn't been a sales culture and looked for chinks in their armour. I was constantly looking for ways in which I could apply what I knew about business to what I knew about recruitment.

My experience of recruitment companies in the eighties had been that they were essentially order-takers. Clients rang in vacancies, and they simply matched requirements to candidates on their books. I was wondering what would happen if I hired the kind of salespeople the financial services industry hired. In an industry that was very average saleswise, what difference could brilliant sales skills make?

In those days, salaries in recruitment were very mediocre in relation to what you billed. The average recruiter probably took home £10k to £12k a year. With the margins recruitment agencies made, I was thinking that you could comfortably pay a consultant who billed £100k a year as much as thirty or forty grand. So then I started imagining the calibre of consultants you would attract if you paid that kind of commission. I started to get really excited because I'd seen what Reid Trevena had done with its staff: if you put them into the right environment with the right spirit and the right culture, they performed. And, of course, I knew exactly how to recruit the right kind of candidate.

At that point in the mid-eighties the recruitment market was very specific: you had high-street operations like Alfred Marks doing clerical and manual recruitment and typically charging 25 per cent of the first year's salary as their fee; then you had the mid-range agencies offering executive selection, where they adver-tised vacancies and selected a few candidates for interview by the client. These agencies charged for the advertising – often as much as £10k for a big ad in the *Daily Telegraph* or the *Financial Times*

– on top of the 25 per cent fee. Then, at the top end, you had executive headhunters who poached chief executives from one company for another and charged 30 per cent of the first year's salary. What I was trying to do was figure out where I could enter the market and what USP I could offer. I needed a reason to make a company use my agency instead of someone else's. So I kept doodling until I found my USP.

Then one day I remembered a situation at Reid Trevena when we had been looking for a finance director. I'd given the task to the Michael Page agency and they had run an ad, but no one good enough had applied and we had been left with the advertising bill but no FD. I reckoned that kind of thing must happen all the time, meaning companies were landed with the ad cost even though the agency had failed to find them the right candidate. So then I started thinking that there must be times when it would be cheaper to pay the headhunters' 30 per cent fee than pay the selection agencies' fee on top of the advertising. Then I reasoned that this would be even more attractive to clients as they would only pay if the agency had been successful.

I instantly knew I was on to something: there was a gap in the market to offer a headhunting service at the mid-range. Let's say I had a supermarket client that was looking for a manager for its new branch. I could place an ad and field the applications, or I could just call up the managers of other local supermarkets and ask them in for an interview. And, given my skills, I knew the latter approach could pretty much guarantee that I'd place a candidate in the job. Not only would I be providing a service that didn't exist at a price that was more competitive than the traditional selection process, but I could guarantee that the client wouldn't pay unless I delivered. I was saying to myself: *This has got to work, why would it not work?*

The great thing about recruitment – and the reason why there are 10,000 recruitment agencies in Britain – is that you don't need anything other than a phone to get started. Every half-decent recruitment consultant thinks about setting up on their own because they know how much they bill and that their commission is a fraction of that. However, I knew enough about myself to know that I didn't want to be a one-man band working in the spare room, so I started to sketch out a few figures assuming I would be paying for an office.

I thought maybe I could spend a grand a month on an office, and if I placed two candidates a month on £25k salaries and charged 25 per cent, I could make over £12k a month. That was £150k a year! That seemed too easy, so I asked myself, *What's the worst that could happen?* Maybe I wouldn't place two a month, maybe it would only be one. That was still £75k a year. Then I asked myself, *What would I need to break even?* It worked out at less than one placement a quarter. So the only question left was, *Did I have enough faith in myself and my abilities to believe I could do at least that?* When I put it like that, I couldn't actually see there was any risk at all.

At first that seemed too easy, so I asked myself what was really involved. Was I really capable of placing two candidates a week? I went through my process at Reid Trevena where I would often place eight or ten people a month, so I knew that it had to be possible. Looking at it soberly, I had to conclude that it would actually be relatively straightforward. I wasn't thinking that I had to be the biggest or the best – I wasn't going to place chief executives at FTSE 100 companies; I was just going to start an agency doing something that I knew I could do. It was believable, understandable, logical. I was unstoppable.

I spoke to Aisha about it, and she was really pleased that I had found something I could be passionate about. She could easily take care of the boutiques without me, and as all I was risking was my time and whatever it cost to rent an office she encouraged me to go for it. After we'd talked, I remembered my policy of not taking out of the company what the company couldn't afford, so I quickly downsized my idea of paying £1000 a month for an office. However, I wasn't prepared to do this on a shoestring and work from home.

I remembered everything I'd learned at Reid Trevena about how important appearances are when you're selling a service: it mattered where my office was because I needed to create the right impression. Likewise, it mattered what I called the business because it had to feel like a brand clients and candidates wanted to associate with.

I knew I wanted to start an upmarket business that would make clients and candidates feel like they were dealing with one of those established headhunters in a wood-panelled office in St James's, so I started doodling to come up with a brand that fitted that market. I wanted something that everyone assumed already existed, something that said gravitas, substance, integrity and professionalism.

As an exercise, I asked myself this: if my business was a person, what characteristics would that person have? I came up with dynamic, smart, someone with integrity, who was well educated, had a City background. Then I asked myself, what's this guy's name? And I came up with Alexander. And as that's quite a long name, I wanted a short one to go with it. I chose Mann because it was masculine, which fitted my executive market, but it also had echoes of other agencies, notably Manpower. In my mind, it sounded as if there had been an agency called Alexander Mann that had been established for years, and that was exactly what I wanted.

I decided that, ideally, I wanted Mayfair offices to go with my company's sophisticated name. I thought paying for the location was actually a sound investment: the more that people believed Alexander Mann was an established company, the easier it would be to get their business. When I talked to a couple of friends about my choice of location, they thought I was barmy, but I remembered what my father used to say when he was running his business: observe the masses and do the opposite. I hadn't actually thought of that line for a couple of years, but in the months to come I would find myself repeating it more and more. Sometimes, he'd always told me, doing the unexpected brings the rewards. Logically I couldn't justify the expense of Mayfair offices, but I just had a hunch it would be a worthwhile investment.

Once I had decided that it had to be Mayfair, I wanted the best address I could find, and to my mind that was Pall Mall, home of the Institute of Directors. It was near Buckingham Palace, round the corner from the RAC club and a short walk from the Ritz: it was exactly where a company called Alexander Mann ought to be, so I went to take a look and get some inspiration. I took a walk up Pall Mall, turned left into Horse Guards Parade, did a right towards Buckingham Palace, walked through St James's and up to the Ritz, and, let me tell you, it felt great. It felt *right*, and most importantly, it felt 'me'. I was genuinely very excited, and determined to find myself an office there.

I walked up and down Pall Mall examining every doorway and every sign above a bell to see if there was any office space to rent. Eventually I found a building of serviced offices and went in to speak to the manageress. I explained I was setting up a new recruitment agency, and she made all the right noises about the IT support and facilities they could offer.

'How much were you looking to spend in rent?' she asked.

'Oh, about £100 a week.'

She gave me the most disapproving look, as if she'd been a headmistress in a previous life. I've never forgotten what she said next:

'This is Pall Mall, dear, not Petticoat Lane.'

She thought I was wasting her time, but I persuaded her that if everything went to plan I would have a bigger budget for rent in just a few months' time. Somehow she believed me and said that she might be able to find something for me. She showed me a tiny room – it had previously been a store cupboard – that they could put a table in for me. I didn't have a window, but I didn't care. If my hunch was right I wouldn't be in there for long. In fact I was so thrilled with my broom cupboard that on the way home I got new business cards printed: James Caan, Managing Director, Alexander Mann, 50 Pall Mall. It felt good.

Chapter 11

Pall Mall (1985–1986)

'Putting myself in the position of the people taking my call was what turned things around.'

M Y BUSINESS PLAN wasn't much more than my original doodle. Two placements a month meant an income of £13k. I deducted the rent, the phone bill, a few expenses and that was it. It seemed so easy, too easy in fact, that I thought there had to be a catch. The only way to find out was to give it a go.

The weekend before I went to the office in Pall Mall for the first time I spent several hours reading the Yellow Pages, looking at sectors, companies and categories and highlighting pages of companies and industries where I thought there was an opportunity. I decided I would start approaching financial services companies for no other reason than I knew the language and I could talk intelligently about the sector. I knew the jargon and I knew how the industry worked.

I reckon I made forty to fifty calls a day that first week asking to speak to the sales director, the head of HR, the managing director or whoever was in charge of hiring. I've never found cold-calling particularly comfortable, and it didn't help that the person I needed to speak to often wasn't there, and my calls never got returned. It was understandable: no one had ever heard of me, the company didn't have a brand or a track record to trade on. Nevertheless, it was fairly soul-destroying, and after a couple of hours of knock-backs I just had to get out of that broom cupboard. Working in a room without a window made it much tougher, and my need to escape was intense.

Around 11 a.m. I'd take a walk up Pall Mall, go up to the Ritz, past Fortnum & Mason, and maybe dip down into the park. It took about twenty-five minutes, but the fresh air got my brain working again, and the grand buildings and buzzing atmosphere built up my confidence, and I'd get back on the phone until lunch, when I'd repeat the walk and take a detour to pick up a sandwich. In the afternoon I'd take another break so that at any one time it was never more than a couple of hours until I took a breather. It was much easier to look at the clock and think I just had to keep going until 3.30 p.m. rather than see the rejections stretch out until 6 p.m.

'Hi, my name's James Caan, I'm calling from Alexander Mann. We're specialists in financial recruitment and we can help you find the right people. I was wondering if you had any vacancies at the moment that I can help you fill . . .' I got bored with the sound of my own voice and whatever I was saying to them wasn't getting the right response. Still, I recognised that it would have been worse if I had been sitting there saying, 'Hi, I'm James Caan from James Caan Associates' and having the phone put down on me. Having the boss doing the cold-calling would have told the world that I was just a one-man operation, and I took some comfort from the fact that I hadn't named the company after myself. However, after a week of having the phone put down on me I was finding it tough. I tried to change my patter, and when that didn't work after another week I changed it again. But when *that* didn't produce results I had to concede that my pitch wasn't working. Someone once told me that the definition of insanity is to do more of the same thing today that you did yesterday and to expect a different result. I needed to change tack.

I sat in Green Park and went over what I'd learned, doing the same kind of analysis sportsmen must do with their technique. I looked at every approach I'd used and tried to work out where I was going wrong. Why wasn't I getting the results? I had spoken to hundreds of people, all of whom had basically told me to get lost. I went over and over my pitch and tried to think of ways I could make it better, and as I sat on that bench I suddenly heard what I must have sounded like to the people on the other end of the phone. To them I was just another cold-caller wasting their time. So I asked myself, 'When I was at Reid Trevena, what made me say yes when they cold-called me?' And that was the point at which something clicked. Putting myself in the position of the people taking my call was what turned things around.

I realised that if an agency had called me at Reid Trevena and said, 'We're currently working for a number of clients in the financial services sector and I met somebody yesterday who's got five years' outstanding experience in financial services who I think would be perfect for you,' I would obviously have listened really hard. If that candidate had also had an existing client base and was one of the top ten sales people in his company, then I'd absolutely have made an appointment to see him because he could have brought us a whole block of business.

I realised that I had just been giving people a generic pitch. I was basically saying little more than 'Hi, I'm a recruitment consultant and I recruit,' and it was too easy for people to say no to me. Now I'd worked out that I had to ring potential clients with something concrete to offer them.

Excited again, I went back to the office and started to write out my perfect candidate. What would Mr Perfect have? I modelled him on one of the best people at Reid Trevena, a guy who earned a fortune and bagged one referral after another. I decided my candidate was twenty-nine, was an Oxford graduate, had been an investment banker before, and had billed over £250,000 the previous year. All he needed now was a name. I called him Craig.

So now when I called people up I tried to engage them in a conversation about Craig.

'I had this guy in last week, he's at Allied Dunbar and although he's not actively looking to move at the moment I know he'd be perfect for you . . .' I gave them the pitch and at the end of it they'd say: 'Fantastic, we'd love to see him.'

There was a big grin on my face because I hadn't even asked them if they had a vacancy, I'd just got them talking. The fact that Craig didn't exist didn't bother me, because I had also worked out another strategy to find him.

'Hypothetically', I'd say, 'if we were in a position to get Craig to come along and see you, it would be really helpful if you could give me the reasons why somebody like Craig would leave Allied Dunbar to come and work for you.'

So the sales director would start pitching his company to me. Perhaps he'd say something like:

'Well, James, we're one of the largest independents, we won an award from Lloyds Life last year, we have our annual conventions in Hawaii . . .'

'That's great, really helpful. Can you also tell me how the financials would work? Would you guarantee him an income, or is it all commission?'

Effectively what was happening was that I was getting the sales director to write me a job description.

At the end of the call, I'd say: 'Leave it with me. I'll speak to Craig and I'll give you a call towards the end of the week.'

So now I had my first requirement from a potential client, and, of course, the first thing I did was call up Allied Dunbar.

'Hello, I'm quite interested in making some investments and I'd like to get an idea of what products you've got. Is there someone I can talk to?'

'Of course, sir.'

'Before you put me through, can you tell me who you're putting me through to?'

'Sure, it's Stuart, one of our top sales guys.'

'Actually, I've just got another call coming through; I'll have to call you back.'

I would leave it a couple of days before I called back and asked to speak to Stuart.

'Hello, Stuart, I'm James Caan, I work for a specialist head-hunter in the financial services sector, and one of my clients has an opportunity and is looking for somebody with just your experience. They're a really great firm, have an excellent salary package, they recently won an award from Lloyds Life and – I think you'll like this – they have an annual conference in Hawaii. I've told him you're one of the top people at Allied Dunbar and he'd really like to have a chat. I was wondering if you would be free for a coffee this Wednesday at 11 a.m.?'

So we would meet for a coffee, I would find out everything about his career to date and his hopes for the future and then call the client back.

'Unfortunately Craig's been made another offer but I didn't want to come back to you empty-handed, so I've looked through the other candidates I'm working with at the moment, and I've found Stuart. He hasn't got Craig's five years' experience, but he's been there for three and half years . . .' I'd run through his assets and then say, 'and he's available at four o'clock on Tuesday. What's your diary looking like for four o'clock?' Bang. Stuart would be booked in and I was on my way to my commission.

It was absolutely thrilling. You could not have rubbed the smile from my face with wire wool. I was creating the vacancy, and then I was creating the candidate, and I was doing it all on the phone in a broom cupboard. That feeling of creating something out of nothing is unbeatable.

Over the next few weeks I found better and better ways of finding out who the best employees were in any given company. One of my favourites was pretending to be from Porsche.

'We're doing a launch for our new model. I've got five invitations to allocate to your firm, but I really only want to send the invitations to Porsche enthusiasts. Who in your organisation would be the best people to send them to?'

The receptionist would say: 'All the team would love to go.'

'Give me your best people. It's an expensive event so we're looking for people who really do aspire to own a Porsche.'

Needless to say, I'd get the names of her company's top five sales people.

'Great, how do I spell his name? And out of curiosity, how long has he been there? And what's John's position?' I was pretty cheeky, but all I was doing was asking questions and the receptionist was happy to give me the answers.

In a couple of days' time, I would call John: 'Hi, my name's James. I've got an opportunity I want to chat to you about. When's a good time for us to speak?'

I had this enormous desire to make it work and even when I was getting rejections I was never tempted to throw in the towel. After that magic moment when I'd realised all I needed to do was to see things from the clients' point of view and tell them what they wanted to hear, I never looked back. All it boiled down to was having the cheek to tell clients what they wanted me to say. Then I just had to do the same for the candidates: I asked myself what they would want to be offered to take my approach seriously. Every week I varied my pitch and tried a different angle or a different technique to see what worked best.

There was just one problem: I didn't have anywhere to interview candidates. My broom cupboard was so small that when you opened the door it hit the desk: there definitely wasn't room for another chair. So when I got a call from reception saying my candidate was waiting for me, I would go down to meet them rather than having them sent up.

'Hi. I'm really sorry but all our meeting rooms are booked today. Would you mind if we pop up to the Ritz and get a coffee there?'

Some days I was even bolder and I'd tell them that we were running a big campaign at the moment, and that's why all the meeting rooms had been taken! It was important for me to paint a picture of hundreds of people and constant activity. The beauty of serviced offices is that nobody knew who took up the rest of the space, so I let people believe that the whole building was Alexander Mann's.

Whenever I talked about the business, I always said 'we' instead of 'I'. It was natural as I was trying to create the impression of an established company, but I think it had other benefits, too. There might have been those who thought that a company run by a twenty-five-year-old was too flaky to deal with, and I had no problem with people thinking I had a boss somewhere. Being able to say 'I'll just have to run that past Mr Alexander' was quite a handy negotiating tactic. Equally, saying 'we' took the focus off me. If I had used 'me' I would have come across as egotistical and, although I have always believed that appearances matter, my ego doesn't need that kind of stroking. 'We' sounds gentler, less arrogant.

When I was in Claridge's or the Ritz with a candidate, I was keen to make the candidate feel wanted by the client – 'They are really looking for someone with your sector experience . . .' – and it was important that they sensed the vacancy hadn't arisen in response to a cold call. I wanted them to feel excited about their prospective employer so that they would be incentivised to perform well at an interview, and more likely to say yes if they were offered the job. It really mattered to me that they were excited about the opportunity.

Every recruitment consultant feels disappointed when their candidate doesn't take up a job offer, but in those early days I was gutted. It was a lot of work and if a candidate decided to stay put I obviously wouldn't get paid. Having already spent several hours with a candidate, if I thought there was a chance I could persuade him to change his mind I would always call him up and ask him for a coffee.

I needed to understand why he wasn't taking up the opportunity and to do that I had to know where he thought his career was going, how well he thought he was doing in comparison to his peers, or if he was financially secure. I would keep digging and digging and digging until I found out his real objection. Perhaps one of his colleagues had been at his company for a shorter period of time and had been promoted ahead of him: he didn't want to leave until he'd got that experience on his CV. I think this is something most recruitment consultants don't usually bother with, and yet just a bit more effort to understand what candidates really want is all you need to get a result.

I was then in a position to call the client back:

'John's really interested, but he's still undecided because one of the things that's really important to him is management experience. If he were to come to you, what kind of opportunities would there be for promotion?'

'Well, there's nothing immediately . . .'

'How long, would you say, before you would consider him for a management position?'

'If he performs, maybe between three and six months.'

'That's great. If you could put that in writing then I think he will come on board.' It was important that the promotion was real, and having it in writing allowed me to go back to the candidate and convince him he had better opportunities with the new employer than his existing one.

'Hi, John, I've been speaking to the team who interviewed you, and one of the things that really impressed them about you is your eagerness to take on management responsibilities.' It was important that I was able to tell him they were committed to putting his promotion in writing in case he thought I was just telling him what he wanted to hear. He had to know it was a genuine opportunity if he was going to give up his existing job for it. I didn't want to put anyone with an organisation that wouldn't deliver its promises: I wanted to build relationships that would help me grow my business. 'What they'd like to do is meet you again to talk through how it might work. How are you fixed for Thursday at 10 a.m.?'

I'd then get straight back to the client and say something like: 'John's been talking it over with his wife and this is definitely what he wants. However, I think what he'd like to do is just explore that whole avenue of management . . .'

Somehow or other I would keep both sides talking to each other until they shook hands and signed a contract. It took me about five weeks to get my first client, another four to fill the position and another six to get paid: it was nail-biting until I received the cheque. First I had to get the offer, then the candidate had to resign – and you never know what an employer will do to keep a good member of staff – then he had to work his notice period: it took so long that unless I monitored every stage closely, the deal could easily have fallen apart and I wouldn't have got paid.

Once a candidate had accepted a job, I would call him up and tell him we should have a beer to celebrate, which again is something I don't think most recruitment professionals do.

'I think your new job is going to be absolutely fantastic. It's a great opportunity. You must be really proud of yourself.' I wanted to get feedback on how I'd done so that I could perform better for the next candidate. 'So tell me, John, are you happy with the way I've looked after this for you? Is there anything I've done that you're unhappy with, or any way the service was not as you'd have liked?'

'No, James, it's been really good, really professional. It's been pretty painless actually.'

'That's great. I'm really pleased to hear that. Listen, do you think you could do me a favour?'

'What's that, James?'

'Would you recommend me to three people?' It was a technique I'd learned at Reid Trevena: you should always be specific. If I had said, 'Is there anybody else you know who would like to change jobs?' it would have been too easy for him to say no. If you ask a specific question you tend to get a specific answer.

'I'm looking for somebody in their early thirties, preferably living in London, maybe two and a half to three years' experience, specifically within pensions and investment.' When you are so specific in what you ask for, the mind is very good at tuning in to somebody. Our brains start filtering through our memory banks in search of matching information. The trick is to give the brain something to look for.

'Actually, I do know somebody like that.'

'Who's that, John?'

'A friend of mine. I used to work with him at Goldman Sachs . . .'

'What's the best way for me to get hold of him?' I would take the name and number and encourage John to come up with another candidate. Within twenty minutes I had pulled three names out of John's mental database, and the next day I would call up his friends.

'Hi, Gary, excuse me calling you out of the blue but I was with John yesterday. We were having a fantastic celebration at the Ritz because John's just got a fabulous new job. While we were talking, he said the one guy he knew who was really ready for the next step was you, so this is just a quick call to see when a good time to have a coffee would be. How's Tuesday at noon looking?'

A few months in, I had the first fee in the bank, a couple more cheques in the pipeline and eight to ten people out on interviews:

the broom cupboard was really getting me down. Not having a window made it unbearably claustrophobic, so as soon as there was money in the Alexander Mann bank account I told reception that I wanted a window and enough room for two desks. By now, I was also ready to hire somebody, not just because I hadn't enjoyed working on my own, but because I'd proved my system could work and that meant I would be able to convince someone to join me.

The first person I approached was a guy called Mike who I'd worked with at Premier. We met for a coffee and I told him about Alexander Mann before suggesting that he came and worked with me.

Mike was very experienced – he was a good ten years older than me – and he could see that I'd barely been up and running for five minutes. I knew exactly what he was thinking: 'If I join Alexander Mann, James is going to pocket 70 per cent of whatever I bill; I'd be better off if I set up on my own.'

So I started to share my vision with Mike about this big company, based on the atmosphere I'd known in financial services, with a big open-plan dealing room with thirty of the best people in the business. I sold the opportunity not the job, and convinced him that this was going to be a really exciting journey. Over the years, I've been told I'm very good at painting everything as a blue-sky opportunity, but I absolutely believed what I was telling Mike. He was very intrigued with my concept of headhunting because he'd never come across it before.

'You can't be serious! You can't just call people out of the blue and get results!'

I knew that Mike had pretty good clients and if he brought some of them with him he'd be billing in no time. I paid him 30 per cent of what he billed – which was way more than any other agency paid at the time – and he billed £8k in his first month, £11k the following month, and £15k the month after that. Alexander Mann was starting to fly.

I picked up my next employee after a candidate told me about a guy called Mark at another agency he was registered with. So I called Mark up and told him I wanted someone to specialise in his field. He was keen to move because he had been his agency's top biller – he'd billed £180k the previous year – but only taken home £15,000.

That created a problem for me: I was pretty sure that if I told Mark I'd pay him 30 per cent commission he just wouldn't believe me and so wouldn't join me. If you tell someone who's earning £15k that they could earn £60k, they can't accept it because the gap is too big: they think there has to be a catch. So I told him that with 'us' he would make £25k and he came on board. I let him work out for himself that he had the potential to earn £60k and we moved to a bigger room.

A few weeks later I overheard Mike interviewing a woman, and because it was an open-plan office I could hear their conversation. She was working for Canon selling office equipment and being interviewed for a position at a rival company. As I listened in, she struck me as an asset to any company: she wasn't overly salesy, just really straightforward and clearly reliable and trustworthy. The office equipment market was huge in those days, and I thought about how many more people we could place if we had a specialist on our team. So I walked over to where they were sitting.

'Hi, it's Sam, isn't it? My name's James, nice to meet you. So, Mike, what have we got for Sam?'

He started going through the opportunity while I read her CV.

'Ever thought about recruitment, Sam?'

There was something about her that I knew would be just perfect in recruitment.

'We're looking for someone to specialise in the office equipment sector, and as you obviously have all the contacts you should join us.'

'It's not what I do,' she said.

I realised I'd been too hasty. I had gone straight to the destination and forgotten to take her on the journey. She'd walked in expecting to hear about opportunities in her field, not ours, so my offer was too difficult to take in.

'Let me tell you how it works . . .' Several hours later, Sam was still in the office but she still hadn't taken me up on the offer of a job. However, I could tell that she really had what it took to be great at recruitment – she could sell but she could also read people – and I didn't want to let her go.

'I tell you what. Come and work with me for a week. If you still think it's not right for you, then I'll drop it, but give me a week.'

Needless to say, Sam Collins came for a week and never left, and in the years to come she would see Alexander Mann through some of the most extraordinary times that any of us had ever experienced.

Chapter 12

Growing the Business (1986–1987)

'If you offer recognition before it's asked for, it has twice the impact.'

A S ALEXANDER MANN headhunted candidates, clients didn't pay unless we delivered; that made us a very attractive option and we did well in our first year. We positioned ourselves as a sales and marketing recruitment company working across all sectors, and clients assumed we had a supply of great sales and marketing candidates. Over time, that became the case, of course, as one candidate who missed out on one position was often right for the next.

I was aware from the beginning that sustaining a business through cold-calling is just too hard and that success would come through building relationships. If you've performed really well and you call the client back with another top candidate, they're going to be interested. If the last guy you placed was a deadweight, you're not going to get the same response, even though the candidate's performance has nothing to do with the agency. Their performance might be down to training, management, incentives or personality clashes, but it would still reflect badly on Alexander Mann, and that's why I always worked so hard to find out what our clients and candidates really wanted. Whether it was flexibility, opportunity for advancement, training or a decent company car, getting the details right was as important as determining salary and notice periods.

It's much easier for a client to use an agency that it's dealt with before – it just makes life simpler, faster, more enjoyable. I was extremely passionate about making sure that our clients came back, and I engendered that feeling in everyone who came to work at Alexander Mann.

Not only did Alexander Mann understand its market better, its customers better and its candidates better, it also employed much better people. In the mid-eighties a competent recruiter at most agencies might have been making £15k a year. We hired the good performers, turned them into really great performers, and paid them a much higher percentage of what they billed. With us they made £30k plus a year. And, of course, when a team is performing well and getting paid well, morale is high and their performance just gets better.

One of the effective and unique things we did at Alexander Mann was develop relationships with the companies who'd just had a candidate leave. If I had just placed someone at a Top 4 Public Accountancy Firm I'd make sure I knew where the candidate had come from.

'Hi, my name's James Caan, I work at Alexander Mann and we're currently looking for clients who might be interested in some exceptionally good candidates we've got at the moment in your sector.' I would describe the guy that I'd just placed and who had just resigned.

'That's really fortunate that you rang me today because our audit manager Bob just resigned! How did you know?'

'I should explain. I'm an expert in this industry and I make it my business to know. When can we have a chat?'

I would then go and meet the client to take the brief about exactly that they wanted. Again, my willingness to ask more questions than anyone else could be bothered to allowed me to tailor my service to their needs. At first they'd tell me about the vacancy and the skills required.

'That's really helpful. Now, if I sent you somebody, what sort of person would I have to send for you to hire him on the spot? What attributes would he have to have?'

They'd illustrate their dream candidate, itemising with qualifications, attributes and experience. Most agencies would take a brief in thirty minutes. I'd take three hours.

'What sort of package do you think your dream candidate is on at the moment? Where's he working now?'

Again, everything I wanted to know was in someone else's head and all I had to do was ask.

He's probably on this salary, with this car, and that bonus at that company, they'd tell me.

I'd always want to know what age range they were interested in because I didn't want to waste my time finding someone who was too old or too young. People were often reluctant to give me an age, so I asked something like: 'What sort of age were the last three people in this job?'

'And were they all graduates?'

'Actually the one before last wasn't.'

'So you would look at candidates who weren't graduates?'

I'd now widened the brief to include non-graduates.

'And tell me, what are you looking to pay for this position?'

'£80k a year.'

'Just out of curiosity, if I found you someone who was spectacular, who had exactly the experience you wanted, but he cost £100k, would you turn him down?'

'Well, it'd be tough but I think we'd go there.'

Now I'd increased the salary bracket, too – as well as my potential commission. Most recruiters would just write down 'Senior Manager needed, £80k salary'. By the time I left the client I would know exactly who their ideal candidate was and what I would have to say to that candidate to tempt them to leave. I'd also know if there were issues that would mean a candidate got rejected.

Sometimes I would meet a client who described the kind of candidate they wanted to attract – dynamic, high achiever, the kind of person who would be an asset to any company – and I wouldn't take the brief. I'd tell the client that we were over-stretched and wouldn't have the time to dedicate to their needs. The truth was that I hadn't been impressed by the client and I just didn't believe the sort of person they wanted to hire would ever agree to work with someone like them. I had learned that the single biggest reason why most people accept job offers is because they like the person who interviewed them. Clearly, by turning down opportunities where my chances of a successful placement were slim, and by widening the brief from the clients I took on, my hit rate was that much better than virtually any other agency's. As I passed these techniques on to the staff, Alexander Mann got stronger and stronger.

In Aisha's boutiques the biggest cheque we could expect was perhaps £500. At Alexander Mann it was several thousand, so I was always interested in keeping an eye on the books. In the early days, I asked the accountant we'd used for the boutiques to do Alexander Mann's bookkeeping, but I could always have told you within a couple of hundred quid what our bank balance was because I was the one collecting the invoices and writing the cheques.

As we grew, I hired an in-house administrator whose job it was to raise the invoices, check they were paid on time, get new employees on the payroll, calculate commissions and log everything in the books we passed to the accountant. He told us what he needed to see to file our accounts and make our VAT returns, and we just did what we were told. It was all done by hand as we didn't have computers then.

If I hadn't already used an accountant who was cheap and reliable, I would have done the admin myself. I think an entrepreneur should be able to do that stuff, and I would strongly advocate that first-time entrepreneurs take on those tasks. It's really not that complicated, especially as the internet gives you so much access to information these days, whether it's a template business plan or a sample VAT form. It might be different in businesses where you have a high volume of transactions, but in an agency situation where you have a modest number of invoices to take care of, doing your own books gives you the opportunity really to get to know your business, to spot patterns and to spot mistakes.

Perhaps the biggest lesson – or maybe the biggest surprise – in the early days was that there really wasn't anyone I could turn to for a definitive answer about anything. I had assumed that lawyers, accountants and bank managers were there to help. I was wrong; they're there to make money.

For instance, when I was considering increasing our rate of expansion – after all, the more people I hired, the more money we made – I went to the bank for a loan to cover the cash flow (even the best recruiters take a couple of months to place their first candidate, and then it takes another couple of months to get the invoices paid; in the meantime I would be paying their basic salary). Given Alexander Mann's flying start, I hadn't anticipated a problem.

'The problem with Alexander Mann', the bank manager told me, 'is that it is a service industry.'

'I know, it means I don't have the expense of production,

maintenance, logistics, storage or any of the problems that manufacturing businesses have.'

'Yes, but you don't have any assets.'

'I know; we have very low overheads in comparison to our turnover.'

'Yes, but there's no security for a bank. What can you offer us as security if there are no assets?'

'The security I can offer you is that in a couple of months my cash flow will have massively increased.'

It wasn't enough: without any assets to secure the loan, I couldn't get a bank to back me.

By and large I found accountants equally unhelpful. I would phone up wanting advice, but they would simply give me the options and then say, 'So what would you like to do?'

'I want you to tell me what's best.'

'All I can do is give you the options. The decision has to be yours.'

'Yes, but which is the best option for me?'

'That depends on your circumstances.'

It drove me nuts: *What was I paying them for?*

The worst were the lawyers. I learned very quickly that lawyers never make decisions or recommendations. What lawyers do is draft documents based on what you tell them. It was a big disappointment because I'd assumed that if I had a legal problem I'd go off to my legal firm and they'd sort it. However, at the end of the day it doesn't really matter to the lawyer what the outcome of a legal situation is because he makes his fee anyway. The minute I sat down and talked to him, the clock was ticking, and the longer I asked questions, the more money he made.

When you ask lawyers for an opinion, they never give you one. What they do is present you with the facts, and leave the decision up to you. I used to walk away from meetings thinking: *What am I paying them £100 an hour for?* What was frustrating was that I genuinely didn't know how to make the decision in question because it was a technical legal matter.

I would sometimes find myself with a bill for lengthy legal negotiations and wondered why I hadn't just picked up the phone and sorted out problems directly. Wouldn't it be great if you could just get lawyers in the same room with their clients and get everything agreed in a couple of hours rather than after weeks of negotiation by fax? But as most lawyers charge by the hour, they have an incentive to drag things out. It was genuinely disappointing to me to find out that lawyers are not exactly what they're cracked up to be, and I had similar run-ins with various accountants. I thought I was paying them to sort things out for me, but they were always reluctant to take responsibility for their work. If the Inland Revenue got in touch about an accounting mistake, I expected the accountants who had done the work to sort it out, but they would never admit they'd made a mistake.

'With all due respect James, you signed the forms.'

'You told me that was the best way forward.'

'It's not for me to tell you what to do. When you sign a set of accounts, you are responsible.'

'I don't understand: I thought that was your job, after all, you're the accountant. That's why I come to you.'

'No James, my job is to point situations out to you and it's your job to make a decision, so when you sign a set of accounts, you are saying that you've checked and agreed with all the numbers.'

'Yes, but you prepared them . . .'

Again, I was really frustrated – what's the point of an accountant if they're not actually accountable for the recommendations they make?

Having the new administrator removed some of these hassles from my day-to-day life, but when she started, we didn't have room for another desk. The solution was to get a cordless phone, and I started sitting at whichever desk was free as there was always someone out on an appointment. It meant I got to sit with all the staff and listen in on their calls, and perhaps more importantly, for them to listen in on mine so they could pick up tips.

We had clearly outgrown the serviced offices in Pall Mall and so we moved to our own space above a hi-fi shop on Tottenham Court Road. It was pretty shabby, but despite my belief in appearances mattering I was nervous about committing the company to huge overheads. I had learned with the boutiques that there could be weeks when our income didn't cover the rent, and now that I had a staff of six and was responsible for six basic salaries – whether or not the team billed – I was nervous of getting into cash-flow problems. I got the office painted, but that barely compensated for the tatty doorway and stairwell. Still, it was a good location and there was room for twenty people or more, so as soon as the last person I hired started billing I took on another member of staff. I arranged the desks in a horseshoe so that we could all see each other: not only were all our desks identical, which did away with petty hierarchies, but there were no separate extension numbers for the phone, so when the phone rang, every phone rang. This might have been noisy, but it was great for team spirit.

'John, for you on line one!'

'Oi, new girl, your boyfriend's on line three.'

'James, someone's chasing an invoice on line two.'

It was impossible to work in that environment and not feel part of the team. Instead of most offices where people work in banks of desks and never get to know colleagues sitting ten feet away, the people at Alexander Mann couldn't help but feel like a team.

Just like at Reid Trevena, I had charts on the walls showing how many vacancies we had, how many candidates were out on interviews, and a sales graph showing how everyone in the team was performing. And when a candidate accepted a position, there was, of course, a bell to ring, which was something no one had ever seen in recruitment before.

By the start of 1987 the business was turning over around £40–50,000 a month: a third of that was paid in commissions. I had overheads of around £5000 for the rent, rates and utilities; allowing for another few grand a month in expenses and professional fees, the profit was over £20k a month. That was effectively my salary, and that meant that Aisha and I had a very nice life and we decided it was time to start a family. When Aisha told me she was pregnant it was one of the happiest moments of my life, and I wanted to ring the sales bell off the wall! I just couldn't wait to be a dad.

Running Alexander Mann was a lot of fun, but it was also incredibly hard work. I was still the biggest biller in the office, and on top of that I was hiring staff, training them, chasing late payers and planning our way forward. I would often have breakfast meetings with candidates as this was the only time they could meet, and in the evenings I would regularly spend two or three hours on the phone after dinner talking to candidates who were too busy to talk during the day. When I talked to them while they were in their office it was so difficult for them to be honest. I was only really able to understand their aspirations and reservations if I talked to them out of hours. A fifteen-hour working day was standard, and there were several days a month when I worked for eighteen hours. We also opened on Saturday mornings (before mobile phones allowed candidates to slip out for a private chat a Saturday service was essential), so I was always busy.

When you run a small company, especially when it's your first, it's vital that you understand every aspect of it, whether that's IT, or the admin, or the sales or the logistics, so I was also spending time on management issues. I was learning that as a small company it was hard to get the best advice because we simply couldn't afford the best lawyers, or the best telephone engineers, and even if I'd had the budget for the best people they would have chosen to work for a blue-chip company anyway. So it fell to me to understand things like the phone system so that I could be more effective in hiring a guy to fix the phones. As the owner of a small business, unless you understand each component of your business, it's virtually impossible to get it to work as a whole. These days I do quite a bit of public speaking and meet aspiring entrepreneurs who just assume they can buy in the expertise; they don't realise that any decent expert would rather be working with a bigger and more established company. The responsibilities of an entrepreneur to their new business are almost unending.

I was always the first to arrive in the morning, and always the last to leave. I think it is important that bosses, and especially owner-managers, set an example. How could I reprimand staff for timekeeping, or long lunches, or any other kind of sloppy behaviour if I was guilty of it, too? If you want people to work hard for you, they have to see that you are working harder.

Right from the beginning my ethos was summed up by the word energy. I wanted to see a lot of activity – candidates coming in for meetings, me walking round, phones ringing, jokes being shared. Whenever I went into that office, it was electrifying. I was very good at creating that energy and encouraging constant activity: I was always painting blue skies; it was my biggest cultural contribution and it was instrumental in what the business would go on to achieve.

When you work so hard it's vital that you enjoy your work; if you're having fun you perform better and achieve more. Making the office fun also meant the staff were incredibly loyal in an industry where staff turnover is pretty high.

I would constantly make sure that something fun was happening. In those days, the Trocadero near Shaftesbury Avenue had a booth where you could go and make a pop video. They projected images on to a screen behind the performers, so a bunch of us would stand there with a mic and mime to one of those eighties power ballads against a backdrop of the Hollywood Hills. We'd then go back to the office and show it to the rest of the team, who of course were all first in the queue when we did it again.

The team got more and more into it and started hiring costumes for the videos, and the game was on to make the best video you could. I met all the expenses, but the team were so enthusiastic they often paid for accessories out of their own pocket.

If we weren't making videos, we'd be going out for a drink or a meal, anything that created that camaraderie that enhanced the work ethic, and that got us bouncing ideas off each other and believing in each other. Alexander Mann wasn't about me, it was about *us*.

The office atmosphere meant we became very close and we all knew a lot about each other's lives: if someone had been on a date, we all knew, just as we knew if the date had been successful or if someone had a flatmate from hell. The team became so close that if there was a situation where someone was buying their first flat and had saved up a deposit but was a couple of grand short of their dream home, I would tell them not to worry.

'I'll lend you the two grand and we'll just take it off your wages.'

Or if someone phoned up to say their car had broken down and they'd be late in, I'd tell them to get it fixed. I'd pay for it and deduct it from their commission.

I didn't have a separate office, I didn't have a title, I was no different from everyone else and billed just as they did. The fact that I wasn't 'up there' and they weren't 'down there' made a big difference. If I'd noticed that someone hadn't stopped for lunch, I'd pick up a sandwich for them: you'd be amazed how those little things make a huge difference.

However, I was still the boss, still the leader, and it was a big part of my job to motivate the team. Let's say that Bob had done fantastically well:

'Bob, what are you doing this lunchtime? I'm thinking of going to Bond Street to get a suit. Do you want to come with me?'

Once we were in the shop and I was trying something on, I'd turn to Bob and ask if he wanted one, too.

'Don't be silly.'

'I'm serious.'

You can imagine? He was like a Cheshire cat for a week!

'Just for a bit of a laugh, Bob. Why don't you wear your suit tomorrow because I'm definitely going to wear mine.'

So we'd stroll in in matching suits, and you could almost hear the little voice in everyone else's heads saying, 'Next month, I'm going to be the top biller.'

I was learning that if you offer recognition before it's asked for, it has twice the impact. Imagine if I approached an employee and said, 'I think your work is fantastic and I want to promote you,' how much more effective it would be than letting that employee have to come to me and say, 'I've been here over a year and I think it's time I got promoted.' Recognising the team's contribution – even their potential to make a contribution – was something I was good at, and it made for a great atmosphere because everyone felt valued.

As the company grew, maintaining that culture, keeping that day-to-day contact with the staff was vital. I absolutely believed in the culture, and I believed that I could manage and lead and motivate. The one thing I was struggling with was having the time to maintain my relationships with clients at the same time.

Chapter 13

Learning to Innovate (1986–1987)

'I'd convinced myself it had to work and, crucially, I'd also put myself in an embarrassing position trying to convince everybody else. The whole office – and pretty soon the whole industry – was looking at me saying: Go on then, show us.*'*

I BEGAN TO BE INVITED to events and seminars for recruitment professionals. I found they were a really useful way of finding out what other companies were up to, for spotting opportunities and to meet people who I might want to work with in the future. As my career progressed and Alexander Mann grew, the network of contacts I built up became increasingly valuable to me. The more you talk to people – the more questions you ask – the better informed you are, and as a direct result of getting out from behind my desk Alexander Mann devised a couple of lucrative new ways to expand its operations.

As I talked to other people who ran recruitment agencies, I noticed they all had pretty much the same concern: they all told me business was booming, and that meant they all wanted to hire more recruitment consultants and expand. The problem was that they were having real difficulty finding good staff.

In the car on my way back to the office I was thinking it was odd that Alexander Mann wasn't having the same problem as the rest of the industry, and I realised it was probably because Alexander Mann recruited salespeople: when good people came in to see us about another opportunity, we could say, 'Have you thought about recruitment?' But an agency that specialised in legal or accountancy work only attracted lawyers or accountants for interviews. So the only way they could hire salespeople who would make good recruitment consultants was to advertise. But everyone else was doing that, and in a buoyant market it was hard to get good people. So I went to talk to one of my managers with an idea.

'Why don't we set up a division that supplies recruitment consultants to recruitment companies?'

He looked at me as if I'd gone mad.

'James, how whacky can you be? Which recruitment agency is going to pay you a fee to do what they're supposed to be good at themselves? Forget it.'

He had a point. But so did I. 'Just think about it – if you're an accountancy recruitment agency, why are you any different from any other client that comes to us because they can't find the right people? They're in exactly the same position as every other client, which means they have to run ads, which is exactly what we tell our clients not to do because our skills get better results.'

He wasn't looking convinced, so I carried on. 'Listen; think of Alexander Mann as specialists in hiring good people, the best people. It's what we're known for in the industry, so why don't we hire for other recruitment agencies?'

'You're being daft. Hiring us would be like admitting they were bad at what they do. James, it just won't happen. Forget it.'

I talked to a few others in the office and I couldn't convince anybody that we should try it.

'You know what?' I said. 'I'll do it myself.'

So I picked up the phone and started canvassing recruitment agencies, and – just as my colleagues had predicted – they started laughing on the other end of the phone.

'Don't be so ridiculous! I'm not going to give you a vacancy to hire recruitment consultants for me. What do you think I do here? That's my job.'

Being a bit pig-headed, I wasn't easily dissuaded. I knew they had a need, so I just had to find a way of making it work. I did what I always did and sat on the phone for days, slightly altering my pitch and assessing the results. I could understand why I was being knocked back – it's the obvious emotional response to say no – but commercially I knew there was an opportunity. I'd convinced myself it had to work and, crucially, I'd also put myself in an embarrassing position trying to convince everybody else. The whole office – and pretty soon the whole industry – was looking at me saying: *Go on then, show us.*

I couldn't lose face, so for six weeks I canvassed other recruitment agencies solidly. If I couldn't convince them on the phone then I went to meet them, but still I couldn't persuade them. I realised I must have the wrong pitch, and so I sat in the office and went back to basics. I asked myself, *What do they want to hear?* What could I tell them that would get them interested? Mentally, I went back to the broom cupboard in Pall Mall when I didn't have a service I could sell, and I'd sold the candidate instead. I closed my eyes and imagined the kind of candidate another agency would be willing to pay a fee for.

Supposing someone had rung me and said: 'James, I've got a consultant who's a specialist in the sales market and he's been doing it for three and half years. Last year he billed £150,000, he's got a very good customer base and he's looking for an opportunity.' Immediately, I'd be thinking – *£150k? That's £50k profit. Is that worth the £6k agency fee? Would I pay six grand to buy £150,000 worth of revenue? I think I would.*

That was my pitch. I wasn't going to sell Alexander Mann, I wasn't going to try to convince them that our service was different; I was just going to ring them up and say: 'Hi, listen, this is just a quick call ... I just wanted to mention we've got a consultant who's been in the industry three years, she's billing at £150,000. Is that something you might be interested in?'

'What sector is she in?'

I had immediately engaged them in conversation, and they started asking questions.

'What's her average fee? Is she permanent or contract?'

They were interested, but they were still confused.

'What's in it for you?'

'Just a standard fee.'

'Let me give you a call back.'

I could almost work out word for word the conversation they were having at their end, and within an hour they would usually call back and say: 'It's not something we've done before, but I think we might be interested in meeting this person.'

I had found the pitch! Now all I needed was a candidate! So I picked up the Yellow Pages, and looked at all the agencies who specialised in that particular field. I also looked at the recruitment ads for those agencies in the papers, and at the bottom of each ad it usually said: 'Ring Jane Smith to talk about this and other vacancies.' So I called Jane Smith.

'Hi, my name's James Caan, I've got an opportunity I think you might be interested in and I'd like to get together . . .' A week or so later, I sent Jane out for an interview, she took the job and I got my fee. Bingo!

When I made that placement I was the first person in the UK to charge a fee for placing a recruitment consultant. Nobody had ever done it before because it hadn't even existed as a concept. Yet precisely because no one else was doing it we became really well known very quickly as the recruiters' recruiter, and by 1987 the recruitment to recruitment market (or rec2rec, as it became known) accounted for half of everything Alexander Mann did. I can't emphasise enough how important this became for the business. Whenever you're in a market where you're the only one, it's like being ten times bigger than you really are. Our name spread so quickly because everybody was talking about us. Several of my consultants realised there was an opportunity to earn more money and moved to our new rec2rec division. That side of things just grew and grew, and my dad's philosophy about the less travelled road being paved with gold was proving to be true yet again.

Not only was it lucrative for the company, but, because we were constantly interviewing recruitment professionals, if anyone really impressed us we could hire them for Alexander Mann. Everyone who walked through our door was a potential recruit, and we started to employ better and better people, and of course that helped us grow our reputation, our client base and our profits. What made this even sweeter was that it meant we had virtually no recruitment costs ourselves, as 95 per cent of the team we hired had initially come in to see us about another vacancy.

We attracted a lot of attention within the industry after that, and I noticed that when I went to industry events and said I worked for Alexander Mann, people paid attention. We were seen as upstarts and mavericks and, although some people admired us, we also got a lot of flak. Not everyone liked us – largely because we were placing their best people elsewhere – but everyone in the sector had heard of us, and a consequence of being higher-profile was that people wanted to work for us. Alexander Mann became a prestige name to have on your CV, and that in turn helped us hire better and better people.

The early years of Alexander Mann were extremely creative as we tried different angles and different techniques to prise open sectors, industries and profits. We spent a lot of time talking between ourselves about other avenues we could take, and one of the innovations we came up with was recruitment fairs.

The economy was so buoyant in 1987 that we were struggling to find enough candidates and we had more vacancies than we could fill. I'd be walking round the office talking to the team, and they'd all be saying the same thing: there just weren't enough candidates to go round. So I started to think of ways we could attract more candidates. One way would be to advertise, but in the days before the internet recruitment advertising was incredibly expensive. An ad in the *Telegraph* was something like £10,000 a page, and I could easily have spent £100,000 a week on advertising. The breakthrough came when I had a slightly cheeky thought: *How can I get someone else to spend the £100k for me?*

I wasn't the only person in the office trying to think of new ways to find candidates, and one of my team, a guy called Nick Baldock, had a brainwave: when he had left university, several blue-chip employers had come to try to persuade final-year students to join them. Nick's idea was to take this concept into the commercial world. As ever, when you come up with something innovative you have to tell people about it in the right way for them to understand exactly what you're offering. So I thought about the right pitch to use and then called one of our best clients.

'What would you say if I said you could hire as many people as you want in a day at a fixed fee, rather than paying me 25 per cent of their salary?'

'Sounds interesting, James, but how are you going to get me several candidates in one day?

'Alexander Mann's going to be holding an event at the Dorchester hotel specifically for blue-chip companies to find the best candidates. We're going to advertise it and invite anyone interested in working for the best companies to come along. We're inviting BT, Glaxo, IBM and others to come along to find out about positions from trainees to senior management. I suppose it's a bit like the milk rounds companies do for final-year undergraduates, and there will be plenty of candidates all looking for a job.'

'And what do you want from me?'

'Just a contribution towards the cost of the advertising.'

'And that's it?'

I asked several clients to make a similar contribution, and then asked another to pay for the venue hire, and another to help out with the costs of refreshments. Normally these clients would pay Alexander Mann a 25 per cent fee, which could often be a five-figure sum. If they only hired a handful of candidates, they would make quite a saving. If they hired several, they'd be quids in.

I then hired an advertising agency to design full-page ads for the press. It was a brilliant campaign packed with logos of companies like BT, Glaxo and the high-street banks inviting jobseekers to a free recruitment fair at the Dorchester, one of the best hotels in London.

The branding for Alexander Mann was incredible, but that wasn't the real benefit: if 800 people turned up and our clients hired 100 of them, we still had 700 jobseekers whose details we could store and find opportunities for. My consultants desperately needed candidates, and in one day we were going to find hundreds of them. Or so we hoped. At that stage we had no idea if the plan would work because it had never been done before.

I turned up at the Dorchester not knowing what to expect: for all I knew, I might have been about to embarrass myself and my company in front of some of our biggest clients. When I pulled up and saw the queue outside, it was an incredible feeling. I didn't quite dare hope the queue was for our event, but I had a sneaking suspicion it had to be.

The key for us was the registration process. Although our clients had footed the bill it was still only valuable to us if we got the names, addresses and phone numbers of all the attendees. So I had a team of temps just taking down those details, and candidates weren't allowed into the main hall until we had their information.

By the end of the day we'd placed over 100 people, which meant the clients were ecstatic. The average cost per hire for them was nothing in comparison to what they could have paid. It worked out brilliantly for us, too, and the next quarter was the best we'd ever had. We went back to the office with stacks and stacks of forms; we broke them down into sectors, divided them between us and then sold them to prospective employers. Our problem of not having enough candidates had been solved, and after that we had a recruitment fair every three months. The candidates were happy, we were happy and our clients were happy: as my dad would have put it – win-win-win.

The recruitment fairs were another innovation that helped Alexander Mann get a reputation for being different, and maybe a bit awkward. We were a young company that was turning conventional wisdom upside down and taking business away from other agencies. In the years since, people have come up to me and said things like: 'You were really pissing me off in those days,' or 'You had some front. Who did you think you were?' Others have told me I was really brave: these could easily have been high-profile failures instead of successes. The way I look at it, if you don't try things, you don't give yourself a chance to succeed.

Alexander Mann seemed to be on the threshold of becoming a really great company, but I was wary of feeling too confident after what was happening to Reid Trevena. I knew there were no guarantees, and perhaps that's why I made just about the most outrageous purchase of my life while I had the money. I sold my Rolls-Royce and promptly bought another. The reason why I say it was an outrageous purchase was because less than two years earlier I had bought a house for £75,000. My new Rolls-Royce Corniche cost £77,000. It was such a massive amount that I felt nervous about it, and there was a little bit of me that worried I'd have to pay for my purchase with something other than money. From then on, I decided that I would only ever buy anything if I could afford two of them.

Chapter 14

Having Fun (1987–1989)

'*My strategy for growth was to invest all the profits back into the company and, when the staff saw where the money was going, their enthusiasm and motivation went up.*'

O N 3 APRIL 1987 I cried for the first time in my adult life. When I held my daughter in my arms, I was overcome. I hadn't expected it to be such an emotional occasion, but the sense that she was a part of me, an extension of me in some way, set off fireworks inside me and the feelings of love, of joy, of pride were so immense that I wept.

We had spent a long time discussing names before she was born and we both wanted our children to have names that would bridge the culture our families were from and the culture they would grow up in. We chose Jemma-Lia, and from the very beginning there was no doubt that Jemma was her father's daughter. She had my features, my curly hair, and as she developed it was weird to see that she had my mannerisms, too.

Aisha was not the kind of woman who was going to give up her career for motherhood, and after a couple of months at home with Jemma she went back to managing the boutiques and we got a nanny. By then, I knew enough people who had employed domestic staff and seen how having the wrong people in your home could easily become a nightmare. Even people I know in recruitment spend less time and effort finding someone to work in their home than they do in their business. I went to great lengths not just to get the best nanny for Jemma, but to find one who was right for us.

At weekends we used to take Jemma for a walk in Winchmore Hill, where there's a road called Broad Walk. It's a very wide, tree-lined road which has to be one of north London's most desirable streets to live in. There's hardly any traffic, a fabulous park, and palatial houses with huge gardens and swimming pools. Someone told me that Rod Stewart lived there, and you could easily see why. It was the kind of road that you would drive down really slowly just so that you could get a good look at the houses!

On this particular trip we saw a For Sale sign and started wondering if we could afford to move there. The last house, in Mill Hill, had cost £75,000, and this one was going for £550,000 – several million in today's market – which was a very big leap, and I didn't know if I was ready for that kind of debt.

Alexander Mann was doing well enough for me to realise that, actually, I was really pretty good at recruitment, and I was also good at running a business. So I asked myself: *Do I believe Alexander Mann will continue to be successful?* When I realised the answer was yes, I also realised I could afford the repayments on the mortgage for what would be anyone's dream house.

It was fabulous. You could have parked ten cars in the drive if you'd needed to; it had more bedrooms than I remember, so many reception rooms that I could put a full-size snooker table in one without it getting in the way, and really extensive gardens. In fact, it was such a gorgeous house that it was almost too much, and when friends and family visited I occasionally felt slightly uncomfortable. We were undoubtedly the youngest couple in the street, and in many ways it was the kind of house you aspired to live in when you retired, rather than when you were in your twenties. When my parents came back from Pakistan to meet Jemma for the first time, my father was clearly impressed and I realised that ever since I had left home I had been wanting to find out what I could achieve on my own. That house was the first purchase that made my success real. It was tangible, it wasn't P&L or accounts, or a bank balance. Success isn't about those things – it's about what you do with your money – and to me that house was a representation of what I had achieved in business. I didn't think life could get any better, but then Aisha told me she was pregnant again. *It's like buses*, I thought! *I wait all this time to be a father and then I get two children within a year!*

There was a big part of me that really hoped our second child would be a boy. Not because I wanted a son to take to Chelsea or anything like that, but simply because I was curious to see how different it would be to have a boy. When our second daughter arrived, however, I had no sense of disappointment, just absolute love. We chose the name Hanah as it's a name that's in the Koran as well as the Bible and it bridges both cultures. With only eleven months between them, it's not surprising that Jemma and Hanah have always been close. What's fascinating is that Hanah is as much like Aisha as Jemma is like me in terms of looks and mannerisms. As babies I found them absolutely enchanting, and if I got home after Aisha had put them to bed I would drive her nuts by waking them up just so that I could spend some time with them.

'Don't you dare! I've only just got them to sleep!'

But I couldn't help myself, and as they grew up I loved spending every moment I could with them – teaching them to swim in a pool I'd had built in the garden, teaching them to ride a bike, play football or helping them read. Being a dad was great fun, and I loved every moment I was with them.

With Aisha and me both running businesses we needed more help at home to manage the place. So we got a gardener, a housekeeper, a guy to come and do the pool and a nanny for each daughter. I'd also had the idea that I wanted a butler ever since I'd seen John Gielgud in *Arthur* – he played a real old-fashioned gent who called Dudley Moore 'sir' and was as discreet as he was indispensable – but I was told that you just couldn't get them any more.

By the end of 1988 Alexander Mann had grown to about twelve people, and it was giving me an income in excess of £250k a year. With the house and the cars I had everything I could ever want materially, and, if nothing were to change, the business could have given Aisha and my daughters a fantastic lifestyle for ever.

I felt like I had a choice: either I could keep Alexander Mann as a lucrative boutique, or I could try to grow the business. My dream had been to have a big open-plan office like Reid Trevena with hundreds of employees ringing the sales bell all day long, and I realised that I still wanted that.

When I meet entrepreneurs at my public-speaking engagements these days, the one area of my career that gets the most attention is how I turned Alexander Mann from a boutique into a corporate organisation. History is littered with companies that tried and failed to expand, as there are so many pitfalls: if you move too fast your overheads can gobble you up, and if you move too slowly your competitors can steal your thunder.

Most entrepreneurs are control freaks and they want to be involved with everything from ordering the stationery to hiring staff to negotiating the lease, as well as actually doing the deals and winning the contracts. If you try to manage every little piece of your company, it can never get any bigger than you are. I realised that if I wanted to grow the business I couldn't do everything: there were going to be some areas of the business that I would have to let go of.

Although I was able to delegate to Sam Collins when I was out of the office, it wasn't fair to ask her – or anyone else for that matter – to give up her clients and, crucially, her commission, to take over some of the administrative tasks that would have freed up my time. The only way I could see to grow the business was if I concentrated on those areas, but that meant that I would have to stop billing.

At the time I was the company's biggest biller, bringing in over £200k a year in fees. If I stopped billing, Alexander Mann's cash flow would lose around £20k a month, and for a small business that's the kind of hit that makes you vulnerable. Making the decision to stop billing was probably the biggest one I had faced in my career, and I just wasn't sure what to do.

I had to ask myself a couple of questions. Firstly, did I believe my team could bill the difference? And, secondly, did I think the changes I would be free to implement would earn more than I could by billing? These were questions I couldn't have asked twelve months earlier, but now that the concept of mid-market headhunting had been proven, now that I had recruited and trained able and motivated people, it was possible to look to the future. I lay in bed at night tossing and turning: I was excited about what could be achieved, but I was nervous of taking such a big risk.

By this stage, the eighties economic boom was in full swing. The papers were full of dealers making fortunes overnight, young entrepreneurs like Alan Sugar were making the headlines, and *Dallas* and *Dynasty* were the biggest shows on TV. There was a culture of thinking big, and maybe somewhere in the background that was influencing me.

By now, I was talking to my dad every week on the phone. The damage I had done to our relationship when I'd left home had been completely repaired, in part because now that I was a father myself there was a new dimension to our relationship. Talking every week had brought us really close again, and he was a useful sounding board for most situations, but this was something he had never dealt with in his career.

I decided to take my family on holiday for a couple of weeks – my first proper holiday in years – to think over my options. I knew that if I spoke to any of my friends, they would tell me I was stupid to walk away from that kind of income, so I wanted to go somewhere where I wouldn't be influenced. One of the things I have been very good at in my career is making uncluttered decisions. Don't listen to your friends; don't read what the papers say: just look at the facts and assess what you really want.

We went to Greece, and as I sat on a beach I considered all my options. On the one hand Alexander Mann felt like a company in the right place, at the right time, in the right market, and I started to believe the business could grow. I started to believe in the future. I could visualise it being a real player in British recruitment. On the other hand it was a massive risk and if I got it wrong it could be game, set and match. It felt like playing roulette, like putting it all on red, and I don't like that feeling. Although a lot of entrepreneurs are very risk-tolerant, I'm actually not one of them. I now see that a big part of my career has been about risk management: I have always considered the odds and the options, and it's only when I've calculated that the risk is minor, or even non-existent, that I've pushed forward for things. The risk here was pretty big, however: once I stopped billing, within three to six months my clients would find another agency and we would have lost the business for good. Not only would I personally have to take a huge drop in earnings, but it was even possible that the company could get into serious cash-flow problems and go under.

Normally in these circumstances I ask myself, *What's the worst that could happen?* I suppose you might say that the worst was that I would have to start from scratch again, but being successful was now part of my identity, part of how I saw myself, and the fear of losing everything was really quite palpable. I had just seen Reid Trevena fall apart, and I desperately didn't want the same thing to happen to my company. Failing at that point would have felt like knocking on my parents' door two weeks after I'd moved out and saying: 'You were right, I'm useless, I can't make it on my own.'

I knew I couldn't bill *and* offer that strategic leadership, and I also knew that unless I had the time to get to grips with the accounting and legal side of things I wouldn't really be in charge. I came to the conclusion that I believed in the business, and I believed in me and my team enough to do it: I was going to stop billing. When I told Aisha my decision she was totally supportive: she believed in me, too.

When I got back to the office, I called everyone together for a meeting.

'I think this business could really become something special, but to do that I think it needs some strategic leadership, someone who's job it is to drive us forward.'

'Who have you hired?' someone asked.

'No one. I'm going to do it.'

'Really?' They couldn't believe that I would stop billing, that I would stop having the contact with the clients that I so clearly enjoyed.

'Listen, this business isn't just about me, it's about you, and I want you to do well, I want us all to do well, so I've decided that means I should stop billing and focus on the strategic side of things.'

It took a little while for my announcement to sink in, but it didn't take long for some joker to pipe up: 'Can I have Glaxo, then?'

'Sure.' That *really* surprised them. 'If I'm going to stop billing then you're all going to have to start billing more because the only way I can replace my income is by increasing yours. So we're going to divide my clients between you and I'm going to take you out and introduce you to the key people, because the first step is to get you all billing more.'

Of course, the more they billed, the more they would earn, so this went down well. 'I'm going to spend time with all of you making sure that my clients are taken care of, and together I believe we can build something to be proud of.'

Everyone likes to feel that the company they're working for is on the up, and the team responded brilliantly. It was now my job to look to the future, and mentally I sketched out a new job description for me as managing director. I wasn't an accountant, I didn't really understand balance sheets, but I knew that if I was going to build the business I had to learn: that was my job now.

I started to look at new sectors: should we be in IT, for instance? Or should we offer in-house training programmes, or company cars, or BUPA cover, or pensions? I considered every aspect of the business and looked for ways I could turn it from a boutique into a corporation. I found it strange not always worrying about how my candidates were doing, but I was finding my new challenges very stimulating, which meant I was enjoying myself. I actually found dealing with the monthly management accounts really interesting, and seeing patterns in our billing, our costs and our margins was a revelation. Slowly, things that had always baffled me a bit were coming into focus simply because I had the time to concentrate on them.

I was working out things such as how much it really cost me to hire someone. When I hired a new member of staff, it took them three months to place their first candidate, and it would be another six to eight weeks before the invoice was settled. That meant I had to know exactly how much money was coming in to be sure of expanding the team. This was stuff I had known instinctively, but now I had concrete figures and processes that would help me grow the business.

I was also spending a lot of time walking the floor, moving from desk to desk, and checking in with the team to help them solve their problems. Fairly quickly, the company's performance started to rise, and within eight months of me stepping back we had grown to eighteen members of staff.

My strategy for growth was to invest all the profits back into the company. Aisha and I had everything we needed and if there was money in the bank it was spent on the business. First there was money to computerise, then to advertise: everything was an investment in the future, and, when the staff saw where the money was going, their enthusiasm and motivation went up.

The office was a great place to be, and I was finding more and more interesting ways to keep the atmosphere at fever pitch. A good example of this is the day I gave away my Porsche.

I had just hired a guy called Mike from the Michael Page agency. I'd admired him for a while and was really pleased that he'd joined the company. He'd had an important client to meet and he asked if I'd go with him. We drove there in my Porsche 928 S4 and all the way there he was talking about the car. He clearly loved it and was playing with the gadgets, like a kid in a toyshop, for the entire journey.

The meeting went really well, and on the way back I asked him:

'What are you going to bill this year?'

'I don't know, James. I guess at least £300k.' To put this in perspective, even I had only be able to bill £200k: this guy was good.

'That means you'll be making £100k. What were you earning at Michael Page?'

'About £40k.'

'So you'll be £60k up by the end of the year. You could afford a car like this.'

We carried on chatting when we got back to the office and my brain started going at 100mph. I could feel I was about to do something dramatic. As he turned to go back to his desk I called out:

'Mike.'

'Yes, James?'

I grabbed my car keys.

'You know what you said about billing £300k?'

'Yes?'

'If you're going to bill it anyway, you might as well take the car now.'

I threw him the keys.

'What do you mean?'

'Look, you just spent twenty minutes telling me what a fantastic car it is, you told me it's your dream to own a Porsche like that. Why don't you just take mine?'

'James, you've completely confused me.'

'You say you're going to bill three hundred grand, so you're going to make £100k. I don't know what the car's worth exactly, but let's say it's £60k. To me that's £5k a month. You'll be earning £8k a month for the next twelve months, so I'll just take it out of your wages.'

He looked really confused.

'How are you going to get home?'

'I'll take the bus.'

'I'm just going to ask you again, James. Are you telling me I can take these keys now and it's my car?'

'Yes.'

'What's your wife going to say?'

'She'll think I've completely lost it.'

'You're giving me the car?'

'I'm not giving you the car, Mike, you're going to earn it, you're going to pay me. And when I've got the £60k I'll give you the logbook.'

'What happens if I don't bill?'

'We'll have to have a chat then.'

'So it's mine?'

'It's yours, now get back to work.'

You can imagine what happened in the building for the rest of the day: the place was on fire because the boss had given a guy who'd only been in the company four weeks his brand new Porsche.

Mike paid me for that car by month eight. My philosophy of giving recognition before it's asked for made him realise I believed in him, and so he really started to believe in himself. In giving him the car I had given him a tangible target to aim for and he raced towards it. The car crystallised what he was working for and his billing started to soar: by the end of the year he'd actually billed £460,000. That's 50 per cent more than he'd predicted.

I hadn't really been in any doubt that he could do it. After a month working with him I was convinced he could bill, and when I tossed him the keys I said to myself: 'If I gave him a reason to bill at a level he's never billed before, would I take a bet he could do it?' The answer was yes. I didn't think he'd ever had something to aim for like that, something to believe in, and my dad's maxim of always doing the opposite was really playing in my head. Most employers would offer the car only when the guy had billed the £300k, but I just thought: imagine what he'd do if I gave him the car now. What are the chances of me giving him that car, and him turning round in twelve months' time and saying: 'James, I'm really sorry, I had a shit year . . .' That just wasn't going to happen: there was no way he would ever give that car back to me. His family, his girlfriend, the entire office were all impressed. Imagine what he would feel like if he turned up in his old Mini one day? If I gave him the car, I knew I could be absolutely certain he'd bring in that £300k. The extra £160k he billed wasn't entirely a surprise either. Win, win, win: he won, Alexander Mann won and I won.

The impact of that sent ripples through the business, and everybody's motivation levels increased. Everyone wanted to know what Mike was billing and if he was going to keep the car. I can't tell you the amount of business that generated, because Mike was billing at such a prolific rate and everybody else tried to catch up. Mike broke every target we'd ever had – highest single fee, best ever month, best ever quarter. It was definitely worth a lot more to me than the Porsche that I replaced within a month anyway.

I was now pretty well known in the industry and I was often taken out for lunch by people who thought getting to know me would be good for their business. One of those people was David Head, the publisher of a trade publication called *The Interviewer*. As a regular advertiser I was a valuable client, and it was his job to know who was doing what in recruitment. He clearly knew everyone in the business and had a lot of experience, and as we were talking I had an impulsive idea.

'Have you ever thought about setting up on your own?'

He was quite shocked that I'd asked, and so was I – I'd only just had the idea.

'All the time,' he said, 'but I haven't got the money.'

'Tell me, David, if money wasn't a problem, what kind of magazine would you launch?'

I liked David and I suddenly saw an opportunity to create a nice little business. As he talked, the idea of owning a recruitment magazine started to appeal. People really would think I was an upstart! It became clear that David had a firm vision of a different kind of trade publication, and the more he told me about it, the more I could see how it would appeal.

'I tell you what, David, you work out what it would cost to launch and I'll back you.'

When he broke it down, launching a magazine didn't cost much: it was no more than a rented office, David's salary, a PA plus the print and postage costs. We knew what the going rate for advertising was, so it was straightforward to come up with the figures: David reckoned he'd need £20k to see him through to break-even, which meant my investment wouldn't amount to much more than paying in advance for my advertising for the first year. The only question I had to ask myself was whether I believed he could sell the advertising, and I only had to look at how many pages he sold at *The Interviewer* to know that he could. It would never be a huge business, but it was a solid one and I thought it would be fun.

Recruitment International launched in 1989 and it was different from other trade publications because it had a photographic cover. In time I realised that appearing on the cover was so good for people's profiles that we could charge them for the privilege. A year on, I found myself looking at our back issues and was pretty impressed by the calibre of people we'd featured. Then I started to think how great it would be if we could get some of them to speak at a conference. I thought recruitment professionals would pay good money to see them all on the same bill. So I gave David a call.

'If we set up a conference called something like "World Leaders in Recruitment", do you think you could get some of our cover stars to speak?'

'I think with that title they couldn't refuse. Their egos mean we probably wouldn't have to pay them either.'

'How much do you think we could charge?'

'I'll ask around, but my hunch is around £300.'

'Could you set it up fairly easily?'

All David had to do was book the venue and advertise tickets in the magazine which, of course, cost him nothing. I got my PR person from Alexander Mann to work on it and we got one of our biggest clients, Arthur Andersen, to sponsor it. We sold 420 tickets for the first one, and David has run 'World Leaders in Recruitment' ever since.

David still runs *Recruitment International* out of a leased office with a PA. The business has hardly changed apart from the fact that I no longer own a piece of it. Five or six years after launch, David offered to buy me out. We agreed an amount that he borrowed from the bank and repaid through profits. As far as I know, he's never sought to launch another title or offer a whole range of events: sticking to the one magazine and landmark annual event gives him a very nice income with none of the hassles of staff, investors or premises. He has proved that running a successful business doesn't necessarily mean running a big business.

Although I had very little to do with the day-to-day operation of *Recruitment International*, it still added to my workload and, as I was working late one Friday, I said goodnight to one of the guys as he was leaving. I couldn't help but notice he looked as exhausted as I felt. I didn't want my team to go home on a Friday night thinking, 'I've got to get away from this place.' I wanted them to leave on a high, so over the weekend I started thinking about what I could do on a Friday afternoon that would create a sense of fun and lift their spirits at the end of a hard week.

The following Friday I said to everyone, 'Let's knock off early tonight. Instead of finishing at 7 p.m., let's turn the phones off at 5 p.m., we'll get a few beers in and we'll just take it easy. How does that sound?'

When 5 p.m. came round, I heard people saying – with delight in their voices – 'I'm sorry, we're closing early today, can I call you back on Monday?' and we opened the beer and just talked to one another. I can't remember who told the first joke, but it soon turned into a joke-telling competition and by 5.15 we were all in hysterics. The whole team was there – the admin and support people, not just the sales guys – and it was clear that people were starting to talk to colleagues they hadn't really got to know before.

When people left that evening, many were off to the pub to carry on the fun, and everyone left with a smile on their face. I decided to make fun on a Friday night Alexander Mann's new creed. 'From now on,' I said to one of the consultants on the way to a meeting, 'we're going to close early on a Friday and do something as a team. Apart from drinking beer, what else can we do?'

'I don't know.'

'We're bright people. We must be able to come up with something.'

'Well, maybe we could do a sketch.'

'A sketch of what?'

'How about *Blind Date*? Someone could be Cilla Black, we could have Our Graham making the announcements, get three people to be the dates and someone else to be the contestant.'

I liked the idea, and on the way back to the office we planned it all. We asked one guy on the team who had a fantastic sense of humour to write out all the questions, but we didn't tell anyone else what we were planning. On the Friday morning I told the rest of them.

'I thought we'd wrap up at 5 p.m. again today, and, just so as you know, we're going to do a sketch.'

'Oh, no!'

'There's no debate, you're all coming. It's a *Blind Date* sketch and I've taken the liberty of allocating the roles. You're going to be Our Graham, you're the contestant, and you're Cilla.' I handed the participants cards with their lines on. 'I want you to take an hour at lunchtime, go and sit in the park, learn your lines, and at five o'clock we're doing the sketch.'

'I can't do that!'

'I don't want to!'

'Listen, there's no debate. Five o'clock. We're doing it. We're all doing it.'

Come five o'clock, the atmosphere was just unbelievable, and we had such a good time that night that the team insisted on doing it the following week, too. At five the next Friday, the theme tune to *This Is Your Life* blared out and the sales rep who was being Eamonn Andrews said: 'James Caan, this is your life!' The staff then paraded dressed up as people from my past – my mum, the first girl I kissed, the bank manager – it was hilarious.

One week we had a staff band and they brought in drum kits and guitars and microphones. The talent in that team was incredible and absolutely matched by their enthusiasm. There was a guy in the office called Terry who was able to take the lyrics of any song we gave him and rewrite them on the theme of Alexander Mann. One week we challenged him to do Queen's *Bohemian Rhapsody* and, instead of starting out with the original opening line, Terry's version began with a lyric I have never forgotten:

'Jimmy, I just placed a man . . .'

We had such a good time on those Friday nights that we became really good friends. We even started an annual fancy-dress day, and I will never forget the day that Mahatma Gandhi travelled in on the train from Cambridge, or the time we had a pantomime horse stopping traffic outside the office!

I'm still good friends with a lot of the people from Alexander Mann, and I know for a fact that those years were as special to them as they were to me. We all had such a good time and none of us has ever worked anywhere like it since.

Chapter 15

Kidnap (1988)

'Kidnapping is a business for some people in Pakistan, and if they don't carry out their threats occasionally, then their business will dry up.'

I T STARTED WITH a phone call out of the blue.

Life was going well, the business was great, and Aisha and I were getting ready to go out one Saturday night.

'Nazim?' a voice said on a crackling line.

Nobody called me Nazim any more.

'Yes.'

'This is your uncle. I am calling with bad news.'

I hadn't spoken to my father's brother for over a decade: I barely knew him because he'd always lived in Pakistan. Whatever he was calling me about had to be very serious. Was my mum OK? Or my dad? Or had something happened to one of my sisters? My heart was in my mouth.

'Your father has been kidnapped.'

'What?' *Kidnapped?* He had to be making it up. This was some kind of joke, wasn't it?

'He was jogging in the park yesterday when a car pulled up and four or five men got hold of him, put him in the car and drove off.

They rang today and said if we didn't pay the ransom we will suffer the consequences.'

'How much is the ransom?'

'They will call at four o'clock tomorrow to tell us how much and give us instructions on how to hand over the money.'

I was completely freaked out. People didn't get kidnapped. It was something you read about in the papers, not something that happened to my family. Still not sure if this was some kind of prank, I called my brother Adam.

'You'll never guess what . . .'

Adam called our uncle and satisfied himself that it was absolutely genuine.

'What should we do?' he asked.

'I'm going to call the police.'

'The kidnappers said we mustn't.'

'They were talking about the police in Pakistan.'

I called Scotland Yard and was put through to an officer who had experience of several overseas kidnappings. 'What should we do?' I asked.

'Honestly? You should pay the ransom.'

This really frightened me. 'You're seriously saying that if we don't pay the ransom the kidnappers will kill my father?'

'There is a real chance that will happen. Kidnapping is a business for some people in Pakistan, and if they don't carry out their threats occasionally, then their business will dry up.'

'What about dealing with police there?'

'I wouldn't bother. It's a politically unstable place and kidnappings are quite common there. There's a chance they're involved somewhere down the line anyway, and if they're not involved there's probably a reason why they don't want to be involved. Seriously, if you have the money, I would pay the ransom.'

I couldn't believe it. The concept was just so alien to me, and I was quickly realising just how big the cultural divide was between

Britain and Pakistan. I couldn't believe Scotland Yard was telling me to pay up. There had to be another way, so I called a Pakistani friend who worked for one of the major banks and was much more in tune with Pakistani politics and culture.

'I think you should give them the money.'

I couldn't believe he was telling me this, too.

'And should I call the police?'

'Absolutely not.'

I didn't know what to do but I just wanted to do something. Perhaps I should get on a plane? I called another friend for advice.

'Don't do that.'

'Why not?'

'How do you know you're not the real target? You've been featured in the press a few times. Anyone can see you live in a nice house and drive a nice car. Maybe someone from the community knows that your father has a wealthy son; maybe they're actually targeting you.'

Oh, my God. I hadn't thought of that. I couldn't think straight. Aisha didn't know what I should do for the best either. Emotionally, I wanted to go to Pakistan and be there for my father because our weekly phone calls had brought us really close again, but I was scared that going there would make things worse. Maybe it wasn't the right time to leave Aisha and the girls alone.

Nevertheless, the one thing I couldn't do was nothing, so Adam and I met at Heathrow the following morning and got on a flight to Karachi. I called an old family friend who said we could stay with him, but he was adamant that we mustn't tell our parents or anyone else where we were because it was too dangerous.

By the time we landed, the kidnappers had made their demands and I called Aisha for the figure. For obvious reasons, I don't want to reveal the amount they were asking for, but let's just say it was significant: a lot of money for the UK, and a fortune for Pakistan. I hadn't been in Pakistan since that family holiday in 1971. It was a country where the culture, the language and the infrastructure were unfamiliar, and Adam and I were dependent on our hosts. We spent a day at their house waiting for the phone to ring with more news while I made arrangements to get the cash with my friend who worked for the bank. He knew I had assets and would be good for the loan, but there was no way I could sign the paperwork.

'You're going to have to trust me.'

'I do trust you, James, but we've got procedures. I'll see what I can do and call you back.'

Every minute was like an hour, and when the bank didn't call I started to panic: if I couldn't arrange the cash, then it would be my fault if anything happened to my dad. I must have looked at my watch every minute, but still the bank didn't call. Eventually the phone rang: it was Aisha.

'Are you sitting down?'

'Just tell me!'

'Your uncle called,' she told me. 'The police have found your dad. He's alive and they're taking him to the house.'

'Really?'

The relief was intense, but instantly I had so many questions – how had they found him? Was he OK? Had the kidnappers been caught?

'I don't have any details, only that he's alive.'

Thank you, God.

Even though there was a risk that the kidnappers were laying some kind of trap, there was no way I wasn't going to the house: I had to see my father.

We knocked on the door and, of course, as no one knew we were in the country they were amazed to see us. When I saw my father I was just as shocked: he was filthy and unshaven and I realised I had never seen him with a beard. And it was a *white* beard: it had been so long since I'd seen him that he had started to go grey. It made his appearance seem ten times worse to me than it probably was. All my life he had got up before me and had always shaved first thing. It's funny how the little things make such a big impact, but the sight of him with a white beard has stayed with me ever since.

'What are you doing here?' My dad was obviously very excited to see us, but confused that we had appeared unexpectedly. 'How did you get here?'

We hugged each other and we were all tearful, euphoria mixed with exhaustion and relief.

'We couldn't sit there and wait. We had to come.'

He told us how he had been taken to desolate marshland and been tied to a tree. Eventually he had been left alone and for an entire day he'd rubbed the rope against the tree until it frayed. He showed us his hands and the skin on his wrists was raw and I noticed the blood on his torn shirt. Eventually he had been able to snap the rope and ran until he reached a farm. The farmer called the police and he was picked up and brought home.

'I'm so glad you two are here,' he said, 'but you have to go now. The kidnappers might come back.'

'We've only just got here. I'm not leaving you. And if it's not safe for us, it's even less safe for you. You can identify them. You're the one who should be leaving.'

There was a big debate: my father had been through enough and didn't want the kidnappers to drive him from his home, but to protect our mum and the kids he accepted that going to Lahore and staying with his family for a few weeks was probably a wise precaution. Reluctantly, Adam and I got back on a plane and headed for London.

It was such a weird experience: it was so intense, so bizarre, and the fact that it was over so quickly made it almost unreal. I was so focused on whether or not my father would live or die that I didn't have the capacity to take in much about the country of my birth. I was pretty shocked at how differently things worked in Pakistan – it was all about personal contacts rather than institutions, and you turned to friends ahead of the authorities – and on reflection I realised that I felt far more British than Pakistani.

It was an incredibly confusing few days. Aside from the cultural divisions and the anxiety about what was happening to my father, in the back of my mind there was the thought that they were actually after me. And not having seen my parents for so long, and then only seeing them for a matter of hours, was emotionally hard to deal with. From one minute to the next we hadn't known what might happen. The kidnappers might have killed him, or the bank might have phoned and I would have had to collect the money. Would I have needed protection? There were so many different scenarios playing out in my head simultaneously that I would have been completely disorientated, even without those strange couple of hours with my parents and my brothers and sisters. On the plane on the way home I had to keep asking myself if these things had really happened. When I went back to the office the next day and carried on as normal, it felt increasingly surreal.

For several weeks my anxiety levels were higher than normal as we waited to see if the kidnappers would come back for my father. After six or seven weeks, he got fed up with hiding in a friend's house. It was no way to live his life, and so the family moved back to Karachi and got on with their lives.

Despite my relief, I could not relax. At this stage in my life I was working so hard – I would be in the car at six in the morning and not leave the office until eight at night – and I wasn't spending nearly enough time with the girls. There were days when the only chance Aisha and I would get to talk would be over the phone between meetings. Even when I got home, the phone would ring or there would be accounts to look at or the trade press to read.

As I don't drink – except the odd glass of champagne at celebrations – I was finding it increasingly hard to unwind. I smoke

– I smoked a lot more in those days – and cigars and cigarettes helped ease my stress, but that only made my lifestyle even unhealthier. Regular meals, fresh food, a balanced diet – these things just don't happen when you work as hard as I did, and the only way I found to unwind was massage. Several times a week a masseuse came to the house and pushed and pulled at my muscles to release some of the tension.

We had a tennis club at the back of the house – you could reach it through a gate at the end of our garden – and I found playing a couple of sets helped to get me focused on something other than the business for an hour, and, of course, when I was with the girls I would forget about the hassles and excitement of work. They were utterly delightful toddlers, and I loved taking them out for day trips or just watching them play together in the garden.

Building a business was so demanding, so time-consuming and so engrossing and rewarding that when I look back on those years I don't remember much else. I couldn't be sure who was Prime Minister half the time, let alone Chancellor. I don't even know how Chelsea did for entire seasons in the eighties and nineties. Royal weddings came and went, elections passed without me knowing, and I even had nieces and nephews I didn't get to meet until they were toddlers.

The business was fantastic, but building it came at a price. It was one I was prepared to pay, but I am well aware that there are people who have worked just as hard as me and paid a much higher price. I've met entrepreneurs who have turned to drink and drugs to get them through; some of them then lost control of their businesses and were left with nothing. Building a business is great fun, but it is also the hardest thing I've ever done in my life.

Chapter 16

Life in the Office
(1989–1991)

'I almost certainly should have computerised, but I just didn't understand computers enough to know how important they were.'

A T THE END OF THE 1980s things were going very well for Alexander Mann. The recruitment fairs meant we had a constant stream of candidates. We also ran advertising campaigns on Capital Radio in London that helped to boost our profile and our supply of quality candidates. The booming economy also meant that picking up vacancies was relatively easy.

I was making good money and as the sole owner of the business I could do what I liked with the profits. My accountant encouraged me to expand, but I made the decision to pay my mortgage off instead. It didn't make much sense to do that as the cash could have been used to create value elsewhere in the business rather than clear a debt that I wasn't struggling to repay, but I just wanted the security of knowing the house was paid for. I suppose I've always been a bit cautious like that.

My accountant also suggested that we should move to bigger offices. I still had this fear of incurring overheads, but his comments did make me think that maybe it was at least time to redecorate the offices. I remember the day the decorators came in and took the sales charts off the wall, leaving big white rectangles. We had smoked so much that the walls had gone yellow. That we smoked in the office seems so outdated now, but in those days pretty much everyone smoked and I'd pity the one or two who didn't.

What was interesting was that when new people joined, within a couple of weeks they had started smoking Rothman's, which was my brand, and my packet of cigarettes was deemed a communal packet. It's an example of how – despite my efforts to grow the company – it was still a classic owner-manager business and my personality ran right through every layer of the business. Although Alexander Mann had doubled in size since I'd stopped billing, I was still struggling with my ambition to make it a corporate entity. It was now just a bigger boutique, and its success was still heavily reliant on me being there.

The thriving economy encouraged a few of the team to think that they could set up on their own, and every so often one of the really able consultants would not only resign and set themselves up in competition, but they would take several members of staff with them, not to mention a few clients. Emotionally, I found that very hard to deal with – it was impossible not to take it personally.

Although the admin side of things was now computerised, the recruitment side of the business was still reliant on boxes of file cards. Of course, this made it very easy for members of staff to take their clients with them when they left, and because having Alexander Mann on your CV was considered prestigious we had quite a high turnover. Some people – like Sam Collins – were loyal both to the company and to me, but a big part of my job was still hiring and training new staff.

I had really come to rely on Sam, and she was great at mentoring new recruits; if I wasn't around people knew they could turn to her. Two of my other managers were also women, Elaine and Cathy, and I remember having lunch with the three of them when the subject of pregnancy came up.

'What would you do if we all got pregnant?'

'Oh, you're not allowed to do that!' I joked and the conversation quickly moved on. Then a couple of weeks later Sam's husband came to pick her up, and by then I'd got to know him quite well.

'Sam tells me she's not allowed to have kids,' he said.

'That's right.' I thought I might as well continue the joke. 'I need her here.'

It seems Sam may have thought I was being serious, because a couple of years later she actually came and asked me if it was OK if she started a family. Of course I was absolutely delighted for her, but I wasn't at all sure how I'd cope without her in the office for several months.

Things change all the time when you run a business. Virtually every day there would be a mini crisis or a new situation I would have to face up to. Whether I needed a lawyer to sort out a dispute with a client, a cleaning company to service the office or a branding agency to improve our corporate image, I was always learning. I often get asked by aspiring entrepreneurs these days how you wear so many hats – after all, none of us can be an expert in every field – but when it's important to your business it's vital that you get the information you need to succeed.

What I typically did in those situations was call three people in to pitch to me for my business. The first person would come in and give me his pitch and by the end of the meeting I would have a pretty basic grasp of what a branding agency could do for me, or a PR agency or an advertising agency.

When the second company came in to see me, I knew a bit more and could ask more pertinent questions. By the time the third company came in, I was well placed to assess its strengths and weaknesses. I had learned that everything I wanted to know was in someone else's head and I just had to keep asking questions until I uncovered the information I was after. My strategy was – and still is – just to say '*How does that work?*' until I found the nugget I needed to make a decision.

I meet a lot of senior executives in business who are uncomfortable asking questions because they perceive that someone of their status and position should already know the answers. I'm the complete opposite: I am very comfortable asking questions and I don't have the kind of ego that worries about whether people think I'm smart or not. So with every situation, my routine is the same: *What do you do? How do you do it? What do you charge? How does it work? How will I know if your work has been successful or not? What would I measure you with?* I'm very comfortable being direct or inquisitive, so I just ask.

After I'd asked my questions, I would have enough information to call the companies I liked back in or would have gathered leads to find better companies. By the end of the process I'd be pretty well informed about what I was really looking for: I'd know what the going rate was, I'd know what the broad options were, I'd know how I would be able to tell if it'd been successful, I'd know how long it would take a team of x to do the job well. There's no situation in which that strategy doesn't work, whether it's seeking investment advice or finding someone to fix my guttering.

Sometimes, of course, I drilled down into the external agency's business and realised they weren't offering anything we couldn't do in-house. Did we really need external accountants? Or PR? Or car leasing? When I knew what people really did for their fee, I could make an informed decision about what was best for Alexander Mann.

This technique also subtly allowed me to work out what

someone was making on a contract. 'So you say the materials are £15,000 and it will take a team of fifteen people twenty days?'

'That's right.'

'And what's the day rate for each worker?'

'£150.'

'So, let me see, that's £15k for materials, plus fifteen people, times twenty days, times £150, that's . . . £60k for the job. But you quoted me £75k, what's the extra £15k for?'

And if they couldn't justify the extra, I would negotiate hard: they'd already told me what their costs were, I'd worked out their margin so I knew how hard I could bargain.

I still believed wholeheartedly in my dad's strategy of win-win – I still do, of course – but my negotiating position changed depending on whether I was negotiating for a commodity or a service. If I was simply bargaining with a stationery supplier, I would be looking for the best price, but if I was buying the services of something like a PR agency then price wasn't my only consideration.

If, let's say, an agency had quoted me £2k a month to handle my PR, what would be the point of bargaining them down to £1500? They would have been demoralised, angry even, and they wouldn't work as hard for me. I might as well have thrown that £1500 away.

The other thing I learned to do in negotiations was always to ask one final question when we shook hands: *Are you happy with that deal?* Mostly, people said they were.

'Good, because what I don't want is for you to go back home and feel bad. I want us both to feel that we're going to get what we want out of this deal. So if you're not happy tell me now, don't call me tomorrow saying you've changed your mind.'

Probably about 20 per cent of the time, people said: 'Actually, James, I'm not very happy with it.'

'Great. You've done me a huge favour. Let's sort it out now. If you could change one of the pieces of this deal, what would it be?'

The remarkable thing is that when you ask this question, the answer you get is very rarely about money. It might the timing of payment, or the deadline for delivery, or a clause that allows for renegotiation after a certain period. Sometimes, though, it is about money. So I would ask them what a fair price is.

'I know it's not right for you to do it for nothing. I don't want to work with somebody who has no margin, so tell me at what price the deal starts working for you.'

I always wanted to make sure that when they walked out of the door they were happy with the deal, and, you know what, no one's ever asked me the same question! It's something that we just don't ask in business and yet to me it makes perfect sense. If you're going to be working together on a project that's important to both of you, isn't it just common sense that you will work better together if you're both happy with the deal?

I was getting a lot of things right, but, looking back, I can see that I also made one pretty big mistake. If I had invested in properly computerising the company, then I probably would have found it easier to grow the business and break out of the boutique trap. The truth is, I almost certainly should have computerised, but I just didn't understand computers enough to know how important they were. When I'd started in the mid-eighties I'd made sure I understood every aspect of my business, but as technology became more important there was a whole element of the operation that I neglected. I let my personal disinterest in computers affect my business, and, if I had taken a different stance and tried to get to grips with what computerisation could have done for Alexander Mann, maybe the company could have been twice, if not ten times, as big.

I was still working long hours – on average probably fifteen hours a day – but I always made sure I had time for my family. If one of the girls was giving a performance at school, I was always there; if there was a sports day or a parents' evening I made sure

I was there on time. Sometimes these school events would cut into my working day, but I would just get in the car and leave Sam in charge.

Jemma and Hanah both went to school in Hampstead, which was on my way to work, so I sometimes took them there in the morning. I loved our car journeys and always tried to make them fun. When they were little I used to get them to give me the names of a country starting with the letter A and go through the alphabet. Or capital cities, or vegetables, or fashion designers. When they got a bit older we'd play a game with number plates. If a car's registration was A815 TNH, I'd ask them to multiply eighty-one by five. They became good at doing large sums and they really enjoyed it. If it was ever possible for me to work from home, I would try to pick them up from school, too. They were such good company that I wanted to spend as much time as I could with them.

Although most of the staff enjoyed working at Alexander Mann, not everyone coped with our boisterous, noisy office where practical jokes were a matter of course, and some people found our sales environment intimidating. One of the jokes was that people called me Jesus, for no other reason than my initials are JC, but sometimes new recruits would – naturally enough – think that just too weird. Some people struggled to fit in, and when one person finds it difficult to cope it becomes hard for the people sitting near them not to be affected, so I would have to have a chat with them. With no meeting rooms or private offices, these delicate discussions took place in full view of the rest of the team.

'I see you've been here nearly six months now and you've not made a placement. Why do you think that is?'

'Well, it's taken me time to find my feet, and I've come close a few times. I don't think my first placement is far away.'

'Our top billers are placing eight people a month. Do you think you could place eight people a month one day?'

'I don't know about eight, James. Can I just start with one?'

These chats were known in the office as 'Come to Jesus' meetings, and everyone knew when they were taking place.

'How are you finding it on the phones?'

'To be honest, it's tough; I'm just not getting through to people.'

'I tell you what; give me the people you were going to call this afternoon. I'll make the calls and you listen in. Do you think that would help?'

'If you would do that for me, James, that would be fantastic.'

Sometimes, even with help, the odd person still struggled and they'd have to have another Come to Jesus meeting.

'You still seem to be struggling, and I can tell from your body language that you're not enjoying yourself.'

'It's difficult sitting here seeing other people make placements while I'm getting so many rejections.'

'I know it's tough. If there's anything I can do to help, just say.'

'Thanks. I will.'

'You know, I don't like seeing you like this. You might just have to come to the conclusion that this isn't the right job for you. It's not for everyone. Maybe you should give it another couple of months, and if you still feel this way, maybe you should think again?'

And do you know what? After that conversation, 80 per cent of the strugglers resigned within two months. There was no disciplinary procedure, no dispute, just a recognition from all parties that it hadn't worked out. The other 20 per cent started to look for something else because they just couldn't survive on their basic pay. And, of course, there is no better place to find a job than at a recruitment agency, and we would actually place them ourselves, and earn a nice fee in the process!

It was about this time that my mum and dad came over for a visit. They absolutely doted on Jemma and Hanah, though my dad thought it was a shame we hadn't had a boy. Much as I loved having two beautiful daughters, I still hankered after a son, and I tried to persuade Aisha that it was time to have another kid. But Aisha really didn't want any more children, and even though I pleaded with her for a couple more years, she wanted to balance a career with a family, and that meant keeping our household to a manageable size.

While my parents were in the country, dad came to visit me in the office and I couldn't resist showing him a cheque that had just arrived from a client for £22,000 for placing a single candidate. His first reaction was that it was a mistake.

'This is crazy. Do they know what they're doing?'

'This is what we do. We're actually really good at finding the best people.'

To him, the idea that someone would pay us £22k for one piece of work was like a joke, and he saw me as just a young guy who'd come up with a flaky idea. I could almost hear him thinking 'It'll never last.' He still didn't take it seriously at all.

That same trip, however, our conversation got very serious. I had just returned from abroad and was putting my travel documents away. When he saw my passport he asked me a question I'd thought I would never have to answer.

'What's the name on your passport?' he said almost casually.

As I turned round to face him, the look in his eyes told me that my answer was going to hurt him deeply. A few months before I had made my name change official with a Change of Name deed. I instantly realised I had made a huge mistake in not telling him earlier.

'It's James Caan.'

There was silence for quite a while. He was really upset. In fact, to say he was upset is an understatement. He was angry. A nickname was all right, he said, but don't lose your identity, don't lose your family name. It was quite a lecture, and I completely understood his point of view. In Asian families tremendous importance is attached to carrying on the family name, and, now that I had become successful, the problem was compounded. The name that got written about in the recruitment press wasn't his name. He was proud of me, but he clearly wasn't proud of my choice of name.

I was a bit ashamed that I hadn't thought about how he would feel. The decision to change my name officially had been one of convenience. All my credit cards had been in the name of Caan, as were all my assets, and professionally it was how I was known. It was only ever a problem when I needed to use my passport as I'd check into a hotel as Nazim Khan and pay as James Caan. It looked a bit dodgy, so I decided to tidy up what I saw as a small administrative problem with a short legal declaration. I hadn't given it any more thought until that conversation with my father.

I realised that I'd been insensitive and really felt I had let him down. It was an absolutely awful moment, and, if I'm being completely honest, I did toy with the idea that maybe it was something I shouldn't have done. But it was too late to go back: my wife knew me as James, my kids knew that was my name, and in the industry I worked in James Caan was a name people recognised.

In recent years a couple of people have accused me of changing my name to fit into British society. I tell them that changing your name doesn't help you integrate: it's not what you're called, it's what you do and who you are that make a difference.

Getting cheques for £22,000 was an indication of how well the company was growing. When I'd started the business, our average fee was £5 or £6k. The economic boom had seen wages skyrocket, and we were now getting 25 per cent of much bigger salaries. That meant I could still afford to help out staff who were struggling to get a deposit together or needed cash for an emergency, but the problem with being that kind of boss was that I was seen as a soft touch. People knew I was pretty laid-back; and as the expenses claims started to add up they just assumed I would pay for things like parking tickets accrued while they were on company business. I was so busy myself that I didn't have the time to go carefully through every expense claim, and so they were just paid.

Of course, the expenses were processed by an accounts executive, but it was only his job to pay them, not to question them. I decided that what I needed was a general manager, someone who could take care of the day-to-day stuff. And as an expert in executive recruitment, I was pretty sure I had found the right guy.

I hired someone completely different from me, someone who was organised and efficient, but this meant there was a culture clash between the new general manager and the team. Whereas I had always tried to help out staff in difficulty, he took a hard line.

'We're not giving them loans to buy a flat,' he'd say. 'If they've got a problem it's up to them to deal with it, not you.'

I knew he was right, and even though his officious presence seemed to affect morale I decided that I'd hired the guy and I had to back him. After a few months, key team members handed in their resignation and, when I asked them why, a few of them told me it was the GM.

I still thought I had found the right man for the job and it was only natural that there would be a transition period, so I accepted the downturn as temporary. But after nine months I realised I couldn't let things slide any longer.

We agreed that it wasn't working out and he left the company. But when I stepped back into the operational side of things I was stunned to see how badly we were doing. Billing was down, clients we had relied on hadn't given us any business for months, and my team of thirty-six motivated people had become twenty-four demoralised individuals. I knew that this couldn't just be down to the GM, though: to my horror, I realised that Alexander Mann had just walked slap bang into a recession.

Chapter 17

The Recession

(1992–1993)

'*It's amazing how changing your state of mind can change everything else.*'

IN 1990, ALEXANDER MANN had made a profit of over half a million. In 1991, that figure dipped to £256,000, a decline I'd put down to the troubles we'd had for the previous nine months. In 1992, however, my profits were just £1475: the economy had fallen off a cliff.

I couldn't believe that you could work as hard as I had, absorb that much stress, create that much energy and end up with £1475. I knew the economy had been going through a tough time, but I was still absolutely stunned when my accountant brought me the end-of year-figure. I was spending more than that a year on petrol.

The recruitment industry is a mirror of the economy as a whole, because the first thing any chief exec in trouble will do is trim his staff bill. No new staff meant no new business for the recruitment industry. When people resigned, they simply weren't replaced. Entire branches of organisations were shut down, and several tiers of management were stripped out: no one was hiring, and the recruitment industry nosedived. The value of shares in recruitment companies virtually halved overnight. The phrase we kept hearing on the phones was 'headcount freeze', and the more it got repeated in the office, the more it started to grate.

I had never experienced a recession before and had no idea how you ran a business in such a climate. All I had known was seven years of fantastic growth and I was completely stunned by it, and utterly clueless about what I could do to change things. After all, I couldn't make my clients hire people for whom they didn't have a budget in that kind of environment. When I asked my accountant for a projection of where we might be in a year's time he said: 'Making a loss.' That really scared me.

Previously, when things had gone wrong I'd been able to try a different approach, find a different angle, but the economy was so bad – unemployment was high, interest rates were high, repossessions were at a record level and the stock market was reeling. The economic boom that had underpinned our success in the eighties had gone spectacularly bust, and there wasn't anything I could do that would make a difference. I called up all my old contacts but no one was hiring, and if there weren't going to be any vacancies for the foreseeable future then I thought we really might as well have turned off the lights and gone home. I found myself in the car driving into work in the morning wondering if it was worth it – there just wasn't anything to do. I started to get resignations from the staff who – naively, as it turned out – thought that things wouldn't be as bad at another agency. The office that had once been full of noise and banter and bell-ringing was now eerily quiet, and it got so bad that I really didn't see a future for Alexander Mann.

We used to have these productivity boards on the walls of the office. When we picked up a vacancy it was marked up in green marker pen; when we had a candidate out on interview that was marked up in red; and when they were hired it was marked up in black. For years I had sat and looked at those boards and seen the green dots turn to black ones, and now I was looking at them and seeing the colours fade away. The thing that struck me was how quickly it had happened: three months before the boards had shown evidence of all the activity, but as the weeks passed they became increasingly empty. I had spent seven years working unbelievably hard to make it a success – I *had* made it a success – and the sensation of having it taken away was really quite crippling and I just didn't want to be there.

I found myself in the very strange position of driving a Rolls-Royce and living in a mansion but I wasn't making any money. I had achieved what it takes most people a lifetime to achieve and was still only thirty-one. Although I knew we wouldn't starve or become homeless – we could always have moved to a smaller house, or downsized to a smaller car – I felt like a complete failure, as if my dad had been right all along. It was the business that paid for everything, but it wasn't just that I wondered how I would pay the bills – my fear was more fundamental than that. When you live in a house like that and have a lifestyle like I had, without the income to support it you actually feel *wrong*, as if you don't belong, and that feeling of insecurity started to eat away at me.

It's a strange sensation to own a Rolls-Royce and not be sure if you can afford to fill its tank. Even without a mortgage the bills were massive: there was the pool guy, the guy who cleaned the cars, the insurance on the cars, the gardener. I don't know how else to describe my emotions at the time except to say that it felt *wrong* to live in that house and say, 'You know what, I'm not going to use the Rolls this weekend,' or 'Let's not have that birthday party for the girls.'

Knowing I didn't have the income to support the lifestyle was emotionally damaging. I was disillusioned, disheartened, and I was ready to throw in the towel and close the business down. That in itself felt weird because I had never thought of myself as a quitter. But I didn't see a way out, so what else could I do? Then I discovered that giving in to those feelings of failure made me feel even worse and I started spiralling downwards. I became moody, I didn't eat, and, looking back, I can see that I was deeply depressed.

What I found difficult to deal with was that friends, colleagues and even family had come to see me as the kind of guy who could sort anything out. They saw me as resourceful and successful, and I suppose that was how I had started to see myself. Everyone thought I would come up with an answer, but I just couldn't find one. Without a secure future in recruitment, I felt emotionally lost. Who was I if I wasn't successful in recruitment? That was my identity, not just my occupation, and without it I felt very unstable.

I started frantically looking round for another business in another sector that wasn't so vulnerable to the economy as a whole. I talked on the phone to my father and talked things over with Aisha, and she was really worried about me leaving recruitment, because what else did I know?

'Well, I know a bit about fashion. People will always need clothes.'

By now she had sold the boutiques so as to be able to spend more time with the kids, but she knew – we both knew – that fashion is actually one of the first things people stop spending money on when money gets tight. So I started looking around for a business that could buck the trend.

With property prices low it seemed there might be an opportunity to shift some of my capital into the property markets, and so I started spending time with some friends of mine who were property developers. If I had been a mature, experienced property investor I might have had the inclination to say it was a good time to buy, but my research was telling me the risks were too high. Borrowing was expensive – interest rates briefly hit 15 per cent in 1992 – and it would have taken too long to make a profit, so I rejected that idea.

The next business I investigated was a sandwich shop. Chains like Pret A Manger were just starting to appear, and I wondered if there was an opportunity to open a rival. People might not always need clothes, but they would always have to eat.

I went to see a friend who ran a sandwich shop and started looking at premises I could lease, but the more I looked into it the less I could see myself getting up at 5 a.m. to be ready for the breakfast trade. I was used to deals where I made £10k a time and I just couldn't get my head round making margins of 50p. It wasn't for me.

I enjoy business, so, although I was motivated by fear and panic to find an alternative to recruitment, I actually found this process of analysis quite interesting, and it helped me keep a sense of myself and what I was good at. So much of business is the same regardless of sector – maintaining good relationships with customers, getting the margins right, seizing opportunities – and my brain was buzzing with possibilities. In the midst of my terror, I found I was having fun, which in turn meant I would rather look for something new than sort out the ever-increasing troubles at Alexander Mann.

I looked again at fashion; after all, Aisha and I made a good team, and if the retail climate wasn't right maybe the wholesale one was. We started talking to old contacts, people who had supplied the boutiques, and I soon realised what a cut-throat business it was. If you agree to supply a garment for £6, there will always be someone who will do it for £5.50. Even if you had a supply deal with a major retailer, the payment terms – they sometimes paid months after you'd delivered the goods and paid your suppliers – meant cash flow was a nightmare, and that was something I just didn't have the appetite for.

By now I had spent several months searching for an alternative business and had really taken my eye off the ball at Alexander Mann. I was rarely in the office, the staff weren't being led or motivated, and their incomes were in freefall because we couldn't make any placements. Every week someone else resigned. There really couldn't have been a worse time for me to take my hands off the wheel, and now the company was in a far worse state than it had been when I'd found out about the profits of £1475. I was now really lost and I just couldn't see a way forward.

I continued to speak to my dad on the phone and he could tell how confused I was. In the previous few months I had practically given myself whiplash from trying to change direction so many times, and what I needed was for someone to tell me what to do.

'Of all the options you've looked at, which is the less risky?'

'I'm not sure.'

'You've spent months looking at other things and none of them is any better than where you are. You think the grass will be greener, but in a recession it's just a different kind of grass.'

As we talked I realised the least risky option was actually sticking with recruitment.

'Why is that?'

'At least I know recruitment and in the other areas I risk capital in industries where I don't know the pitfalls.'

'You're right: you've already made your investment in recruitment, so you're not risking any new capital. And in recruitment', he pointed out, 'you have a brand that means something. That's got to be valuable to you. You wouldn't have that if you started something else.'

He was only saying what I had started to work out for myself, but when someone else says something it tends to crystallise and, as we talked, I began to feel more positive and my affection for Alexander Mann started pulling me back to the company I had been neglecting.

'The best advice I can give you is just to ride it out. Don't expect a lot, don't expect a great year, batten down the hatches, cut your costs as much as you can and just ride it out.'

Although his conclusion was pretty downbeat I actually put the phone down feeling more positive than I had for months. For the first time in ages I had some certainty: I knew what I was going to do, I had some purpose again and I knew that I was going to make Alexander Mann work because there was no alternative.

Knowing that there weren't any greener pastures made me look hard at Alexander Mann. I was now completely focused on surviving the recession and getting the company in the best shape it could be in so that when things started to pick up, as they were bound to do one day, we would be perfectly positioned to take off again. I had gone from being really quite depressed to being fairly optimistic: I was beginning to understand that I do well when I've got something to prove.

It's amazing how changing your state of mind can change everything else, and everybody in the office knew the minute I walked through the door that Monday morning that something had happened. I was in early, I had a smile on my face, and all because I had accepted the situation I was in. I wasn't going to fight it, or torture everyone with 'Why did it have to happen to me?' sob stories. I was going to lay the groundwork for future success.

I called everyone together and levelled with them. And by now 'them' was only eleven people. One of the benefits of paying people on commission is that if they can't earn the commission they generally leave for a job that pays more basic. At least that meant my overheads had dropped significantly, and that was a saving grace, as was the fact that I had ignored my accountant's advice to rent more expensive offices.

'Look, it's tough, and it's going to be tough for a while. None of us is going to be making much money for the next few months, and I don't think we've got any choice but to accept that. If any of you want to move on, then you do so with my blessing, but this won't last for ever, and, in the meantime, we're going to offer some discounts to our clients, maybe do jobs for 15 per cent commission if we have to, pick up whatever work we can, keep our eyes peeled for opportunities and hang in there.'

It wasn't much of a pep talk, but the team responded really well to it. Maybe it was the spirit of the Blitz, but somehow we rallied each other. If I'd told them I had some grand plan, I think they would have panicked, knowing full well I was lying to them. They appreciated being told how it was; it made them feel it was their company, too. Together we'd have as good a time as we could for the foreseeable future and wait for the storm to pass. A big part of my job for the next year or so would be to inject some atmosphere, and make it as much fun as possible: if the team had a good time, it gave them a reason to turn up and stay loyal.

People who had been taking home £30k or £40k a year before were now living on £15k or £18k and working just as hard to get it, but in a recession that's what happens, and once we had all accepted it we put our heads down and got on with doing the best job we could. It was bloody hard work – we sweated for every pound we earned – and although the business wasn't making very much money at all, we just about kept ourselves afloat.

By the end of 1992, I got the sense that we were through the worst. We didn't have to offer such deep discounts to get the business, and it was getting easier to persuade people that if they invested in the best people they'd get through the worst of it sooner.

The first sector that showed signs of recovery was IT. Technology had been developed for the past few years that made computer systems more affordable and more effective, and several companies now saw the chance to start or upgrade their IT departments. The only trouble was, Alexander Mann didn't have any contacts or profile in IT recruitment. There wasn't even anyone in the office who understood the jargon.

Changing our area of operation was almost like starting all over again. It was back to the Yellow Pages and cold-calling and using every trick we knew to get our clients to give us the information we needed to recruit successfully for them.

'So where do you think your ideal IT manager is working now? And which university did he go to? And which software packages are absolutely vital to your organisation? Are you prepared to train the right person in the specific software you use? So he wouldn't need previous knowledge, just demonstrable aptitude?'

The constant questioning opened up tiny opportunities, and, once we had a relationship with the IT departments and IT companies, we started to make contacts and create a name for ourselves and things began to get easier. I sensed it was time to hire again, and although everyone around me was telling me to wait until the economy had strengthened, I knew that it was the perfect time to attract great people. If I waited until everyone else was hiring I would have competition. Observe the masses and do the opposite. It had worked before for me and it was about to work again.

Chapter 18

Fightback (1992–1993)

'*The recession had taught me not to put all my eggs in one basket: I had come so close to being wiped out and I never wanted to be in that position again.*'

I WAS A DIFFERENT sort of person after the recession: I'd had a good ride, I'd been knocked down, but now I'd come back. The exhilaration of survival, of not going under when hundreds of other recruitment agencies hit the wall, gave me so much energy that Alexander Mann actually bounced back with a vengeance. I was determined to build a bigger, stronger, better company, something that could capitalise on any opportunity the new economic cycle created.

At Alexander Mann I still placed a huge emphasis on making work fun. Seriously, if you're not having fun, why would you turn up to work? But the problem I had was that it was very hard for me to say no when staff asked me for a loan or a favour. I realised that if the company was going to grow it also had to grow up and I could no longer run it like a family business. Part of the reason why I didn't do things like query parking tickets and expenses for lunch with clients was because I just didn't have the time, and, because people knew their expenses weren't being scrutinised, it was pretty hard to stop them filing fairly creative claims. What I needed, I decided, was someone who cared enough about the business to dig down into the expenses, but someone who was also removed enough from it not to worry about upsetting their colleagues. I knew the perfect person.

Aisha was loving being at home with the girls, but she had never wanted to give up work entirely, so she came to work part-time at Alexander Mann. Not only did we get to spend more time with each other, but she saved me a fortune in parking tickets because she, quite rightly, told staff that they wouldn't park on double yellow lines in their own time. We would pay for parking, she said, but not for parking tickets.

For months after she started, the staff would come up to me and said, 'James, you couldn't just pay this fine for me? I was late for a meeting and I just had to park . . .'

'Speak to Aisha.'

'But she'll say no.'

'Speak to Aisha.'

I found it hard to say no, but I knew if I paid the fine Aisha would see it in the books and tell me off! It was fantastic to know that someone who cared about the details was doing such an important job. It was also Aisha's job to look at all our expenditure and manage the company's cost bases. She scrutinised everything from our rent to the stationery supplies and, while economic conditions were still pretty tough, the money she saved us made an enormous difference. For years, like a lot of women she had been balancing the household budget and she was brilliant at forensically analysing our costs. She was yet another senior female manager in the company and, looking back, I think having women like Sam, Elaine, Cathy and Aisha around was a key ingredient in creating Alexander Mann's successful atmosphere. For me personally it was also a lot of fun to have Aisha around. Even driving in together in the morning made a difference to me,

Above My father, my inspiration

Above My favourite film starring my favourite actor James Caan *(Everett Collection/Rex Features)*

Above With Aisha on honeymoon in Venice

Above Daddy's girls

Above With Aisha and the girls at my book launch party

Above My 'Graduating' Class at Harvard in 2002, Warren Buffett is in the centre of the picture

Above Me with my wife, Aisha, at my fortieth birthday masquerade ball

Above Doing business on the move in my Maybach

Above Aisha, Jemma, Hanah and I hit the slopes

Above *Elegance* the Caan family yacht

Above Avoiding the rush hour in the helicopter

Above Me, Ian Wolter and Tristan Ramus at our successful investment in Eden Brown

Above The Dragons together at the book signing of *Success from Pitch to Profit*

Above Andy Harsley and I wrapped in a Rapstrap!

Above Vanessa and James Buckley, Father Christmas (Ed Balls) and me

Above and Right My school in Lahore, named after my father, The Abdul Rashid Kahn (Ark) Campus

Above Lahore schoolchildren and me enjoying each others' company

Above Gordon Brown and I at the Labour Party Gala Dinner

Above Me with Cat Stevens (Yusuf Islam) on our trip to Bosnia

Above The dog treadmill: my first investment at *Dragons' Den*

Above Julia Charles and D4M artists, another *Dragons' Den* investment

and the work she was doing freed me up to spend more time with clients, to train the staff and to keep the motivation levels high.

As Alexander Mann got back on its feet and we built back up to a team of about twenty, my ambitions for the company grew. I've found that entrepreneurs break down into categories: the guy who's great at getting a business from nought to £1 million isn't always the guy who can get the business to £10 million, and the skills needed to get a business from £10 million to £100 million are completely different again. I'd been good at the start-up stage, and I'd also been good at the next stage, but I knew if the company was to become a major brand I would need to hire someone to drive it. My attempts so far to make the business more corporate had always hit a ceiling I realised I wasn't able to break through.

One of the reasons why I knew I would personally have difficulty expanding was my experience of trying to expand Alexander Mann on to a second floor. When the floor above our office in Tottenham Court Road had become available, I'd thought it was a chance to give everyone a bit more space. The office had never been plush – in fact it was so grubby that we would sometimes hear candidates come up the stairs saying 'This can't be right,' and turn back; sometimes we had to chase them out on to the street and bring them in! – but the location was right and we'd needed the space. As soon as I put some of the team on another floor, it was immediately apparent that the atmosphere on the main floor was different from the one upstairs. The productivity on the main floor was better, the morale was better and we had more fun. The other floor felt like another business and I just hadn't known how to spread the culture that was so crucial to our company. Despite having had a bad experience bringing someone in previously, I knew I needed someone who could develop systems and procedures that could be replicated whether I was part of the set-up or not. I'd become very conscious of the fact that the business shouldn't be about me, because if I wasn't around, if I got sick, it would have affected too many people. People had to identify with the company, not with me. It was time for Alexander Mann to grow up, and I knew that meant becoming corporate. And, as with a lot of entrepreneurs, that's not my natural style.

I had another reason for finding a general manager: I wanted to start another business. I had really enjoyed looking around at other opportunities during the recession and it had got me thinking about what else I could do. I was good at recruitment, but I thought I had more going for me than that. I thought my experience was more valuable in business in general than it was in one specific sector.

I had learned that I was good with people, at managing and motivating them, and I knew how to drive for profits. Whether it was persuading Sam Collins that recruitment was right for her or uncovering the innate desires of sales reps at Reid Trevena, I trusted my assessment of people. I had spent over a decade placing people in jobs and I knew how to get the best out of the best candidates, but I had started to wonder what could happen if, rather than finding really talented people and then placing them into a job, I backed them to start a business of their own. The business could be their idea if they were passionate about it, or an opportunity I had spotted. I had a tremendous sense of curiosity to see if I could apply my skills outside Alexander Mann.

The recession had taught me not to put all my eggs in one basket: I had come so close to being wiped out and I never wanted to be in that position again. If I had several businesses in several markets, then I reasoned that I wouldn't be as exposed. I became really excited about the possibilities ahead and my mind was made up: I would invest my time and profit from Alexander Mann and back brilliant people, just as I had done with Aisha and the boutiques a decade before.

Around this time I was considering expanding Alexander Mann through the acquisition of a smaller agency, and a guy called

Jonathan Wright came in to advise me on the best way to proceed. As Jonathan talked, I realised that I had found my general manager – he had previously worked in recruitment and he was now in private finance – and all I had to do was convince him he was the right man for the job.

I painted a bit of blue sky and told him my vision for the company and that I thought there was a real opportunity to make Alexander Mann one of the big names in recruitment. 'Our turnover was over a million before the recession; Michael Page used to make £100 million and I think that's the level we should be at.' However, Jonathan said he really didn't want to go back into recruitment.

'Really, why is that?'

I kept questioning him until I had got to the bottom of his reservations, and, needless to say, five hours and a parking ticket later Jonathan had got himself a new job and he started a few weeks later. I realised Jonathan could do such a good job that I would soon be able to step back. However, I wasn't going to make the same mistake I had made before: this was going to be a gradual handover, and only he and I knew that the ultimate plan was for him to become the chief executive. The staff had reacted badly to Peter, and I thought it was important that Jonathan be given a chance to get to know the business, and for the staff to trust him, before he took the senior role.

After his first week, we had a chat about his initial observations, and one of the things he told me was that he thought one particular staff member wasn't pulling her weight. More than that, he said, she was disruptive and demoralising.

'What do you think we should do?'

'To be honest, James, I think there's only one option. We should let her go.'

I wasn't sure if he was right, but he probably was, and it was important he knew that I trusted his judgement.

'Look, Jonathan, it's a Friday. No one should get sacked on a Friday. Let's leave it to Monday. Set up a meeting with her at 9 a.m. and we'll give her the news together.'

At about 8.50 on the Monday morning I walked into the coffee shop opposite the office and ordered a cappuccino.

'Jonathan? Hi, it's James. Listen, I'm stuck in traffic. You're OK to take that meeting on your own, aren't you?'

It wasn't that I didn't want to be the bad guy; it was just that I wanted the staff to know that Jonathan had that kind of authority and that level of trust from me. If I had told Jonathan on the Friday that I thought he should have handled the meeting on his own, he would have spent the weekend dreading it, and tried to persuade me to be there.

Jonathan became quite effective quite quickly. For the first couple of months people would still come to me with queries, and I would tell them to take their issue to Jonathan. Of course, pretty soon they just went straight to Jonathan. It was really weird: it was like having your child pay more attention to their uncle than their dad, and I was like: *Oi! Stop it!* I'd spent six months wanting him to be seen as the chief executive, but as soon as he was I couldn't help feeling a bit left out.

Chapter 19

An Amazing Day
(1993)

'*It was the most effective staff-bonding exercise. The atmosphere in our office that day was electric as the entire team pulled together.*'

I WAS STUCK IN TRAFFIC on my way to work one morning and was listening to LBC on the car radio. The DJ was talking to a woman from Barts hospital as the deadline for lodging an appeal against the closure of its Accident and Emergency unit was that afternoon. They were £75,000 short of the cash they needed for the legal fees and unless they got the money by the end of the day the unit would close.

As I sat there listening, it seemed inconceivable that they hadn't been able to raise the funds. It had been a fairly high-profile appeal, and as Barts is the nearest hospital to all the City firms' headquarters, I couldn't believe that one of the big corporations hadn't made the donation they needed.

'Someone should help her,' I said to myself. And as I said it, I realised that that someone should be me.

For years I had made donations to charities but had always found the process unsatisfactory. Subsequently I might have discovered that the funds had gone elsewhere, or that the charity's overheads meant that only a fraction of my money got to the people who needed it. I'd been invited to countless black-tie events where I'd felt obliged to bid at charity auctions for things I didn't want, and I'd realised that I wasn't interested in that kind of giving: from now on, if I was going to give to charity I was also going to get involved.

I got on my car phone and called Jonathan Wright.

'Jon, there's a woman on the radio trying to raise £75,000 to keep Barts hospital open. She needs the money today and we're going to get it for her.'

'How are we going to do that?'

'Not sure. Just off the top of my head, how about we don't work today; we just get on the phones and get donations from clients and candidates?'

'You're crazy, James.'

'Have you got any better suggestions?'

'I suppose your idea could work.'

'Tell you what, Jon. Why don't you call up the radio station and tell them what we're going to do and get their support.'

About fifteen minutes later I was still stuck in traffic and still listening to the radio when Jonathan was introduced. He had only called up to speak to a researcher but had been put through on air! By the time I got into the office, the place was in a state of pandemonium. Every member of staff was on the phone talking to their clients and their candidates asking for donations to save Barts. We then went back through every candidate we'd placed in the past year and every client we'd recruited for and told them about the campaign and asked for a contribution.

'Hi, I'm calling from Alexander Mann. We've dedicated the whole day to save Barts from closing. The A&E unit is so important to us in the City, it's the oldest hospital in London, it's vital for the capital and we shouldn't let this happen. We're really committed to doing this today: what can you donate?'

By 10 a.m. there was an LBC van parked outside our office: they wanted an update for the next bulletin. By 11 a.m. it had been joined by a van from Capital Radio. It seemed as if the whole of London wanted to know if we were going to raise the money by the end of the day.

'We're crossing over live to the offices of Alexander Mann where the race is on to save Barts' A&E unit. What's the latest?'

'They're up another £3000 and I've got the chief executive James Caan here with me now. Do you think you'll make the total, James . . .?'

I didn't realise it at the time, but the publicity we were getting was phenomenal. Every half-hour our company was on the news, and everything they were saying about us was positive. I spent the rest of the day with about three microphones shoved in front of me at any one time as journalists from newspapers and other broadcasters turned up. Then a camera crew arrived and we were on the local London lunchtime news on BBC1. I said to one of the journalists: 'You couldn't give out our phone number, could you?' And once the media started doing that, members of the public started calling up and making donations.

As the bids came in I became a little concerned that members of the public were pledging money that they would never send in. Barts needed the money immediately and, while I was happy to write the cheque to cover the pledges, I wanted to know that the public's money would actually arrive. So I called one of the courier companies we used and asked them to donate their services in lieu of a donation and they agreed to collect cheques for us.

The atmosphere in the office that day was unbelievable, and as the total started to creep up we began to believe that we really might manage it. By lunchtime more than £20,000 had been pledged, and I spent the day walking round the office picking up any phone that rang. After lunch, I took a call from a woman who said she wanted to donate £11,734. I remember the figure because it was such a precise amount and I was a bit worried that it was a hoax.

'I've heard what you're doing and I think it's fantastic.' She sounded like she was in her eighties. 'My son was treated at Barts, as was my aunt, and I've got some money and I would like to donate it.'

'Do you mind me asking why it's such a specific amount?'

'It's what's in my savings account, darling.'

I couldn't let a pensioner give away all her money, even if it was for Barts.

'You can't give it all. Give a grand, but don't give it all.'

'I want to.'

'Well, that's extremely generous of you. Would you mind writing out a cheque today?'

'Not at all.'

'And would we be able to collect it from you today?'

'Well, I'm going out to meet a friend for lunch right now.'

'Where are you going for lunch?'

'We're meeting at Harrods.'

'If I send a courier to Harrods in fifteen minutes' time, will you give him a cheque?'

'Of course, darling.'

We were featured in the later editions of the *Evening Standard* and as the day went on the total crept up, but I was still concerned we wouldn't meet the target. Privately I had said I would top up the donations if necessary, but it was important to me that Alexander Mann rose to the challenge: I didn't want us to fall short. Staff even went out on to the street and started shaking buckets, and a couple of our clients made donations in excess of £20,000, while several members of the public made donations of over £1000. I was completely blown away by people's generosity, and by the end of the day we had raised over £100,000. Although the entire team was exhausted, we were also elated: it had been a fantastic day – absolutely fantastic – and, as well as giving the money to Barts, with the extra funds we were also able to make a donation to the Great Ormond Street hospital.

That evening we were featured on the *Nine o'Clock News* on the BBC and the *News at Ten* on ITV, and the following morning we were on the front page of *The Times*: HEADHUNTER SAVES BARTS. A friend of mine who worked as a media buyer told me the publicity we generated that day would have cost £1.8 million in a planned advertising campaign. But the truth is, you can't buy a slot on the *News at Ten*, and the only figure I can put on what that day did for Alexander Mann is priceless. It was absolutely incredible how in one day the name Alexander Mann went from meaning nothing to most people in London to being something everyone had heard of. It was an extraordinary day.

Apart from the good publicity, it was the most effective staff-bonding exercise. The atmosphere in our office that day was electric as the entire team pulled together and rallied everyone they knew to contribute. It certainly beat paintballing or weekends away at an expensive hotel. The place was buzzing for weeks after that, and in the months that followed our increased profile helped us attract better candidates and better clients. But, of course, the best thing was that we lodged the appeal to stop the closure of the A&E unit and I got to know some brilliant doctors and nurses at Barts who wanted to thank us for what we'd done. I couldn't have known it then, but the following year I would have another reason to be thankful that we had saved the unit from closure.

I now had a reputation as someone who gave to charity and I was approached by the NSPCC. Although it was one of the biggest and best-known charities in the country, I didn't really know much about their work, so I was invited to visit one of their call centres where they counselled children in need. Within a few hours of listening in on some of the conversations I knew I had to help. I was invited to join their fundraising board, which meant attending meetings once every six weeks to discuss ways I could use my knowledge and contacts to bring funds in for the charity. I knew from the letterhead that the patron was Prince Andrew, but I didn't think for one second that he would ever actually attend any of the meetings.

I turned up for my first board meeting and was introduced to some of the most impressive people I had ever met. Stanley Kalms, the chairman of Dixons; David Svenson, who ran Microsoft in Europe; the head of Goldman Sachs in the UK: these were some of the most high-profile and successful business operators of their generation, and I was somewhat of a minnow in comparison. And then Prince Andrew joined us.

Working with such a high-calibre board was an amazing experience for me because I learned so much from the others. For ten years I had been so wrapped up in running my own businesses that I had never really looked at how others ran theirs. I was getting an up-close masterclass in how some of the most talented people in business operated and I gained insights into what it takes to run really large corporations. I was a bit of a maverick, a cheeky outsider, but they were Establishment stalwarts and watching them operate was an eye-opener. Just as I had observed the effective habits of Tom at Reid Trevena all those years before, I now took my chance to learn from some of the brightest and best in British business. And what was even better was that we were using what we had to raise millions of pounds. There was always this terrific motivation in the room because we were trying to help the NSPCC, and that made everything we did really enjoyable.

I remember once someone suggested having a tennis tournament with all the old greats playing each other. 'Let's have Borg v McEnroe: the rematch.' There are a lot of charity tennis events, so we had to find a way to make ours better. Could we really get Borg and McEnroe? Such was the calibre of the people on the board that one of them knew Borg and another knew someone who was very close to McEnroe. But that still wasn't enough; we decided that we had to make our tennis tournament unique.

The obvious venues in which to hold it – Wimbledon or Queen's – were often used for corporate entertaining, and we thought there would be a limit to how much we could raise in those venues, assuming they'd let us play there in the first place. Then someone hit on the idea of holding it on the tennis courts at Buckingham Palace.

'Do you think we'd be able to?'

We all turned to Andrew. 'I'll ask Mummy.'

I served three years on the board and personally raised over a million for the NSPCC before my work commitments meant I had to step down, but before I left a letter arrived from Prince Andrew saying he was really proud of what the board was achieving and thought it would be a good idea for us all to have dinner to see if there were other options we could explore. When the Queen's son invites you for dinner, it's a big deal, especially when the venue is Buckingham Palace!

I'd never been to the Palace before, but I knew lots of people who had been invited to garden parties there so I was aware that it was often used for social events. Nevertheless, it was pretty exciting and I was really intrigued to see inside the place. I had driven round Buckingham Palace countless times, and it was an odd sensation to turn in through the gates instead of looping round the Victoria Memorial. A security guard signalled that I should stop.

'Good evening, Mr Caan.'

How did he know my name? It was only later that I remembered my PA had been asked in advance for my licence plate details for security.

'If you will just drive through the arch there and park where you see the other cars.'

I followed the instructions but thought there must be a mistake as there were only two or three other cars. Had I taken a wrong turn? It's a big place, I told myself, there are probably lots of places to park a car.

I got out of the Rolls and was greeted by a butler, the kind I had always wanted to hire but had never been able to find.

'If you will come with me, sir.'

As we were walking up the stairs he told me that we would be eating in the Chinese Dining Room. I thought that sounded fabulous, but I was surprised that I couldn't hear the sounds of a party coming from down the corridor. It dawned on me that maybe this wasn't going to be a big function after all. No cars, no noise: maybe it was just a small dinner.

'How many of us are there for dinner tonight?'

'There are a few, sir.'

A few? Was that a handful or a hundred? There was no way of telling. He escorted me to the Chinese Room and, as I'd suspected, it was just the board members and Prince Andrew. Suddenly, I was really nervous. I was at a private dinner in Buckingham Palace. *Oh, my God! Am I dressed right?* And when I looked at the table there were so many pieces of cutlery I started to panic: I regularly eat curry and chapattis with my fingers!

I calmed my nerves by talking informally to Andrew – we called him Andrew, not Sir or your Royal Highness – and Stanley and me started to have a laugh and I began to relax. For the first course I was sitting opposite Andrew, but he switched seats for the main course and came and sat next to me. It was hard not to be struck by what a natural, friendly guy he was and what great company he is. He was also pretty tactile. I remembered all the techniques I had learned at Reid Trevena about using body language and touch to reassure people: had he been taught these skills, too, or were they just natural for someone in his position?

The guy was brilliant. When he took on the role of patron, he promised he would hold the position until he had raised £250 million pounds for the Full Stop campaign to stamp out child abuse. That's an awful lot of money, but he was as good as his word and somehow he managed it. Consequently, he's someone I have a lot of respect for.

It was at about this time that I also accepted an invitation to join a group called the YPO, the Young Presidents' Organization. I had learned that hanging out with able and dynamic people rubbed off on me and so I took the opportunity to join. It's a pretty hard club to get into because you have to be chief executive of a company with a turnover of so many million and a pretty healthy bank balance – and you have to be under forty-four when you join. The annual subscription is no small sum, but I found I was meeting several people a year who told me it was the best money they'd ever spent.

YPO is essentially a networking organisation that brings together the most successful operators of their generation. They organise events where you can meet other entrepreneurs as well as politicians, business leaders and power brokers. When I went to my first meeting, I realised I had a lot in common with the other members. Because of the entry requirements, we were all of a similar age, at similar levels of success, and our outlooks had a lot in common. I even found out that most had children who were the same ages as mine, and that they had the same problems with balancing home and work life: with so much in common I made many great friends really quickly.

One of the elements of YPO membership is forums made up of CEOs of non-competing companies who meet up every six weeks to discuss their businesses, their plans and their options – it sounded like some kind of informal board meeting to me. I'd met other YPOers at conferences, and I was amazed when I got talking to an American in London who flew back to San Francisco every six weeks for his forum meeting.

'Why don't you just join a London forum?' I asked.

'You haven't joined a forum, have you?'

'How can you tell?'

'You just wouldn't have asked the question if you had.'

He convinced me of the value of belonging to a forum. In business, you are so often concerned with your shareholders, your directors, your customers, your rivals or your staff that you don't often think of yourself. Forum discussions, he told me, helped you make decisions that were right for you. Being in sole charge of an organisation is a big responsibility, and it was helpful to talk to other people who understood that burden. So often there are things you just can't discuss with anyone else either because you will make them worry or because it's commercially sensitive. So I signed up for a forum, and I think I've only ever missed one meeting since. No matter what position I find myself in – being approached for a takeover, approaching someone else for a takeover, poaching a senior member of staff – someone in my forum has been there first. There is a rule that what is said in forum stays in forum, and over the years a phenomenal amount of trust has built up between me and the other members. No matter what stage you're at in life, having a support network of allies is incredibly valuable.

Chapter 20

Investing in People
(1993–1995)

'I don't know why I had so much front. It was like David asking Goliath to come to London, and give up a lucrative corporate career in the process.'

HAVING TRIED MYSELF to make Alexander Mann more corporate, supporting Jonathan was my number one priority for the first six months he was with us. By the middle of 1993, he was starting to take control, and that freed me up to look for new opportunities. In my mind I had the idea that I wanted to start one new business a year for ten years, so I was constantly on the lookout for talented people and lucrative ideas. It was a pretty bold statement to make, but articulating my ambitions for growth had the effect of galvanising the team: if I was talking confidently about the future, they started to feel confident about it, too.

Networking had become very important to my career, and a lot of my time was spent catching up with old friends and colleagues or attending conferences so that I could better assess the market. One of my research trips took me to a recruitment conference in

Cleveland, Ohio. Maybe the next opportunity was overseas, I thought.

One of the businesses exhibiting at the conference was MRI – Management Recruiters International – which had 600 offices across the US. Its techniques were similar to Alexander Mann's in that it headhunted mid-level staff, but its real business was in franchising. They taught people how to headhunt, helped them set up their own operation and then took a percentage of the franchisee's profits. It wasn't just a big operation, it was a hugely successful and profitable one: they had an entire department of fifty-odd people just to collect the money.

I knew a bit about MRI because I had met one of its managers – a guy called Doug Bugie – when he'd come to London in the late eighties to check out the UK market for expansion opportunities. He'd been told lots of stories about this maverick who was doing recruitment-to-recruitment and organising recruitment fairs. He'd called up and asked me for a beer and at one point suggested that MRI should buy Alexander Mann. I was interested in his offer, but after the initial negotiations the deal never happened.

I was really interested in MRI's model because franchising was a concept that didn't exist in the UK recruitment market. I had just one office – and a pretty tired-looking one above a hi-fi shop at that – while they had 600 branches. I was full of admiration for the company's founder, Alan Schoenberg.

I spent some time with Alan at the conference – Doug had taken a sabbatical so that he could run for Congress at this point – and he started trying to persuade me that I should buy MRI's master licence for the UK and start franchising the business myself. I was quite interested until I thought: *What can they really offer me?* They wanted me to buy the brand for quite a big upfront fee, and then pay royalties for the rest of my life. The more I drilled down into the offer, the more obvious it became that, actually, there wasn't much they were offering me – after all, their brand meant little in the UK and there was no infrastructure outside the US to support me. I realised I would have to spend a lot of money to make their brand a name in the UK market. I didn't like the idea of that, but I still liked their business. I then heard that Doug's bid to become a congressman had failed and I sniffed a new opportunity. So I called him up.

'You know you've been saying to me for years that MRI should expand outside the US?'

'Sure.'

'Let's have a coffee.'

As MRI's head of marketing, Doug had personally been responsible for opening 300 MRI offices and the guy was a genius at rolling out the formula. I told him that MRI wanted me to buy the UK licence, and he could absolutely see why I wasn't taking the deal.

Doug is a six-foot-three, larger-than-life guy with one of those booming voices, the epitome of a successful American corporate exec. He came to meet me in a café in Cleveland, Ohio, and I told him what had been on my mind for several days:

'Why don't just you and I do it? Why don't we set up an international recruitment franchise?'

'Are you serious?'

'Doug, let me ask you a question. How long have you been with MRI?'

'Ten years.'

'Did you get any equity in the business?'

'No, I'm corporate. A salary man.'

'You've been telling me for years that someone should do what I'm talking about. You've been convinced for a long time that if MRI had let you, you could have opened offices all over the world. Are you still convinced you could do it?'

'Beyond doubt.'

'Then why don't we set up a new brand of our own rather than selling theirs? Why shouldn't I invest in my brand rather than somebody else's? And why would you want to work so hard and not own a piece of it?'

'Where are you going with this?'

'I'll put up the cash, you come over to the UK and you run the business. You know exactly what you're doing, you know exactly how to create the brand, the systems, the procedures and the processes. You know how to franchise a business. You have convinced me beyond doubt that you know it backwards – so if it's that good an opportunity, why don't we just do it? I'll give you equity in it.'

'I've never thought of that.' He was completely thrown. 'I couldn't do it. I'm an American, I just ran for Congress, for Chrissakes. I've got a great life here, a great house, my friends are here . . . I couldn't.'

I wasn't prepared to take no for an answer, so that evening I rang him from my hotel room. I couldn't get the idea of starting an international recruitment franchise out of my system. Just as with rec2rec or recruitment fairs, I had made my mind up that this was what I wanted to do and, crucially, that Doug was the guy I wanted to do it with.

'Listen, Doug, you know that conversation we had? I really want you to think about it. When I get back to the UK, let me send you a ticket. I'll pay your expenses, pay for your flight, and let me just show you what I'm doing.'

'OK, I'll come over – but don't pitch me. I'm not leaving the States, but I don't mind flying to London and giving you my thoughts on how you could do it yourself.'

'You've got a deal. I promise I won't waste my time trying to persuade you to do something you're clearly not interested in.'

I really don't know why I had so much front. Doug was one of the biggest names in the American recruitment industry and I was, frankly, a nobody out there. It was like David asking Goliath to come to London, and give up a lucrative corporate career in the process. But obviously something I'd said had interested him, and Doug came over. We spent a week together looking at Alexander Mann and seeing if I had a model that could be franchised. The more we looked at it, the more Doug saw the opportunity, and by the end of the week it was clear he was getting excited about it.

'I know you said I shouldn't pitch the idea of us doing this together, but just imagine if everything you're telling me is right, Doug, imagine what we'd have. If I buy a master licence, MRI owns the brand. I want to own the business, Doug, I want to own the brand. And I think you're the best person in the world to run it.'

'What would be in it for me?'

'I'll give you 50 per cent equity: I'll take all the risk, put up all the money and if it works we own it together. If it fails, I'll take the hit.'

I didn't realise it at the time but running for Congress had wiped him out financially. Starting over in a new country began to appeal to him and we shook on the deal. I couldn't quite believe that Mr America was going to swap his massively well-paid job and his sleek corporate HQ to come and work above a hi-fi shop: I knew then that he really believed he could do it.

Doug went back to the States to get his affairs in order while I sorted out his flights, accommodation, his visa, a car – whatever he needed. I decorated the second floor of our office which had been empty for a while, bought expensive furniture for it and created a boardroom: I wanted Doug to have the kind of office he was used to. It was a bit of an outlay, but the bulk of my investment in our new venture would be meeting Doug's expenses until we could make it pay.

I actually didn't really mind what it cost, because to me securing Doug was such a massive coup. To any outsider, it looked like I was trying to play several leagues above my ranking, and it was partly for that reason that we made a very early decision that the franchising operation we were about to set up wouldn't be branded as Alexander Mann.

One of our first meetings was with a branding agency, and we told them we needed a name for our headhunting franchise that would operate all over the world. Coming up with a name that means something in China and Brazil and France – without offending people in Indonesia or Finland – isn't as easy as you might think. The agency suggested 'Humana', which we both liked because it was generic and was easy to pronounce. It also suggested that it was a business about people. We then asked them to come up with a logo and other corporate identity material, because when you're selling a franchise the brand is an extremely valuable part of the franchise package.

Franchises generally work like this: franchisees pay an upfront fee and then a percentage of future profits to the franchiser. In exchange, they are taught how to operate the franchise and given help in managing their business. With Humana, we were going to teach people how to headhunt for a fee of £30,000 and then take 10 per cent of what they billed.

Some of the biggest names on the high street are franchises – McDonald's, the Body Shop, Kall Kwik – and it's easy to see why you'd buy one of their franchises: the chances are you'll do much better selling Body Shop cosmetics than unbranded ones. With Humana, I realised, we had no track record to offer and no brand. It was a huge oversight and I couldn't believe that neither Doug nor I had anticipated it. We'd got so caught up in replicating MRI internationally that we forgot we didn't have MRI's brand.

Oh, my God, I said to myself, I've just hired this guy. I've brought him over here, paid a fair whack of cash to a branding agency and this isn't going to work. So I took Doug out to dinner for a crisis meeting.

'Tell me again how this is going to work.'

'Trust me. I'm not naive, I know exactly what I'm doing.'

I don't know why, but I believed him. In a way I had no reason to, but something in the way he was talking made me believe he was going to make it happen. The guy was and is brilliant, so I did as he asked and trusted him. His pitch was this: we find people who want to open their own headhunting business but don't know how to do it. They pay us for the training, and we supply them with manuals and video coaching and branded materials, from invoices to business cards. We tell them the best kind of office to lease, the best way to find clients, the best way to get referrals: everything so that they can replicate the success of MRI or Alexander Mann. The fact that we were selling a new brand was something I was just going to have to trust Doug about.

After he'd been in London for about six weeks, Doug came and asked if I'd mind if he took a desk on the main floor.

'Why would you want to do that?'

On the one hand I was gutted – I'd spent over £10k on his office – but on the other I realised that it took a very strong person who'd been given that status to say he'd rather sit at a desk next to one of the consultants. As soon as he moved on to our floor, it was clear he really enjoyed the atmosphere, and it was great for me to be able to overhear some of his conversations. He was such an experienced operator and it was a real education for us all.

Doug needed to get the training manuals together, but, unlike at MRI where there had been an entire department to create, edit and update the training literature, at Humana there was just Doug. Writing a manual isn't easy – where do you start? What's the second chapter? What's the third? Writing the manual would have taken up all of Doug's time, so I asked Sam Collins to write the Humana manual with me.

'How am I supposed to do that?' she asked, quite reasonably.

I wasn't sure, so I said to Sam, 'Let's just go right to the beginning of Alexander Mann's recruitment process and start from there. Let's start with canvassing for vacancies and map the entire journey.'

Most salespeople wouldn't have wanted to take on that job because it would have meant missing out on commission, but by then Sam knew I would make sure she was compensated: I didn't have to say anything and she didn't have to ask. Sam's loyalty to the company meant she would do what was right for the business ahead of what was potentially more lucrative for her.

For weeks Sam and I worked together, writing and writing and editing and editing: it was a thousand times more complicated than I ever thought it would be. We couldn't use any of the shorthand that had developed between us, or any jargon. We had to explain how our business worked in such a way that an alien landing in Tottenham Court Road with no knowledge of recruitment could have picked up our manual, followed its advice and created a successful business: everything from how you answer the phone to marketing a candidate to raising an invoice. They would need to know what to do if a candidate turned down an offer or a client changed the brief. Every time we thought we had finished a chapter we found new questions that needed answering. Franchisees didn't just need to know how to raise an invoice, they needed to know how to collect and bank the money. If they placed a candidate, they needed to know where they stood if that candidate resigned within a month, so we had to write out the client dispute procedure. The detail was incredible, and it took three or four months of solid and intensive work.

In the early nineties the biggest name in recruitment training was an American called Anthony Burn. His training seminars sold out in minutes, not hours, and he was an industry legend in America, a real recruitment superstar. We didn't have a budget to create our own training videos and, even if we had, we couldn't have produced anything half as good as Tony's material. His *30 Steps of Recruitment* was an industry standard and there wasn't any point in trying to better it. So I had an idea.

'Doug, why don't we get Tony Burn to do our training videos?'

'You cannot be serious!'

But I was.

Doug had worked with Tony at MRI and he put me in touch with him. I told him about our plans for Humana and suggested it was a really good time for him to break into the UK market. I offered to promote Tony in the UK in exchange for using his training material with our franchisees. If persuading Doug to leave MRI was a feat, then getting Tony on board was something of a miracle.

For the next year Anthony Burn based himself in the office above ours and I hired a PR expert to promote him, booking him to talk at conferences and conventions and selling his books and videos. Of course, even the great Anthony Burn wasn't busy every day, and having him in the building lent Humana credibility and inspired the Alexander Mann team to greater success.

Looking back at the start of Humana now I'm stunned at what we were able to achieve: it still seems crazy that we would be able to sell a franchise of a business with no track record, even with Doug and Tony's talent on board, but four months after Doug's relocation we were ready to start advertising Humana franchises for sale. We got a lot of interest as there was potentially plenty of money to be made, but each time Doug fielded a call the conversation stumbled when the potential franchisee asked how many franchises we had already sold. But Doug had the bit between his teeth and he wasn't going to fail. 'Let me buy you a coffee,' he would say, and when the interested party came to our office he introduced them to me.

'This is my colleague James. Basically, the Humana franchise is a replica of what James is doing here with Alexander Mann. James, tell Peter how you got started.'

Peter Denton was our first taker. He was in his forties and had grown tired of his corporate career, was ready to start his own business but too old and comfortable to take too many risks: a franchise was perfect for him. So I introduced him to my team and showed him how much they were billing and how much of that was profit. Doug had been very clever and got round the issue of us not having done it before by using Alexander Mann as the pilot business. For Humana to work, I had to make Peter a star. He shadowed me and I mentored him, and for several weeks Peter was my number one priority. His background was in engineering, so I encouraged him to develop his business recruiting engineers for companies he was familiar with.

'Most people who recruit for engineering companies aren't specialists, Peter. They don't know the language, they don't understand the relevance of the qualifications. You do, and that's why you're going to be better than them and why you're going to make a great living at this,' I told him. With his specialist knowledge and Humana's sales techniques, I believed every word I was saying.

I was right to. After working with me for a month or so, Peter went home to Wakefield to open the first branch of Humana. Sam went with him and advised him on premises and negotiating leases – we weren't going to let Peter fail because we had overlooked anything – and after a couple of months we got our first cheque from him to cover our percentage of his fees. After that, selling the franchises got easier and Doug went into overdrive. For a year or so I don't remember him taking a day off. I didn't take much time off myself, but I had a family to get home to whereas Doug didn't. With Peter's success, it was possible to see that Humana really could become as big as Doug's dreams for it. Brilliant as he was, he would need help, so I asked Sam to move across permanently from Alexander Mann to Humana. With two of the best people I had ever worked with on the case, I was giving Humana the best possible start. Doug soon sold a second franchise, and then a third, and when the cheques started to arrive from our franchisees, I realised that Humana would soon be more profitable than Alexander Mann.

I had been so busy with Humana that it had given Jonathan the chance to make his mark on Alexander Mann, and he was growing the business at a phenomenal rate. We were starting to burst at the seams in Tottenham Court Road, and if the company was going to expand, as Jonathan predicted, we would need new offices, so I started looking for new premises. After several years living with flaking paint and a doorway you could miss even if you were standing right outside it, I was ready for the Alexander Mann Group to have a proper HQ.

I had always been nervous of paying high rents – one of the reasons we'd survived the recession was because I'd kept our overheads low – but the business was doing well and there was over a million in the bank. The business could afford an entire freehold building in Lincoln's Inn, near Holborn: we would have a permanent base but without rent or a mortgage undermining our performance. Buying property doesn't normally feel like risk, but in 1995 the fallout from the recession meant that the phrase 'negative equity' was still something you heard regularly. Nevertheless, I took a bit of a gamble and wiped out Alexander Mann's reserves to pay £1 million for the building, which was renamed Alexander House. Now I really felt that I had delivered on my childhood dreams of starting a business: I had two companies that were turning over tens of thousands of pounds a month and a freehold building in central London that was so big we turned one floor into an indoor football pitch.

By 1995, Jemma was eight and Hanah was seven. I could have afforded to buy them anything they wanted, but I didn't want to be one of those dads who just buys presents for his kids to say sorry for not being there. I rearranged my working day to make sure I always saw them in the evenings before starting work again after they'd gone to bed. I loved just the four of us spending time together; nothing has ever been more important to me than knowing my family is happy.

I remember picking the girls up from school and in the car on the way home I asked them how their day had been. Jemma had had a good day, but Hanah was clearly fed up and it dawned on me that she'd actually been fed up for a while. It was important for me that both my kids liked school: they were clearly bright and I wanted them to make the most of their education, so I was worried about Hanah's attitude to school.

'Why don't you like school any more, darling?'

'It's just really boring.'

Hanah was slightly more academic than her sister. Jemma had to work a bit harder to get results, but for Hanah it was just too easy and she was starting to switch off. Aisha and I decided that she needed to go to a school that would really push her, and she sat the entrance exams for City of London School, near St Paul's. She passed easily, but that presented us with a new problem: the commute. Dropping the girls off in Hampstead on the way to the West End hadn't been a problem, but now I had to take Jemma to her school, then Hanah to hers and then get to Alexander House in Holborn. Whether I did it or Aisha did it, and no matter which route we used, the journey was about an hour and half in the rush hour.

Jemma also got into City, but even without the detour to Hampstead it was still taking its toll on us. Reluctantly, we took the decision that we were going to have to leave the house in Winchmore Hill and move closer into the centre of London. We all loved that house, but nothing was more important than making sure the girls weren't too exhausted by the early starts and long commute to get the most out of school. We put the house on the market and moved to St John's Wood, just the other side of Regent's Park from the West End.

One other thing happened around this time: my mum came home. As soon as my younger siblings had reached the age of eighteen, they had all come back to England and, with her children gone, my mum saw no reason to stay in Karachi. My dad, being as stubborn as they come, refused to leave. It was still his dream to live in Pakistan, even if his family was on another continent.

I bought my mum a house in Chingford, and it was great to have her nearby again, although it was weird having her around without my dad. She was happier in England without him because it meant she could have her kids with her. It was a difficult adjustment for all of us, and it was particularly hard on my dad. I still spoke to him every week on the phone, and at first he put a brave face on it. For years I had ended every phone conversation with him with the same question: 'When are you coming home?', but even with Mum in England his answer was still the same:

'I am home, stop asking me that!'

Nevertheless, I got the feeling that with Mum gone he wasn't happy on his own. One day, I sensed he'd come back, too. As it turned out, it would be sooner than I thought.

Chapter 21

What Goes Around

(1994)

'All I could think of was that I'd let my dad down.
I was thirty-five and I still felt it as keenly as I had when I
was a kid.'

AFTER ASKING DAD the same question for ten years, I was both relieved and worried when in August 1994 he finally told me he was thinking about returning to London.

'Why's that?'

'I haven't been feeling too well. I've got a cold, I think, but I can't shake it and it would be nice to have you all around.'

There was something in his voice that was telling me it was more than a cold, and I was worried. If I hadn't had so much on at work, I would have got on the next plane to Karachi, but I couldn't take the time off so I called my brothers.

'Something's not right with Dad. I don't know what, but one of us has got to get on a plane straight away.'

My brother Andrew said he would go.

'Can you get me a ticket?'

'Not a problem. Just do me a favour.'

'What?'

'Go now. Literally, get to the airport and get on the next plane. Charge it to my card, just get there.'

'OK.'

'And no matter what he says, all you're going to do when you get there is pack his bags and bring him home.'

Two days later, I went to see Dad at my mum's house in Chingford. He looked really weak but because he wasn't registered with a GP I didn't know what to do with him. He was so bad that we wondered if we should take him to casualty. I wasn't sure; all I knew was that I wanted to talk to a doctor I trusted.

'I'm going to take you to Barts,' I said.

Ever since that day when Alexander Mann had raised funds for them, I had maintained a great relationship with the hospital and I was often invited to events there. One of the doctors I had met there was Professor Besser, who insisted I take my dad to their private facility on the top floor of the hospital.

My dad thought it was very weird that everyone in the hospital seemed to know my name, but he was took weak and jet-lagged to ask me about it. Professor Besser came to greet us and then took my father away for some tests. Half an hour later, the professor came out to see me.

'Let me show you something. I've got two test tubes. This is what normal blood looks like.' It was a tube of regular-looking red blood. Then he showed me a test tube with a black liquid in it. 'This is your dad's blood.'

I was stunned.

'Why is it like that?'

'When both your kidneys stop functioning the blood stops being cleansed, and then it gets poisonous, and then, well, you're done.'

I couldn't believe what he was saying. Without treatment he estimated my father had two or three days to live.

'I don't know how he got here, but by rights he shouldn't be able to get out of bed and we need to operate on him right away.' He said they needed to make an incision in his neck so he could be hooked up to a machine that would cleanse his blood for him.

'That's the bad news. Would you like some good news?'

I didn't need to answer.

'This hospital is a specialist in renal care. There isn't anywhere better in the world that your dad could be right now.'

What were the chances that the hospital I had helped keep open would be the one that would save my dad's life? The coincidence was overwhelming and I just sat there unable to take it in. *Look at the way God pays you back*, I thought. I was given a tour of the renal unit and met all the specialists, but all I could think about was that test tube of black blood. It looked like it had been taken from a corpse.

My dad's treatment took about six hours, and as I waited for him I realised I was scared, relieved and stunned all at once. What if my brother hadn't got on a plane? What if we'd taken him to Mum's GP? What if I hadn't heard that appeal on the radio for Barts a couple of years earlier? It was too much to get my head round.

I stayed with Dad until midnight and then went back the next morning. He had been such a force in my life for so long and seeing him so weak was difficult to adjust to. After three or four days he had visibly brightened, even though he knew he would be a dialysis patient for the rest of his life.

He was taken to a general ward to recuperate, and on his way there he passed a framed copy of the paper reporting on the day Alexander Mann had raised the money. The next time I went to see him, he asked me about it. Can you imagine how proud he was of me? It was one of the most emotional conversations of my life.

When he'd been back in the country a couple of months my dad asked me to do him a favour.

'Sure.'

'This is really important to me. I really want you to support me on this.'

'OK. What is it?'

'I want you to have supper with me every Sunday.'

'OK.'

'I mean *every* Sunday and I don't want any excuses.'

'And this is because . . .?'

'Because you're my son and I want to spend time with you, and I want to know I'm going to see you every Sunday.'

'OK. I'll come.'

He was worried that now we all had our own lives he could be living within a few miles of all his children but never see them. He might as well be in Karachi as Chingford unless we visited him.

For the first couple of months, I turned up for supper every Sunday without fail. And because I was popping over, a couple of my brothers and sisters would usually turn up, too, and these Sunday evenings turned into a bit of an event.

The time came when I had to take a trip to the States. It was due to end on the Friday and I would have been home on the Saturday in plenty of time for supper with my dad. However, I ran into someone who was really worth having a meeting with, and we arranged to have lunch on the following Monday. I changed my flight and stayed the weekend.

I called my dad from the hotel: 'Listen, I can't make this Sunday, but I'll be there next week.'

'Why can't you make it?'

'I'm in New York, Dad. I've got an important meeting on Monday.'

'Important, you say?'

'Dad! I'm on the other side of the Atlantic, not the other side of London.'

'We had an agreement. You promised.'

'Be reasonable!'

When I put the phone down I felt weird. I wasn't going to enjoy a day off in New York now. All I could think of was that I'd let my dad down. I was thirty-five and I still felt it as keenly as I had when I was a kid. So I called him back and my mum answered.

'He doesn't want to talk to you.'

All that Saturday I couldn't get my mum's words out of my head. By the evening I was completely distracted and wasn't thinking about my meeting on Monday at all. *This is silly*, I said to myself. I went back to my hotel, packed my bag and got a cab to the airport. On the way I called my meeting off and arranged to do it by video conferencing and called Aisha to tell her I was heading home.

'I'm going straight to my parents when the plane touches down.'

'Come back and see the kids. They've missed you.'

'I've missed them, too, but I just have to be there.'

I couldn't explain it any better than that. I got a night flight and arrived back at Heathrow around lunchtime on Sunday. I called my mum.

'Tell Dad I'm on my way.'

When I walked in, he had this big smile on his face because, basically, he'd won. He came up to me and put his arms around me.

'Don't ever let me down again.' I couldn't quite tell if he was joking.

Needless to say, from then until the day he died I never missed a Sunday with my father. Even if we went on holiday, I would fly back early so that I could be there.

As the months passed, these Sundays became a bit of a family ritual: I would turn up with the girls, my brothers and sisters would arrive with their kids and partners and it became a lot of fun. My relationship with all my family was brilliant, and we became as close as we'd been when we were kids, closer probably because I'd left home when the younger ones were so little.

Over the months, each of us would talk about our plans: one sister wanted to open a beauty parlour; another had been encouraged to start cooking professionally. Sunday nights became a family board meeting, and we would help and advise each other on the best way forward. My father, as you'd expect, was the chairman of this board, and if we thought any of their business ideas was the right move, then I would back them. Together we'd decide how much money was needed, and my father would write a cheque when he was happy that the plan was right. I would make sure he always had the funds for the cheques to clear. All but one of my siblings is now involved in business in one way or another: Adam runs an outsourcing business in Pakistan, Nazima's catering business – Nisa Foods – supplies Indian food to corner shops throughout the UK, Nahid has opened her beauty salon, Andrew now runs a business that does tailoring alterations for high-street fashion shops, and my youngest sister runs a division of a business I recently invested in.

Chapter 22

Serial Entrepreneur

(1995–1998)

'*The cash I invested was only one component of what was becoming an increasingly lucrative investment strategy: my experience was more valuable than my capital.*'

A T ALEXANDER MANN, Jonathan was given the title chief executive and I became the group CEO of both Alexander Mann and Humana. When you hire someone to take over your company, you take an enormous risk because so much of a business is about the personality of the founder. When you bring in an outsider, someone who hasn't been a part of the Cilla Black nights or the fancy-dress days, your business is vulnerable: if you lose the culture, do you also lose the key ingredient that makes your business successful?

You only have to look at the statistics in the recruitment industry to see how difficult it is to turn a boutique into a corporate business. There must be 10,000 agencies in the UK, but

I reckon fewer than 10 per cent of them have more than ten employees. Getting beyond the founder's personality and sphere of influence is something that few agencies ever manage.

Ever since I'd failed to transmit the Alexander Mann culture to a second floor in our old building – it was so different from the main floor that it may as well have been in a different city! – I had known I wouldn't be the person to take it into the big league. Jonathan was different, and his systems, procedures, processes and strategies were just what were needed, and it was fascinating to observe the differences between how I had run the business and how Jonathan was starting to run things.

Apart from 'to do' lists, which I compile every morning, I don't write anything down. I would go into a board meeting with a jotter pad, but Jonathan would arrive with a board pack – P&L, operational reports, strategy papers. Everything had outcomes and objectives attached to it, and this enabled every layer of management to know what was expected of them. And with an efficient management structure – I had given people all sorts of job titles to reward them for a good month – the company really started to motor. We had moved into Alexander House with about 25 people, pretty soon we were at 50. Not long after that we had 100.

The difference in the company's performance after we moved to the new office was incredible. Between 1995 and 1999 our turnover doubled every year. Jonathan obviously made a huge difference, but I can't underestimate the boost that having our own building gave us. I had always known that appearances mattered, and it was clear from the way the team and clients responded to our new HQ that if we had moved out of the smoky room on Tottenham Court Road sooner our performance would have improved sooner, too. I was kicking myself that I hadn't invested in a better office for Alexander Mann, but consoled myself with the thought that we might not have been able to survive the recession if I had.

One of Jonathan's first decisions after the move was to take me off the sales floor. He took me out for a coffee and suggested I have my own separate office.

'Do you mind?'

'Actually I do.' I was surprisingly hurt. I thought it was good for the team to see me work and for them to learn whatever they could from me.

'This isn't easy, James, but I don't think it's still good for the business to have you so close to the sales team. We've got trainers now; it's not down to you to teach the new recruits any more.'

'But I enjoy working with the guys . . .'

The truth was, as long as I was visible I would undermine Jonathan's authority. As long as I was on the sales floor, he was never going to be in control. We debated it for two hours, but whatever arguments I put up, he persuaded me I was wrong. It was time to cut the umbilical cord and move into my own office.

I took a large room on the ground floor and went to town fitting it out. I got furniture handmade for it and when I was in Harrods I couldn't stop myself from buying the biggest and most elaborate fish tank I'd ever seen. It was completely over the top and everyone who visited the building commented on it. Being a fan of practical jokes, I kept a plastic fish behind it and when meetings got dull I would wander over to the fish tank and 'catch' the plastic fish and throw it at people, all of whom assumed a real fish was heading their way!

To celebrate Alexander Mann's tenth birthday, some of the staff clubbed together to buy me a present. I was extremely touched but when I opened it I was a bit confused: it was a beautiful frame to hang on the wall of my new office, but instead of a photograph or a picture they had mounted a miniature pot of paint and a paintbrush. It was only when I saw that the shade of the paint was 'Blue Sky' that I got the joke.

My other CEO's accessory was my new PA. Jan Parker had previously been Estée Lauder's personal assistant and she had an impeccable CV as an executive assistant: she was several leagues above the average secretary or PA. When she took up her desk outside my office door, I was sure I had hired the best in the business. However, after a week in the job, she told me she was leaving.

'But you've only just got here!'

'James, at the pace you work it's impossible for me to do my job. You come in with a phone clamped to your ear and have seventeen meetings in a row – most of which aren't in your diary – and by the end of the day you can't remember what happened in the first one in any detail. How am I supposed to help you if we never talk to one another?'

'I take your point.'

'I think you should save yourself my salary. You're fine as you are.'

'I'm not, you know. I shouldn't be having seventeen meetings a day. That's inefficient. I need help.'

Her solution was to move her desk inside my office rather than sit outside it. That way she could listen in on my meetings, and if someone asked to see the '91/'92 accounts, she would just arrange for them to be sent rather than me remembering that they'd asked, and then remembering to ask Jan to sort it out. At first I found it very strange having her there during confidential meetings, but I realised that she needed to be there to be able to do her job. It was great for me because we could update each other between phone calls and nothing slipped between the floorboards. The girl was brilliant, and through her professionalism and efficiency she created a great impression when clients met her. I suppose you could say she enhanced my personal brand, and having her working closely with me allowed me to work more efficiently and achieve much more.

Each week, Jonathan would send me printouts of how Alexander Mann was doing – how many placements, the average size of our fee, the names of new members of staff – which meant I still felt involved in the company, even if it was more of the week-to-week operations rather than the day-to-day stuff. If I saw that one of the sales team was having a bad run, I would go and have a word with him and see if I could help out. A few days later, Jonathan would call me.

'I hear you spoke to our IT team leader about performance.'

'Yeah, the printouts you gave me showed he'd been here eight months and hadn't billed anything. I thought I could give him some pointers.'

'Do you know what point you're making, James?'

'That he was losing us money.'

'And what's that got to do with you?'

'I pay his wages!'

'Why didn't you come to me about it? If you had, I would have told you to check the note I sent you three months ago about it. He's trying very hard to break into a new market and it's taking him time to build up the contacts. I talk to him about it every week and I'm convinced he'll deliver for us soon.'

That put me in my place.

'Either you want me to run the business or you don't, James, but we can't both run it.'

It wasn't always easy for me to keep my hands off the steering wheel, and Jonathan deserves credit for persevering when others might have told me where I could stick my interference, but the fact was that Jonathan's systems and procedures were already paying dividends and I could see I wasn't helping. From then on I was there for Jonathan, not for everyone else. I spoke to Jon most days discussing options and strategies, but I kept out of everybody else's hair. It was clear he was doing a good job, and as the two markets in which we had the highest profile – financial services and IT – took off with the dotcom surge, the profits got healthier and healthier. The fear that the Y2K bug would cripple computer systems at the end of the millennium also boosted the demand for IT professionals, and Alexander Mann kept expanding. As Jonathan grew the business, the building started to fill up with people I didn't know and who didn't know me. If I hadn't been so busy with other projects, I might have felt left out.

One of the few major problems Jonathan had to deal with was our success. This might sound odd, but our staff were so much better and billing so much more than the competition that they were often lured away with offers of grand job titles, benefits and big basic salaries if they could just bring a little of the Alexander Mann magic with them. So I decided to introduce a stock option scheme that gave employees a stake in the company. In the back of my mind, I thought this might help if I ever floated Alexander Mann as it could lock in key members of staff and guarantee continued profits – the kind of thing I knew investors liked to hear. I didn't yet have a plan as to what I would do with Alexander Mann, but I sensed flotation might be an option at some point down the line. At the time the markets were valuing recruitment companies at ten times profits, and, as we were clearing £1 million a year, that meant the business was worth at least £10 million. However, many people assumed that we had already floated as we were called Alexander Mann plc.

During a conversation with my accountant he'd told me in passing that you could register any company as a plc without issuing shares, so I told him to do that for Alexander Mann. It didn't change anything about the management or ownership of the company – I think they were simply listed as unauthorised shares rather than authorised ones – but I felt it gave us kudos. Just as I had let visitors to my Pall Mall office think Alexander Mann owned the entire building, I now let people think we were a publicly owned company.

While Alexander Mann flourished under Jonathan's steward-ship, Doug also had Humana under control. Within a year or so he had sold ten franchises, then twenty, and then he started selling them overseas. We had branches in Singapore, France, Germany and Brazil. He understood the business completely and was brilliant at his job. He worked so hard – trips to recruitment fairs, meetings with potential franchisees all over the world – and also spent hours in the office. With so many overseas partners, it made sense for Humana to base itself closer to Heathrow, and we used some of the early profits to buy an office in Windsor, which is about twenty minutes from the airport. This speeded up our expansion, and after a couple of years Humana was producing the most amazing revenues in royalty payments from the franchisees. The income was spectacular, and it meant I could use some of the profits to invest in other ventures.

There was just one problem: Doug was homesick. He was working extremely hard, but I sensed his enthusiasm was waning. I was genuinely concerned that, despite his early successes, he was going to turn around and tell me he was moving back to the US. There was no way I could let him do that, so I hit upon an ingenious way to persuade him to stay: my friend Jill.

I had known Jill since we'd worked together at Reid Trevena and I just had a hunch that she and Doug would get along. It helped that she lived in Windsor.

'What do you think I am?' She was quite furious at my suggestion they should meet.

'I'm not asking you to sleep with him! Just meet him for a drink. He's lonely, he needs a friend and I think you'll really like him.'

I introduced them at the office and then 'popped out' for something 'urgent' and left them alone for twenty minutes. The next thing I knew they were having dinner, and before long Jill became Mrs Bugie. Matchmaking isn't something I've done a lot of, but it certainly worked on that occasion, and it meant Doug was happy to stay in the UK.

With Jonathan and Doug motoring ahead with their respective

companies, I had time to think about where I wanted to go next. I had met a recruitment consultant at an industry event who told me his average fee was £35,000. Ours was £6k or £8k; we had the odd £20k fee but consistently to take a £35k fee was phenomenal. It was because he worked in the investment banking sector, where the salaries are legendary. I decided to investigate if I should start a specialist headhunters in the investment market. I could simply have started a division within Alexander Mann, but Humana had taught me just how powerful my strategy of backing people to run their own businesses could be. If I found the right person and motivated them the right way, I would create a much better business and have a far more lucrative investment.

For three months or so I immersed myself in the world of investment banking. Like any sector, it had its own language that needed to be learned, key players who had to be identified and gaps in the market that might be exploitable. I did what I always did: I met lots of people and asked lots of questions, and slowly but surely I built up my own picture of what was needed and what would work. I also met the best people in the field and found the best man for the task. Like Doug, I gave him equity in the business, found him space in Alexander House and was on hand for anything he needed. That business was Alexander Mann Financial Markets Ltd, and it was soon joined by Alexander Mann Technology Ltd and Alexander Mann Finance Ltd, all led by the best people I could find who were motivated by a sizeable equity stake.

It didn't cost me a vast amount to get some of these ventures going. The office space didn't cost me anything because I owned the building, the overheads – pay roll, accountancy, etc – were covered by in-house expertise, and in some cases the biggest cost was actually the chief executive's salary until the revenue streams started kicking in. I could offer new partners an exceptional environment in which to be successful at Alexander House and I could also open doors for them and mentor them. The cash I invested was only one component of what was becoming an increasingly lucrative investment strategy, and in many cases my experience was more valuable to these new ventures than my capital.

I was getting a good reputation as an investor and my next investment came to me. I got a call from guy called Mike O'Flynn who ran a small IT recruitment firm called Franklin Human Resources. He felt it had reached capacity and wanted to chat. There was no doubt that the technology sector was booming. Companies I hadn't heard of two months before – like Freeserve, AOL and Vista – were swallowing up new employees and I could see that Mike was operating in a potentially lucrative area. We became equity partners in a joint venture that we called Humana Consulting. By this stage, Humana had more than thirty offices and was advertising every week in the quality papers, so giving the joint venture the Humana brand was very valuable.

Talk about being in the right place at the right time. With Mike's contacts and my strategic help, Humana Consulting went from nothing to a £50 million turnover within four years and made the Virgin Fast Track 100 list as one of the fastest-growing companies in the UK.

Humana Consulting's average billing was higher than Alexander Mann's because wages in the technology sector were skyrocketing. We were hiring people out at £1000 a day, of which we'd pay about £700 to the worker. Imagine we placed 100 people in the past month, and do the maths. But what made it such a ridiculously profitable business was that no one could successfully predict how long their IT projects would last. So people would start a two-week contract and end up staying for two years. The commission was phenomenal, and even people with the most basic IT knowledge and qualifications were in demand. At the dotcom height, Humana Consulting had 600 people placed in jobs with an average commission of £200 a day. Mike was ecstatic. I was over the moon.

What was even better was the valuation of Humana Consulting. Unlike Alexander Mann, where you couldn't be sure how much money you would make from one month to the next because you couldn't accurately predict how many candidates you would place, with Humana Consulting you knew, fairly accurately, how many people you had out on assignments. That predictable level of income meant it was very attractive to potential investors, and the stock market was valuing companies with similar structures very strongly. If Alexander Mann was worth ten times earnings, Humana Consulting was worth eighteen times earnings. I wasn't planning on selling just yet, but it was nice to know we would have no trouble attracting interest if Mike and I changed our strategies.

Chapter 23

The End of an Era
(1998–1999)

'I back people not businesses.'

MY INVESTMENT STRATEGY was clearly working. I was able to use my money, my profile, my building, my payroll department, my lawyer – the entire Alexander Mann infrastructure – and my brilliant team to leverage the opportunities in front of us. I don't know anyone else who did what I did in the nineties, but marrying what we already had with the sector-specific talent we backed enabled us to guide and shape the people who would drive the new businesses forward.

Other ventures we started in those days included Adlam Consulting, a specialist recruiter in the investment world headed by Lyndy Adlam, and QED Recruiting, which operated in the industrial sector and was led by Richard Merrick. We also started joint ventures in Manchester, and in Holland and Turkey, and acquired a business called Nicholson Consulting.

It was a very impressive portfolio of companies, and whether someone needed legal advice, marketing know-how or IT support, it was easy for the organisation to give it to them. With those hassles taken care of, the CEOs of my new companies were freed up to work hard and deliver results. Pretty much everyone I backed was a sales expert. I had realised that the thing that drives companies is getting new customers, and as soon as I found people who I thought could sell their product to their customers, I would back them.

As my reputation as an investor grew, people started coming to me. One of them was an employee. Rosaleen Blair hadn't been with us long but she'd spotted an opportunity and had approached Jonathan with it. She thought there was a business in offering outsourced recruitment solutions to blue-chip clients. We, as an outside agency, could take on work normally done by in-house HR departments, but because we had such expertise we could do a better job.

Rosaleen wasn't one of the stars of our office and not an obvious candidate to back, but when I met her I could see that she really believed in the opportunity. She had previously run her own nanny agency, so she had a bit of a track record, but on paper that wasn't enough to convince me she could run the kind of company she was telling me about. But her passion and enthusiasm were so evident that I decided to back her anyway. As I have always said, I back people not businesses, and there was something about Rosaleen that convinced me.

For nine months Rosaleen worked the phones and went to meetings, trying to persuade companies to use Alexander Mann Solutions for their HR needs. It was a hard sell because companies were making a long-term commitment to a new venture. Nearly a year went by before she got her first contract, because it took so long to get through the layers of bureaucracy before she could talk to the person who could say yes. And once she had some interest, the negotiations were a bit of a marathon because there was so much due diligence to cover, but she did it: her first contract was from ICL and was worth £10 million. With that kind of client, picking up the next one was easier, and the company took off. I believe every organisation has a Rosaleen: the trick is being able to spot them and then giving them the chance to prove themselves.

I reckon that I rejected about 80 per cent of the ideas that came to me. I've never been much of a risk-taker and unless I was convinced of a project's success I gave it a miss. My success rate meant I was getting a good reputation, and more and more business ideas were brought to me. I realised that one of the ways I could minimise my risk even further was if the person I was backing invested some money, too. If they wanted a 50 per cent stake, I asked for 50 per cent of the investment; if they wanted 20 per cent, then they had to find 20 per cent. Some people sold their cars and remortgaged their houses to work with me, but in every case it was worth it: my portfolio of companies grew and grew as did the cash flow and profits from my existing companies.

As a consequence, I started to get interest in Alexander Mann from potential buyers. A couple of private equity firms started sniffing around, and a dotcom in America wanted to use its inflated stock market valuation to acquire Alexander Mann the way AOL had leveraged its market valuation to buy the much bigger, and much more profitable, Time Warner. They offered me £100 million in shares for my portfolio of companies, and it was so much money that I had to take it seriously. It was more money than I had ever imagined making in my life, so I talked to a lot of people about the offer. Pretty much everyone told me to take it, but I realised that it was so much money that I didn't actually *understand* how much money it was. I could only deal with such a figure abstractly, not as a real amount. What would having £100 million mean? What would it allow me to do?

I went to speak to a contact who worked at Goldman Sachs and was very used to those kinds of figures. He said he couldn't tell me if I should accept the deal or not, but he did suggest something I should think about.

'Imagine if you came to me and asked me to invest £100 million of your money in stocks and shares and I turned round to you and said, "I've got this great company and I'm going to put all your money into it," how would you feel?'

I thought about it, and my answer was 'vulnerable'. I wouldn't want all my money in shares in one company. If something happened to the performance of that company or that sector, I could lose a lot of money. I had been stunned how quickly things had collapsed in the recession and I knew shares in recruitment firms were particularly vulnerable to the wider economy, so I turned them down. A hundred million in cash I would have taken, but that wasn't what was offered.

Life on the business side of things was fantastic – absolutely fantastic – and on the home front life was just as good. I had even found myself a John Gielgud-style butler who had recently left service in the royal household. We had a lot of be thankful for, and as Aisha was about to turn forty we decided to have quite a big celebration. We planned a wonderful evening at the Cliveden House hotel in Berkshire and invited forty couples to join us. Aisha's birthday fell on a Friday and it just seemed the perfect day for a party. But the night before the event I received a phone call that would change everything.

My mum called at about 10 p.m. to say that Dad had been taken into hospital. She wasn't sure if it was kidney failure, but the doctors were running tests. I jumped in the car and drove straight to him. By the time I got to the hospital most of my brothers and sisters were already there and the doctors had confirmed that he'd had a stroke. He was hooked up to countless machines, and was pretty much out of it. Seeing him so weak left us all distraught.

I stayed until about 2 a.m., but the doctors insisted he needed to be left to rest completely before tests they had scheduled for the morning. I didn't want to leave him but I was reassured that they had booked him in for tests. If he had tests at 7.30 a.m., I figured that they clearly weren't expecting him to deteriorate overnight.

My phone rang at seven the next morning. It was my brother Adam: Dad had taken a turn for the worse and I should get to the hospital as soon as I could. I looked at Aisha: it was her fortieth birthday, a day we had been looking forward to for so long, and this was how it was starting. I wanted to make it better for her, but I also had to get to the hospital as soon as I could.

'Don't worry about it,' she said. 'Your father is much more important than a party.'

I threw on a tracksuit and the two of us jumped in the car. As it was too early for the rush hour we made good progress and within ten minutes or so we were speeding along the North Circular heading for Whipps Cross hospital. We were about halfway there when my phone rang again. It was still only 7.30 and I just knew it had to be bad news. I was in two minds as to whether or not I should answer. But it might be vital. I answered. It was Adam and there was something in the tone of his voice that made me dread what I knew he was about to say: our father had died.

I was in the fast lane and I remember the road in front of me just blurring. It was as if something had imploded in my head and I couldn't see straight and I couldn't think straight either: all I knew was that my father was dead and I hadn't been with him.

'Pull over.'

I knew Aisha was right but I just couldn't move my hands to change gear.

'Pull over, James!'

Something in her voice brought me to my senses and I pulled into a lay-by. Before I could turn the engine off I had started choking with tears and I could not stop them coming. I just sat there sobbing. All I wanted was to get to the hospital as quickly as possible, yet I didn't feel able to move. I was in shock and I felt as if I was about to collapse. I have this clear memory of desperately wanting to get to the hospital but being utterly incapable of doing anything.

I was just so shocked. *But he was having tests at 7.30 a.m.* That meant he was expected to live, didn't it? No one had said that he might die. It was the first time I had cried since Jemma had been born and for twenty minutes the tears would not stop. Even though Aisha was with me, I felt almost unbearably alone.

Eventually we swapped seats and Aisha took over the driving. When we got there, the entire family was in tears and it really hit me just how much I had wanted to be there for him at the end, not stuck in my car on the North Circular. We had become so close as a family that it seemed unbelievable that one of us had now gone.

A doctor approached and asked what we wanted to do about Dad's body. Islam stipulates that you have the funeral the day a person dies and, although we all knew this was what was supposed to happen, none of us had any experience of losing a loved one and none of us knew what to do. Should there be a post-mortem? Should he be buried? Who should come to the service? None of us had any answers, but we all had suggestions: there was a lot of talking, but what was needed was action.

While we were having these discussions, I remember looking across at Aisha. She was on her mobile calling the guests for her birthday party and telling them it was off. What a way to spend a birthday. We had been looking forward to this day for so long and yet this was how it had turned out.

I called an old family friend who talked me through the protocol of Muslim funerals. Firstly we had to sort out the paperwork. We needed a death certificate from the hospital and some sort of licence from the local council. The doctors gave us the number of the nearest mosque in Walthamstow, and they put us in touch with a nearby Muslim cemetery that had plots available. In such a situation, when someone gives you a simple option you tend to take it, and within a couple of hours the burial had been arranged.

Slowly, we were all given tasks and I really understood why our religion adhered to this practice: we all wanted to feel that we were doing something, and these rituals took us through the first stages of grief and disbelief. When you feel so lost, having traditions to guide your actions is so beneficial. I felt a part of something, and although my religious life probably involved little more than observing the Ten Commandments for most of the year, I was immensely grateful for the guidance of my faith that day.

However, the family friend who was advising us told us of one ritual that I was unsure of: it is a tradition, a requirement, that the sons bathe the body of the father in preparation for burial.

Our father's body was taken to a funeral parlour where they were clearly experienced in Muslim funerals, and we were led into the room where the preparations for burial were made. The experience of washing our father, washing his hair, is beyond description. The four of us – me, Adam, Andrew and Stephen – cried throughout and we all sensed that we were taking care of him, and in taking care, by undertaking this intimate procedure, we were also saying goodbye. It was the most emotional thing I have ever done in my life and it filled me with grief. It was my single worst moment – I have never felt that much sadness at any other time – but through it all there was a recognition that it was part of the healing process.

My father had died on a Friday, the most religious day of the Muslim week, and his funeral was conducted as part of the normal Friday prayers. Our families arrived at the mosque and we all prayed for him. I think Jemma and Hanah were confused and upset to see their dad so distraught. They held on to me, and having them close made me even more emotional.

As the service took place, my thoughts turned to whether or not I could have done more for him. Had I been a good son? I was more emotional than my brothers – the grief just poured out of me

– but I was consoled by the fact that I thought I had been a dutiful son. I didn't feel guilty that I hadn't been there for him. I didn't feel that I had let him down. I hadn't been there when he had died, but I had done everything else I could for him. I wonder if the hurt I caused when I left home at sixteen was actually the foundation of these feelings. My father and I had re-established a relationship as adults, and although I always felt a duty towards him my respect for him was genuine. We had rebuilt our relationship when we could both have walked away. The fact that we hadn't done that, and that we had become close again, told me that he had felt the same way about me as I had felt about him.

After the service my brothers and I had to carry his coffin to the hearse, and when we reached the graveyard we had to lower his coffin into the ground. If bathing him had been traumatic, putting him in the ground was awful. We then had to fill the grave, and every time I had to drop another shovelful of earth on to his coffin I froze. He had only been dead a few hours; yesterday he had been alive, if not well, and here we were now, covering his coffin with earth, carrying on until the coffin was obscured, and then piling on the earth until the burial was complete. It was physically and emotionally exhausting.

It was quite the worst day of my life, but a few days afterwards I was surprised to realise that I felt oddly OK about his passing. It seemed that the rituals had forced so much grief out of me that I sensed I was through the worst of it. In Islam, it is traditional to mourn for forty days, and this is what the rest of my family did, but I was starting to feel that I could almost go back to work. The family thought there was something wrong with me and that I must be in shock or denial, but all the memories I had of my father were good ones, and when I looked back I suppose I was at peace with how I had behaved towards him. I had done what a son ought to have done; I had even enabled him to help his children start businesses of their own. I realised that the rituals and traditions of our faith had allowed me to say goodbye in a way that enabled me to look to a future without him. I would continue to miss him, but I was no longer mourning.

I have lots of Christian friends who say that for them mourning is all about the stiff upper lip, with no expression or emotion. I believe it's so important to let the grief out, otherwise I can imagine you could walk around with it for years. I think the Islamic rituals surrounding death take you through a journey of saying goodbye that allows you to move on.

Chapter 24

A New Beginning
(1999–2000)

'You only have to look at Mike Tyson, or Michael Jackson, to see how a vast fortune can simply be spent. I wasn't about to let that happen.'

MY FATHER'S PASSING added to the sense that I was ready for something new. We were about to start a new millennium and, like everyone else, I was thinking about the future. I realised I had everything I wanted in terms of health, family, wealth and status. If nothing were to change, any outsider would have looked at me and thought I led a charmed life. I could even have employed a chairman and effectively retired. However, I knew I didn't want that. I wasn't quite sure what I wanted other than the fact that I was looking for a change.

I felt this even though business had never been better. Our two biggest sectors – technology and finance – were buoyant with the dotcom frenzy, the Y2K panic and the fact that entire banking systems were being redesigned to cope with the EMU (the European Monetary Unit, which would become the euro). We had never placed so many candidates so easily, and the profits of all my companies were, frankly, spectacular. That year I bought a home in the South of France – an apartment overlooking the Croisette in Cannes – and paid for it in cash.

The dotcom boom was also leading to a stock market boom, and the valuations for all companies were rising. If I was serious about a stock market flotation, this was the time to do it. However, I just had a bunch of companies – it was basically Jimmy and his mates – all owned by different partners on different percentages. For the market to take me seriously I needed to restructure my companies into something more formal. So I hired consultants Arthur Andersen to assess the best way of doing that.

They suggested merging all the companies into one, but when I talked to the individual CEOs of my companies about it four of them told me that they didn't want to be a part of the new organisation. They said that one of the things they most enjoyed in their career was working outside the usual corporate constraints and they didn't want their company to become part of something big. They liked owning a decent slice of their company, rather than the 3–10 per cent of the combined group they would be likely to end up owning. One of those CEOs was Doug Bugie, and I was quite pleased about that. No matter what happened to Alexander Mann in the future, I would still own half of a hugely profitable business: Humana now had over 140 franchises in 30 countries and its profits were doubling every year. In fact it was doing so well that even a couple of the franchisees had become quite wealthy in their own right.

On the advice of Arthur Andersen and the accountancy firm BDO, which I brought in to value everyone's stake in the business, I also appointed a new chairman and a board in preparation for taking the business to the market. Jonathan became the group chief executive and I took the title executive chairman. The combined group had profits in excess of £5 million, and after

BDO's valuation of the contribution that each company made to the combined group, my share was 67 per cent. In my mind, I thought the right time to float would be 1999.

As we were gearing up to float, Doug returned from one of his regular trips home to the States with an interesting proposition. He had been seeing some of his old friends at MRI and the long and the short of it was that they wanted to buy Humana. For years Doug had told them they should expand internationally but they hadn't listened to him. Now that he had taken recruitment franchises global they wanted it! For Doug, there couldn't have been a bigger ego boost, and it was clear he was really tempted by the opportunity to rejoin his old firm with a fantastic salary and share package.

I was so geared up for a flotation that this was quite difficult to get my head round, and I had liked the idea of holding on to Humana. However, it was clear that Doug wanted to say yes to a deal that would allow him to return to the States and give him a fabulous lifestyle. I realised that if I stood in the way of the deal I would be left with a demoralised chief executive and the diminishing returns that would follow such a decision. As long as the price was right, I decided that we should sell.

MRI made us an offer we couldn't refuse, but it just so happened that the week the deal was being negotiated I was attending a conference in the States where I got talking to a corporate banker from Robinson Humphrey, a subsidiary of Salomon Smith Barney, who specialised in mergers and acquisitions. 'Let me handle it for you,' he said.

'The deal's practically done,' I told him. 'Thanks for the offer, but I don't think I need to pay your fee in this instance.'

'Meet me for breakfast tomorrow,' he insisted.

When we met, I told him about the business and the deal on the table and, as I spoke, he realised that there was a way to negotiate a better price. MRI's offer had valued Humana accurately, but what had been omitted was a premium that accounted for the value of the combined company. With Humana under its umbrella, MRI would become the biggest executive search firm in the world, and according to the banker that made the acquisition more valuable.

'Leave it with me,' he said.

We agreed a deal that gave him a percentage of anything he got me above the original offer. I was happy with the deal I already had, but if he could get me more then I was happy for him to share any upside of what I wasn't expecting to get.

MRI were a little thrown when we went back to the negotiating table, and the chief exec called me up wanting to finalise the deal directly. I had to refer him to Robinson Humphrey, and when they restarted the negotiations it soon became clear just how much MRI wanted Humana. By the end of the negotiations, their offer had increased by 50 per cent. Some of that was to be in shares, but I told them that my religion was very strict on what kinds of transactions were permissible and that the offer had to be in cash. I played dumb and told them to make me an offer I could understand. It wasn't true, of course, but their knowledge of Islam was next to non-existent and they came back and matched their offer in cash. Doug decided to take the shares and joined the MRI board. The banker took his fee and we were all happy. I should rephrase that: we were ecstatic.

Although I had been wealthy for a long time, my wealth had been in assets not cash. For the first time in my life my bank balance reflected my status as a millionaire and I found that quite exciting, even though I had received some very good advice from my fellow forum members at YPO that I shouldn't touch the cash for a year. I had been talking to them for a while about the possibility of floating Alexander Mann and what that would mean for my personal wealth. Between them they had a lot of experience of selling businesses and becoming cash rich: with the Humana money in the bank and the Alexander Mann money surely not that far behind, they recommended that the best thing to do was lock it away. When you've never had cash before – and you've already got everything you want in terms of houses and cars – you could end up squandering it remarkably easily: couple of mill on a helicopter, another mill on a racehorse. I took their advice and tied the money from Humana up in a bond for twelve months. My YPO colleagues were also able to introduce me to advisers who arranged for my shares in Alexander Mann to be held in a trust. Not only was this a tax-efficient way of managing my stake in the business, but it was structured so that I wouldn't be able to touch any income from those shares for at least a year, just in case I decided to get seriously flash and buy myself a plane or a million-pound watch. You only have to look at Mike Tyson, or Michael Jackson is perhaps a better example, to see how a vast fortune can simply be spent. I wasn't about to let that happen.

With the Humana deal done, the flotation of Alexander Mann was proceeding nicely. A top City PR firm was hired to market us to investors, and a firm of brokers was appointed that sent me on an endless round of presentations. The company was valued at £60 million, and it was clear that the City loved what we were offering; in fact, in many ways we were the perfect company because we ticked every box. They wanted diverse sources of income. Tick. They wanted exposure in several markets. Tick. They wanted to make sure the founder and CEOs wouldn't leave as soon as the ink was dry: all my CEOs had equity stakes and were in it for the long term. Tick. They liked freeholds in central London. Tick. We all felt very confident about the flotation.

About three weeks before our shares were due to be released for the first time, I got a phone call from a guy called John Singer at a private equity house called Advent International. He had been sent the share prospectus by our brokers, and he liked what he had read so much that he wanted to invest.

'How much of the company are you floating?'

'Twenty-five per cent.'

'Would you sell us 40 per cent?'

I had never considered selling that much of the company.

'I don't think that's something I want to do.'

At this point I was very excited about the flotation. I wanted to look up my company in the *Financial Times* every morning, I wanted the fireworks and champagne on the day of the offering, I wanted to be the boss of a publicly owned company: I really wasn't interested in what he was suggesting.

He rang me again.

'I'm frustrated,' he said. 'We obviously got to you too late, but we really like your company and we really want to invest. We like the sector and we think this is one of the best investment opportunities we've seen all year. Let me come and talk to you.'

'I hear what you're saying, John, but why would I sell to you?'

'Just let me come and see you.'

He talked me through what the flotation would mean for my day-to-day life, and the restrictions shareholders and regulators would impose on my business.

'Every time you want to make a change you'll need your shareholders' permission. You'll be holding extraordinary general meetings just to change a light bulb. If you want more investment, it will take ages, whereas with private finance it would only take a few meetings. Seriously, you have no idea just how restrictive it is running a publicly owned business.'

He was making some valid points, so I thought about what he was saying and tried to imagine me answering to shareholders who only cared about their dividend payments. He was starting to persuade me. His other argument was equally persuasive: the stock market doesn't allow founders to cash in very many of their chips at the time of the offering. Investors like to keep you hungry, and so there would be a limit on the percentage of my holding I would be allowed to sell. If I sold to Advent, I could sell many more of my shares and start investing the money elsewhere.

Believe it or not, I had never thought about these things. I had got so caught up in the razzmatazz of being courted by the City and thinking about my personal situation after the flotation that I hadn't considered these practicalities. The private equity deal was looking more and more attractive. After they had taken their stake, my share would be diluted to 42 per cent, which would mean I would still be the largest shareholder in the company I had founded. That felt comfortable, so I discussed it with the other shareholders and we decided to take their offer. I just had one request: the deal had to be in cash.

'You must be joking!'

'Unless you can tell me why I should leave the cash in the business, then that's the way I want to structure the deal.'

We agreed a valuation that was higher than the level the shares would have been issued at to account for the surge in price we anticipated in the days after flotation. I agreed to put 30 per cent of the cash payment back into the business so that it would be available for growth, marketing, acquisitions or whatever else the board decided to do with it. I didn't think this was strictly necessary as Alexander Mann already had a healthy bank balance, but even without the 30 per cent the Advent deal made me very wealthy. The question now was, *What was I going to do with the money?*

Chapter 25

Kosovo (1999–2001)

'There wasn't any electricity. Everything was black. No one could work without light, there was no TV, no radio, no cars, only darkness. It made me realise how much we take for granted.'

I'D ALREADY HAD everything I wanted before the deal with Advent, so my thoughts now turned to what else I could do with my wealth, and one of my plans was to give some of it to charity. As I've said before, I was disillusioned with simply writing out a cheque, and the thought of writing out a really big cheque and seeing hundreds of thousands of pounds disappear in overheads or mismanagement or, in many cases overseas, corruption, was enough to make me really think about how I could use my money best. I discussed these thoughts with a friend of mine who said he knew someone I should meet: Cat Stevens.

Cat – the sixties folk singer – converted to Islam after a spiritual experience when he thought he was drowning. He had asked God to save him, and when he was delivered safely to shore he spent months studying the scriptures to find a philosophy and doctrine that matched his own. Islam was the faith that resonated with him the most. Since his conversion, he has dedicated his life and his money to charity work.

Now known as Yusuf Islam, Cat is one of the most amazing people I have ever met, and when he told me about his work I knew I wanted to be involved. He doesn't work as part of an organisation; he just boards a plane, sees what needs to be done and then gets on and does it. He'd been doing it for twenty years or more by the time I met him and his results were impressive.

He had been spending a lot of time in Kosovo and Bosnia and the things he told me about the civil war there were almost beyond belief. Massacres of entire villages, rape used as a weapon of war: Europe had let genocide happen on its doorstep and he was doing everything he could to help these shattered states recover.

My life had been so consumed with business for the past decades that all I knew of the situation in the Balkans was the headlines. When he talked to me about the atrocities he had seen first-hand, I was so moved that I readily agreed to help.

He called me up on a Thursday: 'I'm going to Kosovo on Saturday. Do you want to come?'

'There's still a war going on.'

'That's why I'm going. People are being killed. Children are being orphaned.'

I thought about it for a moment. Wasn't this the kind of involvement I wanted? 'How do we get there?'

On the one hand I didn't want to go because I was scared, but on the other here was a guy who was going to show me how I could really make a difference. If I didn't get on that plane with him I would have felt guilty, fraudulent even, so on Saturday morning I met Yusuf at Heathrow. It was just the two of us making the trip: no press, no PAs, no entourage.

There were no direct flights to Kosovo, so we got a flight to Vienna and from there we could get a plane to Montenegro, and from there we could make our way overland into neighbouring Kosovo and the war zone.

We were sitting in the executive lounge waiting for our flight, and I was reading the paper. I looked up for a second and Yusuf had gone. It was only when I put the paper down to look for him that I saw he was on the floor. He'd taken a prayer mat out of his briefcase and was on his knees. Most people would ask if there was a prayer room, but he just prayed in the middle of a departure lounge. I was quite taken aback.

We talked about his conversion and his spirituality for much of the flight, and when we changed planes in Vienna we passed a record shop in the terminal building: his greatest hits compilation was number one in the Austrian album chart! I couldn't believe it. I was very impressed, but Yusuf was clearly used to it.

A few hours later, we arrived in Montenegro and as soon as we were out of the terminal building I was shocked by the devastation. It was all rubble: bombed-out buildings lined the roads and everything was dusty. The roads were sandy and dusty, the buildings were sandy and dusty, the skin of people's faces was dusty and my overall sensation was one of sadness.

Yusuf had arranged for us to be met by an interpreter and a driver who could take us over the border to a couple of villages he had read about in the papers. Most of the vehicles on the road were military ones, and it was unnerving to see so many soldiers. The previous night I had slept in my own bed in my lovely house; now I was travelling through some of the poorest neighbourhoods in Europe. It was quite surreal, extremely frightening and incredibly moving.

The interpreter gave me his perspective on the conflict: Kosovo was a predominantly Muslim province within Serbia, one of the states that made up Yugoslavia. As civil wars in Bosnia, Croatia and other states saw the break-up of Yugoslavia in the 1990s, Kosovo also sought independence from Serbia. A decade or so earlier, the Balkans had been a melting pot where Christians and Muslims had lived peacefully side by side, but the fight for independence had seen the appearance of an ethnic divide – almost from nowhere was how he explained it – and the Kosovans had been persecuted by the Serbians.

On our way to the villages we stopped in a town where we saw a Muslim girl come out of a tower block; she was being attacked by a gang of boys. They were spitting at her, pushing her and throwing cans at her. We got talking to her, and through the interpreter she explained that the boys who had targeted her had once been her friends: they had all grown up in the same tower block.

I asked her why she didn't just take her headscarf off. She wouldn't stand out then.

'I thought about it, but then I thought, "Why should I?"'

I admired her so much for that. I was genuinely touched by her conviction and just wanted to write her a cheque there and then. She continued to tell us of the daily assaults her mother, herself and her sister had had to endure since their father had been killed. I looked to Yusuf for a solution.

'What can we do?' I asked.

'It's up to you.'

So I asked the girl how I could help her.

'Take me out of this hell hole. Me, my sister, our mother, we have no money so we cannot move.'

'How much would it cost you to buy a house? What's the process?'

She explained that there were no houses to buy: they had been destroyed. First she would have to find some land and then they would have to build a house.

'Do you know how much that would cost?'

It was the equivalent of about £30,000, so I told her to go and look for some land.

'When you've found it, send me a picture of it and I will send you the money.'

We agreed that she would then send me a sketch of the house they wanted to build and I would send the next tranche of money.

A couple of weeks after I got home, I received the picture of the land and I released the money. A few weeks after that, I received the documents that said they had bought the land as well as a handwritten report on the construction of the house – it was pretty basic and didn't need an architect even if one had been available – and I sent the rest of the money they'd asked for. Within three months they had moved out of the tower block and to safety.

I couldn't get over the fact that a community that had once lived peacefully had turned on itself. Seeing the way she had been attacked like a stray dog has stayed with me, and I am just so glad that there was something I could do to help.

We moved on to the villages, where we were taken into a one-room house not much bigger than a Portakabin. I was amazed to find a woman living there with eight children. The most striking thing about the place was that there wasn't any furniture in it: no chairs, no tables, only a rug on the floor, which is where I sat and played with the little ones while the interpreter talked to the woman. The story she told still chills me.

She said she had lived in the village all her life: it was a small place of maybe forty families and throughout the war things had been quiet there because it was so out of the way. Then, four months before, the Serbian army had turned up.

'There was a huge commotion,' she said, 'and people started screaming that they had surrounded the village. Then the soldiers marched into the village and started knocking on every door. The noise was terrible.'

Her children were so beautiful – gorgeous little things – and as she told her horrible story I just wanted to protect them. The soldiers then dragged every male over the age of about fourteen – anyone deemed capable of fighting – out of their homes and into the village square where they were lined up in front of a wall. Then, with their children and mothers and wives watching, they were executed.

As she relived the horror, I was looking at the children, trying to imagine what it must be like to grow up having seen something like that. And what would it be like to grow up in a place with no men? Who would bring in the harvest? Who would earn the money? Beyond the impact of the massacre, the economic devastation would last a generation or more. This woman had eight kids and no means of employment: how the hell were they going to survive? I felt so empty yet when I looked up I was amazed – stunned – to see that she had a smile on her face. I asked the interpreter to ask how she could still smile.

'I smile because I am alive,' she said. 'I am still alive and my children are alive. I have nothing else, but this is enough.'

On our way to the next house we stopped at the place where the massacre had occurred. The number of bullet holes in the wall told their own horrific story. The next woman we spoke to had her own memories of that day four months before, and as we talked I just couldn't understand how they were surviving. There was no dole office, no state aid, no employment and no bank. As I looked around, I couldn't see a single building in the village that wasn't a house – no pub, no shop, no café – and I couldn't get my head round how they could survive without an economy. Nor could I work out why they were so friendly and not morbid or depressed. By the fourth house, I knew I had to help.

'What can we do here, Yusuf?'

'It's your call, James.'

'I don't know where to start.'

As we walked around the village we discussed a plan that would see me 'adopt' the village.

'These people don't need blankets or clothes,' Yusuf said, 'they need dignity. Why don't you give them their dignity back?'

The aid agencies in the country were so busy dealing with such a complicated disaster that they thought it would be a year before aid reached the village. I decided that I would fund whatever the village needed for a year until the aid agencies reached it. We devised a plan that trained one person to use a computer who then made a register of every woman and child who was left. Next we devised a budget for each of them – not enough for luxuries but enough for food, for electricity, clothes and transport. It was important to me that the allowance enabled them to live with dignity. I didn't want them to have to sell any of their possessions or to beg, but to be able to live well enough that they could start rebuilding their lives.

Yusuf had funded a similar project in a nearby village and had some contacts on the ground who could help administer the programme and distribute the funds. Each month, every person in the village could collect their money and sign to acknowledge that they had received it. If they needed extra funds to build a store for food or repair their tractor, then I was sent photographs of the problem and I released additional funds. There were as many as 500 kids in that village and fewer than 100 adults, and funding them for a year was a significant financial commitment, but I was learning that there was nothing better I could spend my money on. I was wealthy, sure, but I wasn't Warren Buffett. I didn't have a bottomless pit, but I believe if you're in a position to help and you choose not to, well, I would have found it pretty hard to have lived with myself.

The stories I heard on that three-day trip have never left me, but it's often the smallest things that really stay in your mind. We had spent most of the day inside the villagers' houses, and at around 6 p.m. it was time to make our way to the town where we were staying. When we left the last house I couldn't believe my eyes when I opened the door: it was pitch-black. I have lived in London most of my life, where there's always a street light on or a house light or a car headlight. I couldn't get my head round how dark it was. I really couldn't see anything: no moon, no stars, no lights in any of the windows because there wasn't any electricity. Every-thing was black. No one could work without light, there was no

TV, no radio, no cars, only darkness. It made me realise how much we take for granted.

Going back into the office the next day was a strange feeling. I had just had my eyes opened to a whole new world and I was immediately immersed in my old one. Advent had invested in Alexander Mann because they thought they would get a good return on their money, so the early years of their involvement were spent growing the business so that they, and we, could increase the value of our respective shareholdings.

Having an outside investor changed the atmosphere of Alexander House; some of the fun had gone. We had become slightly more corporate and it felt slightly less like my company. Things really changed, however, in the summer of 2000 when our plans for growth were dealt an enormous blow by the bursting of the dotcom bubble. It sent the stock market into a slump, and our two biggest sectors – IT and finance – were the hardest hit. Thankfully, Alexander Mann was in a good position to ride out the storm, so just as I had done with the recession in the early nineties we battened down the hatches and prepared for a rough time. The recruitment industry was still vulnerable to the wider economy, and we knew we weren't about to enjoy a good period of growth.

Then came September 11 2001 and the world changed for good. Financial companies that had withstood the fallout from the dotcom bubble bursting now fell apart, and share prices plummeted with the economic downturn that followed the attacks on the World Trade Center and the Pentagon. I started to wonder if it was time for a new challenge: it was going to be harder than we'd anticipated and, I realised, possibly harder than I was prepared to live through again. Besides, I was beginning to think I was ready for a new challenge.

After mulling over my options for a couple of months I went to talk to Advent and asked them if they wanted to buy my remaining

42 per cent. I had long seen them buying into the company as the start of some kind of transition and I felt it was probably time to move on. After all, the way the company was structured meant it was pretty much run by the joint-venture CEOs: I had little to do with people they employed as that would have compromised their authority. They were now all individually successful and needed me less and less. I was no longer making the difference I once had, and that was becoming less rewarding for me.

With the way the economy was, my holding was undervalued and Advent saw an opportunity to buy when the market was low. After some protracted legal discussions about valuations and terms we did a deal, and I walked away from the company I had founded, the company I had loved and nurtured and for which I had worked eighteen hours a day. I didn't know what I was going to do, but I realised that my thirst for change in the months after my father's passing had not been satisfied. I was excited about what the future held.

Chapter 26

What Now? (2002–2003)

'*What the hell had I done? And, more importantly, what the hell was I going to do now?*'

THE FINAL NEGOTIATIONS with Advent had taken place over the phone while I was spending some time at the apartment in Cannes with Aisha and the girls. The deal was taking a while to finalise because Advent wanted things like non-competition clauses inserted into the agreement that would prevent me from opening an office across the street from Alexander Mann and poaching all the best staff. I didn't think it was strictly necessary: why would I do anything to harm the company I loved? Besides, I was leaving because I wanted to do something new. It took so long to finalise that by the time I got back to London all the excitement I had felt had been negotiated away. Going back into the office would have been a backward step, so I simply called Jan, my PA, and asked her to pack up my things and arrange for them to be sent to the house. Apart from Jan, I didn't speak to anyone else in the company.

My friends at YPO – several of whom had also sold companies they'd founded – told me that the best way to handle the situation was to make a clean break. It was better for those who still worked there, but, crucially, it was much better for me: if I was still advising members of staff on this contract or that development I would never break free or have the mental space to develop something new.

About three days after the deal was made it hit me – like a sledgehammer. What the hell had I done? And, more importantly, what the hell was I going to do now? For eighteen years my days had been filled by Alexander Mann, and for the past ten of them I'd had twenty meetings a day and an assistant who made sure I was always where I needed to be. If I had wanted a restaurant booked, it had been booked for me; if I had wanted to catch a flight, it had been arranged on my behalf; if I had wanted to take a couple of days off it had required coordinating umpteen people's diaries. I was free now, but I was also really quite lost. I still owned the businesses that hadn't been part of the sale to Advent, but they didn't take up more than a day or two a month. How was I going to fill my days?

I just kept asking myself, *What have I done?* I was forty-two, the age when most people earn the biggest pay packets of their careers and amass the bulk of their wealth, yet I was walking away from my earning capacity. On the one hand, people thought I was mad, but on the other they were jealous: I was effectively retiring twenty years before most people got to think about it.

Obviously, I had discussed it all with Aisha. She had stopped working at Alexander Mann when Advent had bought their initial stake in 1999 and for the past three years she had got into a routine while the girls were at school all day. I think we were both a little bit worried about how things would work if I was hanging around the house all day. But, to her credit, Aisha didn't constantly suggest ways that would get me back into business and out of the house. More than anyone, she knew how hard I had worked and how badly I needed a break. I had worked since I was sixteen, my life for twenty years had been wrapped up in business and she recognised that it would take me time to figure out what to do next. I really didn't know what I wanted, so I told myself I was going to take a 'gap year' and give myself a chance to figure it all out. But unlike most gap years that are undertaken on a shoestring, this would be a five-star year doing all the things I hadn't had the time to do while I was building the businesses.

While I'd been considering whether or not to sell my stake in the company, I'd had an office built in the basement of the house, and on the first Monday of my new life I went into my new office. The first surprise was that the computer wasn't on. I hadn't realised it before, but Jan had always turned my computer on for me, logged on to the system and opened up my e-mail for me. I had no idea how to do these things for myself. It was a little bit like being back in the broom cupboard in Pall Mall: no colleagues, no clients, no atmosphere.

I turned on the TV and watched Bloomberg. At least I felt like I was still connected to the world of business with reports on the markets, companies and share prices. Having it on in the background probably kept me sane, but it was clear I couldn't watch TV for the rest of my life.

I called a recruitment agency – not one I had any involvement in – and asked for a temp to come and show me how a computer worked. A girl called Sam turned up and I had to start by asking her how to turn the thing on.

'How do I set a password?'

Then we moved on to e-mail.

'What's my e-mail address?'

'What do you want it to be?'

So she set me up with an e-mail account.

'So how do I forward an e-mail?'

She burst out laughing. 'Are you really the same bloke who built a global business? How come you don't know any of this?'

Then she taught me about the internet. Strange as it seems, I had never actually surfed the net before. People had come in and said

'You must take a look at this site,' or sent me a link. I didn't know how to find anything, so she explained Google to me. That was a revelation, and I spent several days just looking at golf clubs because I thought that playing golf was what semi-retired millionaires did.

'What else can I do with the internet?'

'You could try downloading music.'

'How does that work?'

I'm not kidding; I spent about three weeks solidly making playlists of the music I had missed out on during the previous eighteen years. Then Sam told me about Photoshop and I spent another couple of weeks touching up holiday snaps. Aisha would ask me what I had been doing all day and I would show her a CD I'd burned or an image I'd made of me meeting George Bush in the White House.

Not only had I not known how to use a computer, but I didn't even know how to use an ATM! If I'd needed cash, I'd always asked Jan to arrange it for me and I'd got used to just having cash in my wallet. When I got down to my last few notes, I didn't know how I would get more.

'Aisha, how do I get cash?'

'You use your card, James.'

'How do I do that?'

I didn't even know about PINs and had to get the bank to send me a new one. It was as if I had this split personality: half of me was capable of running a multimillion-pound business and the other half of me was clueless about some of the most basic things.

Jemma and Hanah were now sixteen and fifteen respectively, and the single best thing about stopping work was getting to spend more time with them. They were really great fun to be with, and instead of just getting half an hour with them before they went to bed, suddenly I was spending whole days with them. Really getting to know these two fabulous young women who I was increasingly proud to call my daughters was the most fun I ever had.

I had always been respectful towards my father; even as an adult I had obeyed him and his word had remained law. I couldn't help but be struck by how differently my daughters talked to me.

'Can we go to Cannes this weekend, Dad?'

'No.'

With my dad, that would have been the end of the conversation, but they would always ask me why not. And unless I could come up with a really good reason, we'd go to Cannes! I absolutely loved their cheek as I recognised it as a sign of a feistiness that would see them achieve whatever they wanted in life. Of the two, Hanah always has to get to the bottom of something, and won't stop until she completely understands a situation: in that respect, she has the makings of a fine entrepreneur, and when she finishes her degree she will be very welcome to come and work with me. Jemma will be, too, but I sense she may follow a more creative path, like her mother. I find it fascinating how I can see both my and Aisha's traits in both our daughters.

The three of us would go shopping together, ostensibly to buy the girls a few treats, but while we were in West End boutiques I saw clothes for me. I no longer needed a suit, and I acquired a whole new wardrobe of ripped jeans and T-shirts. The girls thought it was a bit embarrassing, but I thoroughly enjoyed playing around with my image. I grew a beard and decided I liked it. I started wearing beads and bracelets – things I would never previously have worn. All my adult life I had seen myself as a guy in a suit, but now I could decide for myself how I wanted to dress. It was such a contrast from my previous life that I found the change from loafers to flip-flops liberating. Previously I'd been worrying about cash flow and overheads, but now my biggest concern was how many rips DKNY were putting in their jeans that season or if my beads were the right colour.

A few months after I stopped work I received an invitation to go to the Entrepreneur of the Year awards at the Grosvenor House hotel. I'd been nominated for it in 2000 and I saw these kinds of events as a good night out and a chance to network. That year Hanah and Jemma were both free so the three of us went together, and it was only when I looked at the invitation that I realised I had been nominated once again. As someone who no longer had a career, I didn't expect to win so we went along just to enjoy ourselves.

There were several awards given out that night celebrating success in every sector of the economy but the main award was left until the end of the night. By the time it was announced I was deep in conversation with someone on our table when Jemma tapped my arm.

'Dad, you've won!'

I turned round to see my face projected on to a big screen and everyone in the room looking at me. I was so shocked that I can't remember what I said. I had won a few awards before, but this one was really quite prestigious.

Afterwards, I got talking to one of the panel members who had decided I should be the recipient and I asked him why they had chosen me.

'In the end, there were two reasons. The first was that you're a serial entrepreneur. You've proved that you didn't just get lucky and that you can replicate success time and again. A lot of successful entrepreneurs only ever start one business.'

I thought that was interesting and was curious to hear the second reason.

'You've also exited those businesses. Again, a lot of successful entrepreneurs don't exit their businesses, and, if they do, the businesses often fail without them. You demonstrated that you could create value that didn't rely on your presence.'

It was all very flattering but, of course, the conversation turned to what I would be doing next because 'everyone is interested to see what you're going to get up to'.

'To be honest, I'm not sure. I thought I might learn to fly.'

I wasn't joking: I didn't have a plan, but I knew I wanted to give myself a chance to do things I'd missed out on while I was working so hard and flying a plane sounded like fun.

I went to an airstrip to the north of London and talked to a flying instructor.

'How long will it take me to get my licence?'

'It doesn't normally take more than a couple of months.'

A couple of months? That was way too slow.

'How about I just hire you solidly for a fortnight? Would that give me enough flying time?'

So that's what I did, but after two weeks of intensive flying I was surprised to find out that I hadn't found it quite as thrilling as I'd hoped. The windows on two-seater planes are really quite small, and because I couldn't see much of the ground beneath me I didn't get the buzz I was after. There were also several helicopters at the airfield, and when I saw one which was basically a big glass bubble take off I asked if I could fly one of those instead.

Another intensive course later and I was flying helicopters and had a real taste for thrill-seeking. The next thing to try was fast cars, and I went to Silverstone to race Ferraris. If I had realised flying was my passion, I would have bought a plane; if I'd fallen in love with helicopters, I'd have had one of those; and if I'd thought I would ever be able to race around in a Ferrari on the open road, I'd have bought a sports car, but the thing that captured my imagination was sailing. While we were spending time in Cannes I went to the marina and saw all these gorgeous yachts. I arranged to have a couple of lessons taking one of them out on the open water and I absolutely loved it and so I took lessons to qualify as a skipper. I then bought a beautiful yacht of my own. However, on one of my first trips out I had a close encounter with a cliff! Thankfully I was still close enough to the shore for my mobile phone to work. One of the guys I'd got to know at the harbour was able to whizz out in a speedboat and tow us away from danger, but it was getting so close that I had started to prepare to jump overboard. Ever since then, I have always taken an experienced captain out with me.

All this activity made me realise just how little time I'd had for anything outside family and business for my entire adult life. I couldn't remember the last time I had read a book, or gone for over an hour without making a phone call. Although I was packing a lot in, it was still quite an adjustment to adapt to my new pace of life, and to adapt to my new financial status as well.

I still didn't know what I was going to do with the money. What did it mean to have millions of pounds? What was the best thing to do with it? I have always made decisions fairly easily, but this wasn't something I wanted to rush. I wondered what other people had done with their wealth. I read up about people who have set up charitable foundations – like Bill Gates – and those who have blown the lot, like Barbara Hutton, the Woolworth's heiress who inherited £50 million in the 1920s (which must be several billion in today's money) and died penniless. I read about a lot of people who had inherited wealth and who had become depressed, wasted it or worse: I realised that money could be a burden, especially when you haven't had to work for it. As a consequence I started thinking about my will and my legacy to my family. Did I want the money to be a burden to Jemma and Hanah? Of course not. I will provide for them as I will for the rest of my family, but I couldn't see that leaving them everything was the right thing to do. I still didn't know what I would do with it, though.

I also had time to think about my faith. Since the 11 September attacks, Islam had acquired an unwelcome prominence. The phrase 'British Muslim' seemed to be on every page of every newspaper. Aisha has always been more religious than me, but I have always had a spirituality and there is no doubt that I am a believer, but what did that mean in the modern world? For the first time in my life I wondered if it was the right time to undertake the hajj to Mecca. If the girls had been a little older, we would probably have gone that year.

The girls were starting to think about what university they would go to after leaving school. They were both Oxbridge standard, and I was excited to see how they would flourish at university, which made me realise that if I had one regret – if there was one thing I felt I had missed out on – it was that I hadn't been to university myself. To have those years finding out about yourself, to push yourself intellectually, was an opportunity not to be missed. As I talked to the girls about their options, I realised that I now had the opportunity finally to go to university myself. This was a really intriguing possibility, but what would I study and where would I go?

Should I completely retrain? Could I, for example, become a lawyer? I had enough experience of contract law by this stage. Was that something I could become really good at? Or would I like to do English or History? I started making lists of all the possibilities and then began to narrow the field. The first thing I realised was that I wasn't prepared to study for three or four years to get a qualification that I wouldn't use. That meant studying something to do with business, and the obvious option was to do an MBA. So, I asked myself, if I was to do an MBA where would I like to study? The top three places in the world to study for an MBA are INSEAD in France, the London Business School and Harvard. INSEAD pretty much eliminated itself as I had been told that unless you speak fluent French it's hard to get the most out of it. The London Business School is in Regent's Park, which is about five minutes from my house, so even though I was really impressed with the course and facilities there, it wouldn't have given me the opportunity to experience university life, as I'd still see all the same friends in the evening. So that left Harvard.

Everyone at YPO agreed that the business school at Harvard was probably the best place in the world to study, so I looked into the courses there. YPO held an 'in transition' forum for people who were considering their options, and someone else who had been through a similar transition advised me that the best course to do at Harvard was their Advanced Management Program. One in four of the CEOs of Fortune 500 companies are AMP graduates. 'The tutors are world class, the students are the best in their fields and you will learn more from that course in four months than you will in a year doing an MBA,' he said. It was the most prestigious business qualification in the world, and something about that appealed to my ego. I didn't have a qualification to my name; wouldn't it be something if the first certificate I got was from Harvard?

The admissions officer at Harvard told me I had another choice to make: did I want to do the course for entrepreneurs, or their course aimed at corporate executives and CEOs? The choice seemed pretty obvious, and everyone expected me to do the course for entrepreneurs, so naturally enough I opted for their corporate course! I felt I could learn more being around the kind of people who ran organisations like Intel or Pepsi Cola than I would studying with entrepreneurs with whom I was more likely to share characteristics. I thought I would learn about the skills needed for growing and building really big businesses. I had seen my own companies through the nought to £100 million stage: what was it like to take a company to the £1 billion level?

The entry requirements for the course were pretty stringent – you had to demonstrate a high level of success and recognition and to be able to pay their fees – and this meant I could be guaranteed that my fellow students would be a remarkable group of people. Without any previous qualifications, all I could offer them was the Entrepreneur of the Year award. I found everything about going away for four months to study unbelievably exciting. I was now proficient enough with a computer to know I could have video phone calls with Aisha and the girls every night, and I knew that Stephen, my butler, would make sure they were well looked after in my absence.

Chapter 27

Harvard (2003)

'I had never been a man with a plan. I had always taken life a week at a time and followed instincts rather than a roadmap.'

I GOT ON THE PLANE to Boston without any clear expectations about what I would learn or who I would meet. I was just really, really excited. I wasn't doing the course to get a job at the end of it; I just wanted to learn for the sake of learning and I found that quite thrilling. I had this image of Harvard students – clean-cut preppy types with satchels and floppy hair – and I was eager to experience a little of the freedom and optimism that I associated with being a student. When my plane landed and I told the taxi driver to take me to Harvard, I felt great.

Throughout the admissions process I had been told that the AMP was so intensive that I wouldn't have time for anything else. I didn't believe them. After all, I was the guy who could work eighteen hours a day and do the work of three people. Maybe most people couldn't do anything else, but I was sure I would have time to relax and enjoy the student lifestyle. My God was I wrong! They said it was an intensive course, but, three days in, I had to reassess my definition of intensive.

Not only did classes start at 8 a.m., and in some cases end at midnight, but you have to remember that not only had I never been to university, I hadn't even sat an O level. I hadn't written an essay since I was sixteen and that had probably only been 400 words long. The course assumed you had the ability to write 5000-word reports and analyses: Jemma and Hanah were more familiar with the concept of 'contrast and compare', and I found it tough. It didn't help that most of the other students had degrees, if not MBAs and Ph.D.s. Of the 110 people on the course, 109 had corporate careers and experience of writing reports and analyses for their boards. I had thrown myself in at the deep end, and it got even tougher when one our first assignments involved preparing a set of accounts. I had always had them prepared for me: I knew how to read a spreadsheet but not how to compile one!

I went to see the professor at the end of the class.

'Small problem: I've always employed people to compile these for me. Is there someone on campus I can pay to do this? Are there secretarial services here?'

He raised an eyebrow. 'No problem, James. We run courses here on spreadsheets. I think it's two hours a night. I'll book you in.'

By ten o'clock at night I was completely wiped out. I just couldn't concentrate with enough intensity after that, so I started getting up at 5.30 in the morning and doing two hours of study before I jumped in the shower. Besides, one of the reasons for doing this course was to get to know the other students: if I'd studied all evening I would have missed out.

We were all staying in halls of residence on campus. The AMP quarters are a cut above the average student accommodation, but it was still pretty basic: a small room with a single bed, a wardrobe, a desk and a shower cubicle. There were eight rooms to a floor and they had been designed so that you would spend as much time in the communal rooms as possible: talking about the course and learning from each other was all part of the Harvard plan. I quickly became great friends with the other seven people on my floor. Much like YPO, I found I had a lot in common with the other people who had enrolled there. Within a couple of days, they felt like my best friends in the world. We were all missing our families, all finding it hard, and we were spending every waking hour in each other's company: the conversation never stopped, no matter if we were playing squash at the weekends or sneaking into Boston for a night off.

Among the people on my floor was the CEO of BAe Systems in Australia, the president of one of Mexico's biggest food companies, one of the top people from the Bank of Tobago, and a woman who advised American corporations on their strategies for working in China. All wealthy, all extremely talented and, needless to say, all successful.

Every minute of the day was filled by the course leaders. When I turned my computer on in the morning I was presented with my daily planner: some days I was sent on an outward-bound course with people from other living groups, other times I had instructions to complete a case study with other people on the course I hadn't yet met. Our days were as well designed as our halls of residence, and by the end of the course I had met every one of the other students. Even our desks were allocated when we arrived in the classrooms to make sure we didn't always sit next to the same people.

One weekend a group of us went to Martha's Vineyard, another to New York City. Even though I was missing Aisha and the girls like crazy, I was having a blast. There was one guy – Dan, president of a cigar company – with whom I hit it off. We had the same sense of humour and we soon became the cheerleaders for trouble. We were like a pair of kids acting up in class and playing practical jokes.

When we were sent off to produce a report or a case study, it was absolutely fascinating to see how these hugely experienced and effective corporate operators tackled a problem. I'd say that 50 per cent of the time I looked at situations completely differently to them, approached the solutions in the opposite way and came to different conclusions. Perhaps the most illuminating example was a module we did on decision-making. They all – every single one of them – looked to get consensus from their colleagues before implementing a decision: as the boss of my own company I had simply implemented whatever I thought was best for the business. I listened to my advisers, of course, but ultimately I hadn't felt it mattered if everyone disagreed with my course of action.

I learned so much in those sixteen weeks. The course was planned for people with an understanding of business, so when we looked at the economy of China, for example, our case study posed the question: if China was a company how would you assess its balance sheet? As someone who had had his head stuck so far inside his own businesses for so long, having my perspective yanked towards global markets was a real eye-opener.

I had got used to dealing with pretty big numbers by this stage in my life. But instead of dealing in hundreds of thousands and the odd million, suddenly I was dealing with billions and trillions, and by the end of the course I had an understanding of just what those figures mean in real terms. Just as belonging to YPO and the NSPCC board had introduced me to able and brilliant operators, hanging out with the other students gave me insights into how big companies behaved and how different their challenges were to something the size of Alexander Mann. I was learning what makes a company great, how tiny clauses in deals have huge pay-offs – like Intel's insistence that any computer manufacturer who used their chips had to include their name in the advertising of their products. I found out how you lead a really big company (it comes down to having a clear vision and being able to communicate it to people who execute it) and I was learning how to assess investment opportunities in a global context: things like what political and tax arrangements make for a good operational environment. Unlike the other students, I wasn't applying what I was learning to my own organisation: I was free to pick and choose modules that interested me rather than those relevant to my career, because – frankly – right then I didn't have a career.

I've since recommended the course to several other people who have sold the business they had founded. When you go through a period of transition, one of the hardest things is to get your old life out of your system. It's a bit like coming out of a long-term relationship: it's easy to dwell on what might have been and extremely hard to move on. Doing something so intense, so engrossing and intellectually fulfilling allowed me to put Alexander Mann behind me. It's too easy in that situation to keep going back and see how the team were getting on, but Harvard got me squarely looking forward and not back. It moved me on and, emotionally, that was invaluable. I still didn't know what I would do at the end of the course, but I sensed I was ready for anything.

I came to a couple of conclusions about business that shaped what I thought I might do in the future. I realised that to build bigger businesses takes time. I was impatient and not interested in spending three or four or five years working on something I couldn't be sure would succeed. I wasn't the kind of person who stuck his toe in the water; I just dived in and saw how I got on. I also realised I wasn't interested in starting from scratch all over again: been there, done that.

I was also aware that big corporations find it hard to make good long-term decisions. They have to make quarterly reports to their shareholders and some are guilty of making decisions that benefit their shareholders and not their customers. I felt that limited what could be achieved: oddly, the stock market impedes the growth it demands that companies produce.

I had never been a man with a plan. I had always taken life a week at a time and followed instincts rather than a roadmap. If there's one single thing Harvard did for me, it helped me to start to think long-term. I still didn't have a plan, but I was now able to make decisions for the short term and anticipate the long-term impact of those decisions at the same time.

I wasn't quite sure what this would mean for me, only that these were conclusions that would inform whatever I did next.

Chapter 28

Back to School

(2003–present)

'Imagine if kids were taught to read and write; imagine what that would do for them, for their futures. Now imagine that they were also taught English.'

N OT LONG AFTER I'd left Alexander Mann I had dinner with a very old friend who had just returned from Lahore. As he told me about the place, I realised I hadn't been there since 1971 on that family holiday. It was the city where I was born yet I knew nothing about it.

'Tell me what it's like,' I said.

'The food is amazing,' he said. 'It's a lush, green city with beautiful buildings. The weather is fabulous.' By the end of the meal I had decided I was going to go there, and as it was my gap year and I had no commitments I was going to get on a plane that weekend.

'Hi, Mum, I'm going to Lahore on Saturday. Do we know anyone there that I should meet up with?'

'Are you serious? You've never been interested before.'

'I'm really serious. I want to see where you and Dad – where I – come from.'

'Well, you've got lots of family there. Would you like to me to give you some numbers?'

By this time I was very used to travelling for business. I'd had offices in Australia, Singapore, South America, all over, so taking a long-haul flight by myself was not an unusual experience. I was very relaxed about the trip and when I got off the plane and checked into a hotel I had a completely open mind about what I would do next.

I decided to call the first name my mum had given me, and that presented me with a problem: was I James or Nazim? I'd been James for more than twenty-five years and it wasn't just my name, it was my identity, but in Pakistan I felt a bit uncomfortable using it.

'Hi, this is Nazim, my mum is your father's sister and I'm in Lahore and I would really like to meet up.'

'Where are you staying?'

'The Pearl Continental.'

'I'll be there in twenty minutes.'

My cousin Muneer walked into the lobby of the hotel and started asking around for Nazim Khan. It took me a while to realise that he meant me! So one of the first things I had to tell him was that I had changed my name. Muneer was a really friendly guy and we talked about our parents and our families, and midway through the conversation he called a bellboy over.

'Could you please check Mr Caan out?'

'What are you doing?'

'You're in my city, so that means you're my guest. You've been in England for so long you've lost your manners. When you come to somebody else's city, you don't stay in hotels. It's quite insulting.'

'Then let me insult you. It's wrong; you've only just met me. Thank you, but I'll stay here.'

He turned to the bellboy. 'Go and get his bags.'

I went to check out, but was told there was nothing to pay: the gentleman I was with had settled my bill.

'But it's my responsibility.' It wasn't much, just an early check-out fee, but it was the principle. 'Please don't embarrass me,' I said to my cousin.

'Just come with me.'

It was the daytime, so he took me to his office. It was obvious that he was very successful. He owned a factory that manufactured jeans for clients like Levi Strauss and Calvin Klein, and on top of the factory was an amazing penthouse with a pool and a snooker table: it was beautiful, but it was empty.

'Who lives here?'

'It's for clients. We get these high-powered Americans and the local hotels aren't good enough. You can stay here if you like, or you can stay with my family.'

I couldn't believe how well we were getting on, and after a couple of hours of chatting he took me on a tour of Lahore. He knew so much of the family history and he showed me where I was born, where my father used to hang out, where my grandparents had met, and as we drove around I had the strangest sensation. For someone who had travelled a lot, I was used to just passing through, but I was really starting to feel something; I was developing a real connection to the city he was showing me.

Lahore is probably the nicest city in Pakistan. It's very beautiful, with wonderful old colonial buildings and a real sense of identity. Karachi, the biggest city in the country, is full of families who arrived after Partition, which means it lacks a bit of character; Islamabad, the capital, is like Dubai or a Midwest town in America with gleaming skyscrapers, but it has no soul; Lahore was different, and I was completely charmed by it. All my life I had never really felt anything for my Pakistani heritage, but now that I was in the city of my birth something was resonating inside. The comparison I make – it might sound a little crass, so you'll have to forgive me – is like finding out you are adopted at the age of forty-two and meeting your birth family. I had this powerful connection with Lahore that I had never experienced before. I felt at home in my birth city.

When I tell people in Britain that I spend time in Pakistan, they often ask me if it's safe. The perception is of a war zone filled with militias and fundamentalists. So I tell them their attitude is a bit like an Italian tourist arriving in the Yorkshire Dales at the height of the IRA's campaign and wondering where the bombs were. In Britain, we only hear about Pakistan when there's trouble, but it's a huge country with a population three times the size of the UK, and most people live simple and peaceful lives. Lahore felt like a particularly gentle place, and the more I saw of it the more I liked it.

The next day I met more family members, and I was having such a good time that a three-day trip stretched to eight days. A lot of the conversations I had with relations were about my dad, and I couldn't help but think what an amazing trip it would have been to have done together. I realised how much I missed him, and some of the strong connection I felt with Lahore was tied up with my feelings for him.

On one trip we ventured outside the city and within half an hour we were driving through very rural areas with just the odd farmhouse and a few people in the fields. It looked so . . . well . . . primitive. I talked to my cousin about how things worked in Pakistan. *Who's in charge, how do the politics work, what are the real problems?* Like I always do, I was just asking questions. His feeling was that the country's biggest problem was education. The conflict with India over Kashmir meant a high proportion of the GDP went on defence: the budget for education in a country of 160 million was less than the budget for running the parliament. That meant that kids in state schools were regularly in classes of forty or fifty, often with no books, and sometimes not even desks.

'I'll give you an example of the problem,' Muneer said. 'We need to employ a new security guard at the factory, but we need someone who can read and write. They need to be able to sign for deliveries and make sure visitors are given security badges and the internal post gets delivered. Being a security guard is more of a job than it used to be, but anyone who can read or write can earn good money in the civil service. I cannot find anyone who is willing to do the job.'

I thought about my father and wondered again how he had managed to do what he had done without being able to read and write. Times had changed: being illiterate now meant a life of working for a pittance in the fields. I thought about the Indian economy and how India is on track to becoming a global power. The difference between India and Pakistan was education. Pakistan has one of the worst illiteracy rates in the world. If Pakistan couldn't produce people capable of doing work in the modern economy, then progress was just a dream. I felt I wanted to give something to the country that had given me my start in life, and I wondered what would happen to the village we were in if it had a school. Imagine if kids were taught to read and write; imagine what that would do for them, for their futures. Now imagine that they were also taught English. It would completely transform their prospects. Now consider what would happen if you taught girls, too, because the fact is that girls are often kept at home. A decent education could change the outlook for a girl in Pakistan. But it wasn't just the kids whose lives would be changed: imagine there was a facility in the village with computers and playgrounds and resources. Imagine the children going home and using their maths lessons to help their parents balance the household budgets instead of borrowing from loan sharks. I wouldn't just be educating the kids; the whole village would be changed. I was completely enthused by the idea, and later that night I talked to my cousin about it.

'I think I'm going to open a school.'

'Pardon?'

'I think I'm going to open a school.'

He looked at me as if I was mad.

'Where?'

'In Pakistan.'

He was still looking at me as if I was mad.

'How about that village you took me to? What prospects do kids in that village have? Why don't I open a school there?'

'James, you're crazy. You've been in the country five minutes. Enjoy your holiday, come back with your wife and kids, but stop talking like that. You've got no idea what's involved.'

'I'm serious. I want to build something here. Imagine what a school in a village like that would mean to the people who live there. I want to do it for my father, so that kids always grow up being able to read and write.'

He was still giving me that look.

'Could you lend me your driver tomorrow and I'll go back and see what's what?'

Finally he accepted that I was serious. 'You don't need the driver. I'll take you.'

We went back the following day and discussed between us what was needed, how much land would be required, and whether I would need permission to build or a licence to run a school. While I thought it all sounded doable, Muneer was still sceptical.

'And who will you hire, James? Are you going to come over every month? Building a school is the easy bit. Forget it.'

But I couldn't. The thought of naming a school after my father, of being able to pay for the education of hundreds of children as a direct consequence of the choices he made, was too powerful a feeling to set aside. I was excited about it, but I was also really scared: it wasn't just going to be for a term – this would be a lifetime commitment.

I went back to London and couldn't get the idea out of my head. I talked the idea over with Aisha and used my free time really to work out what I would need. After a couple of weeks, I had thought about the kind of school I wanted to build and had mapped out the logistics in my head. I called up my cousin and told him I was coming back.

'Am I staying with you or at the Pearl Continental?'

'You are absolutely staying with us.'

This time Muneer met me at the airport and did a double take because I had arrived in a suit: I was there for business and had left my casual clothes at home. Actually, that's not quite true: I wasn't there for business, I was on a mission.

I got the names of the best lawyer, accountant and architect and told them I wanted to hire them for two weeks solid. 'I want you to be with me every day I'm here and we're going to look at sites together, because if I have to have a meeting with one of you one day, and another of you the next day, it will take too long.'

We went together to look at sites, and at each one the architect would take me through the construction options, the lawyer would anticipate any legal implications and the accountant would talk me through the impact these decisions would have on cost. It worked brilliantly, and two weeks later I had bought the land, talked through my vision for the school with the architect, decided how many children it would be possible to teach, instructed builders and drafted a management agreement with an organisation called the Citizens Foundation to run the school when it opened.

As a well-connected local businessman my cousin was great at suggesting people to work with, and when I got a quote for a piece of work he was able to tell me if it was a reasonable price or not.

Before I left I asked the architect to take me to an electronics shop and I bought him a digital camera.

'Every Friday at midday I want to open my e-mail and see the latest pictures of how you're progressing, and when you reach the milestones agreed in the project plan I'll release the next sum of cash.'

After that, I went out to Lahore, often with Aisha, about every six weeks to monitor progress. We enjoyed being there so much that we decided to buy a house: after all, once the school was built we would be regular visitors and we weren't comfortable imposing ourselves on relations that frequently.

It was incredible the number of things we didn't anticipate. It's just not as simple as building a school and then having the children turn up. The first problem we realised was that there weren't enough children in the village to fill the school. We were building a facility for 400 pupils, so we were going to have to invite children from the surrounding villages to enrol, and that meant purchasing minibuses, which also meant hiring drivers.

Then I realised I'd screwed up by building the school so far from the city. Stupidly, it never dawned on me that I would have trouble finding teachers, but in a small village there was no one who spoke English – most of the lessons were going to be in English, as being bilingual would transform the children's prospects – or who had any teaching experience.

So now I had to buy another minibus to bring in teachers from Lahore, and with the additional traffic it also meant I had to build a road from the village to the school that wouldn't wash away in the monsoon! The costs kept piling up: books, computers, catering equipment for the kitchen, uniforms. The troubles, pitfalls and delays are too numerous to go into, but suffice it to say that opening the school was a huge challenge, and the first day of term at the Abdul Rashid Khan Campus was one of the proudest moments of my life.

Going there today is an amazing feeling. Every time I see my dad's name above the gate a tear comes to my eye. All the teachers know me and they always get the children to say 'Good morning, Mr James,' when I visit. The last time I was there, the kids recited

'Baa, Baa, Black Sheep', and I couldn't help but wonder what speaking English would do for them, and for the country. If you can speak English, you can get double the salary and you can build a future. I love that nursery rhyme now.

I took my mother to see the school a couple of months after it opened, and when she saw my dad's name, she burst into tears. 'Imagine if he was here, if he could see this!' It was a wonderful moment. There's something so powerful about watching children learn, especially in an environment like that, and knowing that because of you they're getting a life they otherwise might never have had.

I've now been into several state-run schools in Pakistan, so I know how much better the facilities are at my school, and so do the people who live nearby, which means there are always kids outside hoping to be let in one day. Our only entry criterion is that you must not be able to afford education anywhere else, and that means we teach the very poorest kids. When I was there recently, I was in the playground messing around with the kids and I noticed one boy wasn't wearing shoes. He was quite young so I picked him up and I asked where his shoes were.

'It's not my turn today,' he said.

'What do you mean?'

His brother also attended the school and they took it in turns to wear the one pair of shoes that the family could afford.

'Where do you live?'

It was a village forty-five minutes away that the minibuses didn't go to. He was walking for forty-five minutes with no shoes. Sometimes it gets so hot in Lahore that you can burn the soles of your feet. My heart sank because it wasn't just him: the teacher told me lots of the kids had no shoes.

My first instinct was to say, 'Let's buy him some shoes.' I could have included shoes in the uniform I paid for but that meant an extra 400 pairs of shoes, and, as kids grow out of shoes really quickly, so that would mean 400 pairs of shoes perhaps three times a year. For ever. Whenever I thought I could make a simple gesture, it would end up being expensive and complicated and I realised I had to draw a line somewhere. For instance, I might decide that all the kids should get milk every day, but that would be 400 pints of milk, every day of the school year, for ever. There were issues with refrigeration I'd have to think about. What I hope is that within a decade or so the education the kids are getting will mean they will earn at a level that allows them to contribute to their household budgets, and that should mean kids won't be walking to school in bare feet for ever.

Of all the things we failed to anticipate, the biggest oversight has to be what would happen to the kids when they reached the age of eleven. The school is for primary-school-age kids, but, on a recent trip I took with Aisha and the girls, Jemma pointed out that there isn't a secondary school in the area. Without one, the kids would drop out of the system, become dependent on their families again and perhaps forget the skills that would one day land them a good job. I realised we'd only done half the job and that the only answer was to build a secondary school. Construction starts in 2008.

I am incredibly proud of my daughters. They have grown up to be intelligent, thoughtful and beautiful women with terrific futures ahead of them when they finish university. The thing I am most proud of is their dedication to the school: they feel the same responsibility as I do. To make sure the school gets the support it needs, we have agreed that Hanah will be responsible for visiting, maintaining and supporting the primary school, Jemma will be the custodian of the senior school, and I have pledged to fund the university career of any child who reaches the academic levels necessary for higher education.

It is a substantial financial commitment, and it is a commitment for life. I have set up the James Caan Foundation to secure the financing for the school, and all the money I make from TV work, from this book, from my public speaking goes to the Foundation. When I die, money from a trust will continue to fund the school.

My aim is to be responsible 1000 children's education at any one time, and being able to do this helps me make sense of my life. It is also a huge source of joy for me because some days my life is so stressful – I run the business, do the media work, the charity work – and that stress level is maintained from 6 a.m. to 11 p.m., seven days a week. There are days when I can have three conference calls in the car on the way to work, and if there's a spare fifteen minutes in my diary my PA fills them with three people I need to call. My phone rings off the hook: every minute is accounted for. It's exhausting and there are times when it's easy to wonder if it's worth it. When I feel like that, all I have to do is think of the school, of my father's school, and I know that it is.

Chapter 29

Getting to Know Pakistan (2003–present)

'The greatest force for change in Pakistan is commerce.'

AT ONE POINT WHILE we were building the school I was really tearing my hair out trying to find teachers and get the necessary responses from the education authorities: what I needed, I decided, was some advice from someone who already had experience of opening a school in Pakistan. I asked around and I was put in touch with a woman called Seema Aziz, Pakistan's highest-profile female entrepreneur. She runs the country's biggest fashion company, Sarena Industries, and does a lot of philanthropic work in education.

'Hi, I was wondering if you could spare a couple of minutes to give me some advice about a school I'm opening,' I said over the phone.

'Where are you?'

'In Lahore.'

'I'm chock-a-block; how are you fixed for next week?'

'Actually, I'm returning to the UK tomorrow morning.'

'OK, get your driver to bring you here straight away. I can see you before my next meeting.'

Seema was very impressive: I'd guess she had a law degree from Cambridge or Oxford, and it was easy to see why she had been so successful. She told me the story of how she had got involved with education. The village where one of her factories was situated had flooded, and several of the buildings were washed away. When she visited a couple of weeks after the flood she saw all these children running around and realised that if a school wasn't built quickly they would never get an education, and ultimately that would reduce the capabilities of her workforce in the years to come. She knew the government would take years, if not decades, to get round to rebuilding the school so she decided to build one herself. The school originally catered for 1000 children, but now has an intake of 3000. It put what I was trying to do into perspective.

After a couple of years, someone from a neighbouring village had asked if she could build them a school, too, and within a few years she had built several more. The results in her schools were so good that she was then asked to take over the running of state schools; by the time I met her, she was responsible for the management of 180 schools via a charity she had set up called CARE. I knew I had come to the right person for help.

'Would you like to see one of the schools with me? I'm going out on a visit tomorrow.'

'I'd love to, but my flight's tomorrow.' Then I thought again. 'Screw it; I'd love to see your school. I'll cancel my flight.'

'You know what? I'll clear my day, too, and I'll take you to several schools.'

I liked Seema a lot. We had very similar outlooks and I felt I could learn a lot from her. In the morning she drove me round to several of her schools, and there were two things that really surprised me. Firstly, I was absolutely staggered that she knew the name of every teacher we met. She employs 1500 teachers directly and another 1500 for the government, and she genuinely knew the name of each of them. No wonder they worked so well when they were appreciated by a boss like that. The second thing that struck me was that she took a call from a headmistress saying that a couple of computers had stopped working and could she replace them. How could she run the country's biggest fashion house – which had to be an eighteen-hour-a-day job – and manage 180 schools *and* deal with day-to-day problems like broken computers? To my surprise, she didn't refer the headmistress to an IT department somewhere; she simply called up her head office and asked someone to put two computers in a rickshaw and take it to the school. I was very impressed. It reminded me of a lunch I had had in London with the head of one of Pakistan's biggest telecoms companies: a customer had phoned up and complained about his broadband connection. I was learning that in Pakistan it is customary to go straight to the top with any problem. In the UK, the chairman of a company is protected by layers of receptionists, PAs and lieutenants, but in Pakistan the chairman is completely accessible.

Seema showed me a mixture of her schools: some she had started from scratch, some she had taken over five years before-hand, and some she had just taken responsibility for. The difference between them was striking, and from then on, whenever I went back to Lahore to check on the progress of my school, I would call up Seema and she would take me to see another of her schools. As I got to know her, I started to tell her the problems I was experiencing with my school and she would discuss hers. Whatever difficulty I had, she always knew the right person to call to sort it out. I also discovered that running a school and running a business aren't that different. When I have a problem at the school, I find it helps to ask what I would do if it were a business.

Seema asked if I would manage one of the state-sector schools on behalf of CARE, and now, as well as my own school, I also fund a much larger state school, paying for everything from teachers' salaries to uniforms to PE equipment. I also now work with EduTrust in the UK funding schools in some of the most depressed boroughs in the country.

Following on from my work with CARE, I was asked to help Pakistan's Human Development Organization, which takes a different approach to education. It sends teachers or craftsmen into villages to teach skills that can secure people a job, and it's effective because it doesn't wait for schools to be built: classes are offered in people's homes or even simply under a tree. To thank me for the support I'd given the HDO, I received an invitation from President Musharraf to attend a state banquet at the President's official residence.

I had been visiting Pakistan for less than a year by this point and wasn't that well known there, so to receive an invitation from the President was both a surprise and a real ego boost. I bought a traditional outfit to wear – a sherwani with a long black coat and white trousers – and took my cousin Muneer with me to Islamabad where the President's palace is.

The dinner took place in October 2003, and there was something quite strange about entering such an opulent building in what is still, in many ways, a Third World country. It's a modern building with beautiful grounds and magnificent views from every window – it's absolutely stunning – and walking into it is a moment I will never forget.

'I've been here all my life, and I've never had an invite here. You've been here five minutes and look where we are!' my cousin teased.

The dinner was a chance to meet the kind of people you just don't normally get to meet. I was introduced to the Prime Minister, heads of government departments and very senior officials. I found myself talking to a minister from the education ministry and took the opportunity to ask him how his department was going to spend the £100 million in aid the US government had just donated to Pakistan's education system.

'One of the problems we have in Pakistan', he told me, 'is that girls are not encouraged to go to school, so we are going to use the money to persuade more girls to attend.'

I thought that was fantastic. 'How are you going to do that?'

'We are going to give each girl 200 rupees for each term she attends.'

While there was no doubt that this would encourage girls to enrol, it seemed to me to be little more than bribery. What would happen, I asked, when they turn up and find out there are only six desks for a class of 100 pupils and only enough teachers for a few lessons a day? They will get bored and they won't bother going back.

'If we talk in three years' time,' I said to him, 'what will you have to show for the £100 million? Will you have trained any teachers? Will you have bought any desks?'

A few days later, I was staying with a friend in Karachi who had heard similar stories many times before.

'Don't you realise what he's doing?' he said.

I had to say that I didn't.

'He's a minister, right? So that means he's elected. And that means he needs votes. And you can be pretty sure that he's just bought his next term in office. All those families who get money just for sending their daughters to school occasionally aren't going to vote for anyone else.'

I realised I still had so much to learn about Pakistan, and in the years since I have been back on average every six weeks. It is a country with which, despite its problems, I have fallen in love, and, coincidentally, so has my brother Adam. He met and married a girl from Lahore a few years ago, and in the first year of their marriage they visited Lahore so often that Adam really got to know the place. He realised they could have a fantastic quality of life if they settled there, so they bought a house and started a business which is doing extremely well.

Having my brother in Lahore has helped me develop a really good social network out there. That old saying, 'It's not *what* you know that counts, it's *who* you know,' must have been coined about Pakistan. The social network I have established there means I am never more than a phone call away from the person I need to sort something out or make something happen.

In recent years I have started commercial investments in Pakistan, as I believe supporting the economy is better for the country than simply handing out money through charitable initiatives. It's an extension of the work of the HDO, and it means I am in regular contact with the minister for human development. On one trip, I had a really productive meeting with him in Islamabad, and he called me up the following day.

'It was good to talk yesterday, James. Listen, we're having a dinner party at the house tomorrow and I'd like you to come.'

'Thank you for the invitation, but I'm actually visiting friends in Karachi now.'

'I really think you should come.'

There was something about the way he said this that made me think I had better get back on a plane and fly to Islamabad. When I reached his house the next evening, I couldn't help noticing the number of security guards present. In Pakistan, which has been run by the military for almost a decade, seeing men on the street with guns isn't that uncommon, but there seemed to be more guns than usual. It's impossible not to have a flash of fear when you see that many armed men. Still, I reasoned, it wasn't that surprising given it was a minister's house.

There were about twenty people there when I arrived, and I was introduced to one dignitary after another. I had been there about twenty minutes when I turned round and saw the President walk in! Wow! I had never been in such impressive company. Imagine being at a private house party and having the head of state walk in.

President Musharraf wasn't in uniform, which was how I was used to seeing him, and he was surprisingly informal and offered me a cigar. While we were chatting, the Prime Minister walked in.

I couldn't believe it! On one side of me was the President, on the other the Prime Minister. No wonder there were so many security guards! I knew many of the faces from news reports on TV: it seemed half the Cabinet was in the room.

I found talking to Musharraf fascinating. I used the opportunity to ask him why education was in such a mess and why the country has such a bad reputation overseas, and I was surprised to hear how modern, how Western, I suppose, his outlook is.

'James,' he began in impeccable English, 'it's very easy being an armchair critic, but sometimes, unless you're in a position to understand the implications of making the kind of decisions you're talking about, don't judge. Things that appear really simple to an outsider are more complicated than you realise. Let me give you an example: when I came to power, one of the first things I realised is that in a lot of modern economies women contribute more to the national wealth than men. Also, they have had to be resourceful to break through barriers, so I thought an obvious thing to do would be to get more women in parliament. So I introduced legislation that guaranteed 100 female MPs, which, you can imagine, in a country where most women stay at home is a very big statement.'

I agreed.

'It didn't go down particularly well,' he continued, 'but as far as I was concerned we should have more balance. We attracted 100 very professional, well-educated, smart women, and they've had an incredible impact on the country. Within a year of them coming into power, they lobbied the government to change an Islamic law that states if a woman is raped, in order to mount a prosecution she needs to produce three witnesses. You're probably thinking what I'm thinking, that this means women can never bring a prosecution and so rape goes unpunished.

'You would think implementing this new law would be easy, wouldn't you? Who wouldn't support such a simple change that could make such an enormous difference? Guess what, James. It took me six years to pass the legislation. Six years.'

'Why did it take so long?'

'How much time do you spend in Pakistan, James?'

'I visit every six weeks or so.'

'And when you come, look at the people you mix with. If you are doing business here, you are meeting the educated classes, the people with money.'

By and large, this was true.

'You are only seeing 0.1 per cent of the country. The other 99.9 per cent are poor and live in villages. There are fifty million people in Pakistan without electricity. That is the real Pakistan, where people live traditionally with Islam as the only law that counts. If it says in the book that a woman must produce three witnesses, then how can it be right to introduce a law that says she does not need to? People believe what they have been told since birth, not what an official in the capital tells them to believe. So you think it's simple to make changes, in a country this big, with this much poverty? You have no idea how hard it is. Getting the middle classes and the media to support you is easy; getting the country to is another matter.

'In Pakistan a tiny proportion of the population has the loudest voice and their needs are easily catered for. The majority of Pakistanis still live in villages where the entire population is largely employed by one landowner. Those landowners have no interest in educating their employees, because then they'll leave for better-paid jobs and the land will no longer be as profitable. And, of course, because these landowners are the employers, they have power and influence over the entire village, which means local legislators will never take decisions that affect the landowners detrimentally, and so the status quo never changes.

'So when you ask me why things are not changing in Pakistan, I cannot give you a quick answer,' he said.

It is because of the insights he gave me that I have realised the greatest force for change in Pakistan is commerce. Not only does the government have these immense internal problems to overcome, but it is also dealing with the aftermath of 9/11 and the insurgencies that has created. I have realised that economics and entrepreneurs can be a real force for change in Pakistan, and that is where I have concentrated my efforts in the past few years.

I have had similar conversations with Shaukat Aziz, who was the Prime Minister of Pakistan before he stood down ahead of the elections in 2008. He was in London during those elections and I bumped into him at a function. It became clear that even though he was no longer Prime Minister he was still being ushered from one official function to another. He looked like he could use a break, so I called the Pakistani embassy and asked if they would give me his number.

Quite properly, they said they couldn't do that but they could get a message to him.

'Well, would you please tell him that James Caan would like to buy him lunch?'

To my amazement I got a call back from his office saying that he was free the next Tuesday.

So I took him to lunch and we caught up on some of the projects we had both been working on. Obviously the elections were a major topic of conversation. Since the assassination of Benazir Bhutto, who I had also met through friends when she had lived in London, many predicted that the elections would result in civil war.

'What are you doing on the night of the elections?' I asked.

'Actually, I don't think there's anything in the diary that night.'

'Then why don't you come to our house for dinner?'

He accepted, and I also invited ten or so friends who have connections with Pakistan. We had a terrific evening with the TV on in the background as the results started coming through. I couldn't quite believe that the former Prime Minister of the country I had been born in was in my house in London! It was a bit surreal.

I feel incredibly privileged to have had such access to so many influential people in Pakistan, and through events like the Asian Jewel Awards – which presented me with the Entrepreneur of the Year award in 2003 – I also now have a profile among the British Asian community at home. I find it interesting that my Asian heritage is more important to me as an adult than it ever was as a kid.

Chapter 30

Private Equity
(2003–2004)

'I had found the thrill I had been looking for in planes and helicopters and fast cars in an idea for a business.'

I MAGINE YOU WON the lottery. Say you won £10 million. What would you do with the money? Most people would probably buy themselves a nice house with half of it. Then they might buy a holiday home somewhere hot for half a million. Then another million or so gets spent on toys – a couple of nice cars and maybe the trip of a lifetime – before putting the balance into investments that should fund a decent lifestyle for the rest of their lives. After that, what do you need? What can you possibly spend money on that would change anything? Now let's say you won £20 million – doesn't that just mean a nicer or a bigger house and a few more toys and slightly flashier holidays? Sure, the extra £10 million is nice, but it doesn't *change* anything. In the scheme of things, once you get beyond £10 million, the impact of increased wealth diminishes.

Now imagine that you didn't win that money. Imagine that you earned it. I promise you, you're going to be a lot less frivolous with it now. When you know what it's like not to have it, and when you know what it takes to create wealth, the idea that you would fritter it away on depreciating assets or a party lifestyle is pretty ludicrous. The people who spend money recklessly tend to be those who come into it overnight, either via the lottery or an inheritance. When you've earned it, trust me, you want to be sensible with it.

I was starting to find that it was actually quite difficult to spend money. Not only was there nothing I could buy that would make any real difference to my life – if I had moved from St John's Wood to Chelsea, it wouldn't have made my family any happier – but there's often not a clear-cut way to spend a lot of money. Let's take the example of property. Let's say you have £50 million in the bank and you decide you'll buy a selection of central London buildings as an investment. Do you buy them with cash? If you do that, you'll have a huge income from letting them on which you'll pay 40 per cent tax. Is that the best return? So maybe you should buy them with mortgages so that the profit, and therefore the tax, is reduced. And if you are borrowing, who do you borrow from? At what rate? On what terms? Are you better off paying arrangement fees and fixing the rate for a long time? What if your tenants default on the rent? Should it be in your name? Your kids' names? Or held in a trust?

Whatever I thought I would do with the money – whether it was buying a company or giving it away – there were so many options that the natural response was paralysis: it's easier just to leave the money in the bank. But when you're an entrepreneur, leaving money in the bank is frustrating. You want to make it work, you want to seize opportunities: putting your money in the bank is both boring and unnatural. Sure, it's nice to have money put away, but it doesn't *change* anything unless it's doing something. With the basics of my life covered and confident that I had enough money to live on if I never worked again, what became interesting to me was the concept of change. What could I do with my money that would change my life?

When I returned from Harvard, I started looking around at ways I could invest the money I had from the sale of Alexander Mann. At the time I thought I might actually get a job, perhaps as the CEO of a major charity working for a symbolic salary rather than something I could live off, so making sure my cash provided me with an income was important.

Having been hamstrung by the sheer number of possibilities, I made the decision that I would get someone else to invest it for me. At the time, private equity firms were producing the best returns, so I set up meetings with several of London's private equity operators to see what they could do for me. My only experience of private equity had been dealing with Advent when they'd bought into Alexander Mann: I knew how it worked from the target business's point of view, so I was interested to know how they viewed deals from the other side of the fence.

Private equity firms make their money by buying into companies and recommending operational changes that boost profits. They are a lot like venture capital firms except that they invest development capital rather than start-up capital. By investing in existing companies they reduce some of the risks that are inherent in investing in start-ups, but whereas venture capital firms typically invest from £250k to £1 million, private equity deals usually start at the £1 million mark and can involve hundreds of millions of pounds (like the takeover of EMI that created such a fuss in the music industry in 2007, or the billion-pound-plus deal for Sainsbury's). When the figures of the company they're turning around have increased sufficiently, they generally sell up and take their profits.

The money they invest in the first place comes from a mix of institutions and 'high net worth individuals', of which I was one. Typically they charge a management fee of 2 or 3 per cent to cover their overheads – so if they had a fund of £200 million and charged 2 per cent, they'd have an income of £4 million a year – and then take 20 per cent of any gains. So if they buy a company at £100 million, make changes and sell it three years later for £200 million, they'd take 20 per cent of that £100 million gain, i.e. £20 million. That's an awful lot of money, but I had learned that if people weren't motivated with a stake in the profits, they were less likely to produce spectacular returns so I was willing to accept their terms.

I did what I always did: I sat down with one private equity company after another and asked them a bunch of questions. Why should I invest with you? How do you assess opportunities? How do your investments work? Why are you better? How long until I get a return? What's your fee? How do you negotiate the purchase price? Who does that in your organisation? Can I meet him?

Over the course of a month I probably sat through twenty PowerPoint presentations of graphs heading for the sky and was given the CVs of people with backgrounds in banking, investment, accountancy, law and management consulting. One day, I was sitting in a plush office in Mayfair listening to a really good presentation from a great firm and starting to think that I had found the team to trust with my money.

'So, tell me a bit about your backgrounds,' I asked.

One had been at Goldman Sachs, another at Warburgs, another came from the City law firm Clifford Chance, and the accountant came from PricewaterhouseCoopers. This was a very high-calibre team, but there was one component missing: I realised that none of them had ever run a business. It was at that point that a light bulb went on in my head: *Why don't I just do it myself?* Who would I trust more to turn a business around and make it profitable: a bunch of Oxbridge graduates with no operational experience of managing a business, or little old me? It was my eureka moment.

I left their office thinking that maybe I should set up my own private equity firm. I had to do something with my time, and the more I thought about it, the more I thought it was a very good idea. For starters, I wouldn't need to raise the money from investors; I would just use my own cash, which would mean I could make quick decisions and seize opportunities that other firms couldn't. Sure, I didn't have the necessary legal and banking experience, but I certainly knew how to hire the best people with those skills. In fact, I had met many of the best people in the past couple of months, and I started seriously to think about which of those professionals I wanted to employ.

I was so excited about the idea – which is the way you ought to feel when you think you might be about to start a new business – that I had to talk to someone about it. I approached a number of the top accountancy and legal firms in an attempt to understand the structures and legalities of setting up my own fund. While I was sitting with one of the best accountants in the field I told him to come up with all the reasons why I shouldn't do it.

'It's pretty complicated, James. To set up a fund, you've got be regulated. There's a specific legal framework you have to adhere to.'

'That all sounds perfectly understandable, but you could do that for me, couldn't you?'

'It'll cost you.'

'How much? Ballpark. Just give me an idea.'

'At a guess, anywhere between £100k and £500k.'

'OK, now why else wouldn't I do it?'

'Well, most people don't do it because you have to wait for a return. The typical time horizon on a private equity investment is between three and seven years, which means you've got to be able to live on something in the meantime.'

'Not a problem for me. What else should I know?'

'You'll have a lot of costs besides your living expenses. You'll have rent, salaries, and the kind of people you'll need to employ won't come cheap.'

'OK. What else?'

What I was doing with these questions was performing a risk assessment: I didn't need to be convinced of the potential upside; I needed to understand what would happen if I failed. I wanted to know why I would fail and how I would fail: if I knew what the issues and concerns were I could assess the risk. It seemed to me that the biggest risk was the costs I would have until I could sell on my first investment. I did some quick maths: I added up the cost of hiring my team – a lawyer, an accountant, a banker, a secretary, etc. – and the cost of renting an office. I reckoned it would cost me £800k a year, but I also reckoned that with my operational experience I could get a return in three years. So my total exposure would be £2.4 million before I'd find out if I had a talent for private equity. The key questions were these: did I believe in myself enough to invest that £2.4 million to find out? And did I think I could make more than £2.4 million from investments in that time frame? When I realised that I thought I probably could, I became incredibly excited. Not only had I been able to put a figure on the risk, but I had started to map out my next business.

It took me a couple of weeks to realise what was happening: I had stopped faffing about. I was getting up earlier, I had a focus, I wasn't playing. Aisha and the girls were relieved, too: *Finally, he's found himself something to do!* Over the course of those couple of months I stopped being a semi-retired millionaire and embarked on a second career. As I thought about what I could achieve, about the changes setting up my own fund would create, it was a bit like standing in a Savile Row tailors and trying on a suit. Private equity *fitted* me, I felt good when I imagined myself starting a new venture in a new industry, and I started to feel confident about what could be achieved. I had found the thrill, the buzz, I had been looking for in planes and helicopters and fast cars in an idea for a business. I was on an adrenalin high and I had a real sense that I had started the next chapter of my life. I took the research really seriously and tapped into the YPO network. I talked to several people who ran their own private equity firms and asked if I could buy them lunch.

'What issues do you face? How do you broker your deals? How long does the due diligence take?' Questions, questions, questions.

I was formulating a vision of the kind of company I wanted to start, and, just as I had done sitting in Aisha's boutique twenty years before, I was looking for a USP. What could I do differently? What could I do better? Where was the flaw? I looked at the journey of the typical private equity deal and I identified five key skills that were needed: origination, financial analysis, market and competitive research, valuation and negotiation and the legal, due diligence and documentation skills that finalise the deals. In every firm I visited one person saw a transaction through from the beginning to the end. My second light-bulb moment was this: each of those were distinct skills and I didn't think you could be brilliant at all of them. That meant that – taking the deal as a whole – people in private equity would only perform averagely. If I got a specialist to find the deals, a financial analyst to assess the market, a researcher who could investigate the target companies forensically and so on, I could have a team that would be extremely well placed to maximise any opportunity that came our way. However, I was a bit confused. What I had come up with seemed to make so much sense that I couldn't believe someone else hadn't already tried to do private equity that way. I supposed that people were just doing what they had always done and in Britain we're not very good at challenging the Establishment. I'm the opposite: I'm always looking for something to challenge. Still, I decided to talk over my strategy with a friend at a top accountancy firm, just in case I had overlooked something obvious.

'What do you think?' I asked after I'd revealed my plan.

'It's a bit dramatic – that's not how private equity works.'

'Let me ask you a question – do you think one guy can do it all?'

'Honestly? I'd have to say no.'

'If it was your money, would you give it to someone who isn't an expert, or someone who is a specialist?'

'James, you're forgetting that those skills can be brought in on contract. It's not that other firms don't use those skills, they just outsource them.'

'I thought of that, too, but the problem is I'm not really prepared to rely on someone I've paid a fee to to make such a big decision for a company they don't actually work for: that sounds like a compromise.'

'I don't disagree with you.'

After a few more exchanges, he said: 'You know, James, I think you're right. I think your way is better.'

Now I was really excited, and I started thinking about who I wanted to hire, where I wanted an office and what I was going to call the company. I had a vision of an old family firm in an oak-panelled office in Mayfair, something really traditional and, I suppose, very English. Just as with Alexander Mann, I wanted people to think this new business had been established for a very long time. I had in mind a couple of old-fashioned City gents in bowler hats and I asked myself what I thought they were called. The names Mr Hamilton and Mr Bradshaw seemed to fit the bill and that became the name of my new firm: Hamilton Bradshaw.

I took an office in Stratton Street in Mayfair – close to the Ritz, near Lazard's Bank and where the nearest place for a spot of lunch was Michael Caine's Langham's Brasserie. I started having meetings with anyone I thought might be useful, and word got out that I was up to something. To my amazement, the phone started ringing and people started offering me deals. It was time to hire my team. I went back to my notes from all my meetings with other private equity firms and looked at the job titles and CVs. I decided the first person I wanted on the team was a banking professional who had also worked in private equity. I picked up the phone and started looking for likely candidates.

'Hi. You don't know me but I'm James Caan, I'm calling from Hamilton Bradshaw and I'm looking for an investment director. I'd love to have a chat. When's a good time for you?'

I found the ideal person at Close Brothers. Then I hired a corporate lawyer from Clifford Chance. I was like Yul Brynner assembling the Magnificent Seven, looking for an expert in every field of private equity combat. The one skill I wanted on my team that few others have on theirs is a cash expert: someone who can look at a balance sheet and see where the cash is. Cash is different from profit, and from what I had observed the most common reason why businesses get into trouble is that they don't know how to account for their cash properly. For instance, they may secure sales of £1 million and then spend half of that on the production of goods, failing to realise that their sales income only becomes due sixty days after delivery. A cash expert would be key to sorting out companies in trouble, and I hired the best in the business from KPMG.

I found an analyst who had been the chief accountant at Unilever and had just finished an MBA at the London Business School. I also hired someone to originate the deals. I had thought that would be my job, but it was already clear to me that there were more deals out there than I could handle, and to do it well you have to spend a lot of time with people. I could open doors, but I needed someone who could keep them open and I found a great guy who not only had a banking background but who had also run his own business.

In most private equity funds 80 per cent of the profit goes to the investors, but, as Hamilton Bradshaw would be keeping everything it made, it meant I could give my team a very tempting profit-share package. If there's one thing I'm good at it's hiring the right people, the best people, and putting them in positions where they can flourish. Assembling a team was really enjoyable, and I was in my element.

At the same time, one of my YPO contacts called me: he knew a company with a £160 million turnover that was having problems expanding and could use some help. As I wasn't yet working full time, he thought I could give the MD a hand. The company was a financial services firm that operated in the government receivables sector. What this means is that they subbed companies that were waiting to be paid by the government for services they were providing. Say a nursing home was waiting for payment from a local authority for providing care but there was a lag between invoicing and payment: the receivables company would make the payment and claim the money back from the local authority. It's similar to factoring, and they take a small percentage of the bill as their fee. So if a nursing home was waiting for £1000 to come from the authority but it would take six weeks to arrive, they could go to the receivables company who would give them the £1000 less the 2 or 3 per cent fee immediately. For a lot of businesses, having to wait for the cash is a higher price to pay than their modest fee.

I spent a couple of weeks with the MD getting to understand his business and how they could grow and get round their short-term problems. I found myself getting really quite excited about a business where the income is pretty much guaranteed as his client was ultimately the government: his only real problem was how to find more clients. Sales was something I understood, and all he needed in the short term was cash, so I offered to invest: Hamilton Bradshaw had its first deal.

It was exactly the kind of opportunity I was looking for: other private equity firms took too long to make decisions as they had investment boards to report to. I just had to make my own mind up and if I could move quickly I could get a very good price.

I liked the business precisely because I knew that so many companies have cash issues. Ninety-nine per cent of companies create what's called a P&L, a profit and loss account, each month; but, depending on how you account for your income, it might not have any relation to what's in the bank. Let's say you sign a deal for a piece of work in March for £60k; do you log that money in March, or do you log it when it actually arrives in your account in May? And if it's payable in instalments, how do you account for your income then? Some people will put the £60k in March, deduct their costs of a couple of grand and kid themselves they made a profit of £58k in March, when in fact they made a £2k loss. It's a problem that comes up time and again on *Dragons' Den*, but even before I joined the panel I knew that enough companies had cash difficulties: that meant finding new clients shouldn't be a problem precisely because surprisingly few people know how to correlate cash and profit.

I think part of the problem is that spreadsheets make it very easy to extrapolate figures by automatically replicating formulae: to be crude, a spreadsheet assumes that if your profits increase at 5 per cent a month that increase will be constant. In reality, businesses are seasonal or have capacity issues, and they don't grow evenly. It's easy to understand why inexperienced entrepreneurs run aground if they rely on what their spreadsheet tells them. As I suspected, these kinds of errors with cash and accounting allowed the business to grow, and when Hamilton Bradshaw exited the business in 2008 the turnover had increased to £430 million.

The ink was barely dry on the first deal when I took a call that would lead to the next one.

'Do you fancy investing in a property business?'

'Might do. Tell me about it.'

It became clear that the opportunity was to fund a start-up, not what I had set up Hamilton Bradshaw to do, but it seemed like such a good business that I arranged to meet the MD.

David Alberto came to my office and told me about his plan for serviced offices.

'Tell me, David, where are you working now?'

'For MWB, which is number two in the serviced office market.'

'And before that?'

'Regus.'

Regus is number one in the market.

'How long were you at Regus?'

'Five years.'

'And how long have you been at MWB?'

'Six years.'

This guy clearly had experience; I felt I could be pretty sure that David knew what he was talking about. I liked him, which always helps; he struck me as bright, motivated and knowledgeable. What impressed me most was that he had come up with a new concept for serviced offices, which was what was needed if he was going to make a success of a new venture in what had become a mature market.

Having been the tenant of serviced offices myself, I was well aware of their limitations. One problem is that if you're trying to create a sophisticated company it doesn't look very good when clients come to see you and everything is branded with the serviced office company's logo: you want your clients to see your logo, not your landlord's. David's idea was to unbrand the concept of the serviced office, and it was something that immediately appealed to me. You could convince your visitors that the whole building was yours if you wanted to, just as I had done in Pall Mall all those years ago. The difference between the managers of that building and the business David was talking about starting was that his was a scalable operation that could manage several buildings simultaneously. Not only did David's unbranded concept mean that we would be more likely to attract bigger and better companies as tenants, but they were also more likely to hang around.

David also planned to make the most of new technology and leapfrog the services Regus and MWB could provide. Fitting out a

50,000-square-foot office block with up-to-date technology used to leave you with a bill of anything up to £1 million, but recent innovations meant it now cost a fraction of that figure. This would mean David's business would be competitive, but it got better: things like the phone system could be operated remotely, which meant that the same operator could deal with calls in multiple locations, which in turn meant that each of our buildings wouldn't need a receptionist, so there would also be a salary saving.

As David and I talked, I realised I didn't mind that his idea was a start-up: this was the right business at the right time, headed by the right person. He then said something really, really interesting: most of the operators in the serviced sector were themselves leaseholders, and he had worked out a way to make more money – so long as he could find someone to buy the freehold.

He explained that the value of commercial property isn't just in the land and the fabric of the building, as it is with residential property, it's also in the quality of the tenant that you get to sign a lease. You could get two identical buildings, but the one with a quality tenant would be worth more. If you had a blue-chip tenant – a high-street name with a trading record, for example – on a standard commercial fifteen-year lease, banks would lend you money against the value of that lease, as well as the value of the property because your tenant's ability to pay the rent is fairly secure. David's strategy was to buy an empty building, install his serviced office company as the leaseholder, and then refinance the building once he had demonstrated his ability to pay the market rent, which was what the banks would look for before agreeing to additional lending. And that was just the property side of things: the serviced office business was also extremely investible. It was a brilliant plan.

'Let me get this straight,' I said. 'The value of a building correlates with who the tenant is.'

'Correct.'

'The better the quality of the tenant, the more the value of the building increases?'

'Correct.'

'And if there's no tenant the building is worth less.'

'Yes. We buy the empty building because we know who the tenant's going to be – it's me – so there's none of the risk of unpaid rents that other landlords would have. You buy the building, you put me in as the tenant, I sign a fifteen-year lease, you go back to the bank and tell them the building generates an income of x, guaranteed for fifteen years, and they'll lend you 70 per cent of the value of that lease.'

'So the money I spend on buying the building in the first place is recouped from the loan, the repayments on which are covered by your rent?'

'Correct.'

So let's say David finds a building for £8 million which is bought by me. I put down £2.5 million as a deposit and get the rest of the money in a loan from the bank. I refurbish the building to David's specification before he signs a lease and agrees to pay £1,125,000 rent a year. I can then get the building revalued – and this always has to be by a valuer that has been recommended by the bank; typically, valuations assume a rental yield of 7.5 per cent which would value the building at £15 million.

I can then go back to the bank and say, 'My building has been valued at £15 million. What will you lend me against that?'

They say: 'Seventy per cent, Mr Caan.'

That's £10.5 million. I say: 'Thank you very much.'

That figure allows me to pay off the original £5.5 million loan I bought the building with and take out the £2.5 million deposit I had put into the building. The rest more than covers the refurbishment costs and leaves me with around £1 million to put in the bank. David's rent covers the new loan *and* I would still own 100 per cent of the building, *plus* I would still own the serviced office company. Win, win, win.

I knew that financial engineering like this is what frequently enables entrepreneurs and investors to make money. Debt can be a lever that creates profit, as thousands of property owners discovered in the 1990s and early 2000s before the credit crunch hit. They could have bought a property worth £250k with a £50k deposit and an 80 per cent loan, then, when the property was worth, say, £325k, they refinanced with another 80 per cent loan that allowed them to pay off the first loan and take their original £50k back: they had none of their cash left in their investment any more but they still owned 100 per cent of the property.

Although I knew all about these kinds of arrangements, I still couldn't quite believe David's plan would work. Even though I couldn't work out what the catch was, I thought there had to be one. However, if David was right it was a spectacular opportunity and so Hamilton Bradshaw invested. We called the company Avanta and David went looking for his first property. He found it in Victoria and within three months he had refurbished the building. Hamilton Bradshaw then moved in as one of the first tenants and before long the building was at full capacity. Hamilton Bradshaw then went to the bank to revalue the building and we refinanced for the increased amount. Blimey! It had worked!

David had such good contacts in the industry that he quickly hired a team – a sales director, a finance director and regional director – and together they started rolling Avanta out. We opened another one in Great Titchfield Street, then Margaret Street, and the formula kept working. Within a few years, there were ten Avanta centres in Britain, one of which happens to be managed by my youngest sister, Irem. After a couple of years, we started to get approaches from people wanting to buy the freehold of Avanta's first building in Victoria. Freehold buildings with good tenants are seen as sound investments by pension funds and other institutional investors, and when we got an offer that was substantially higher than what we'd paid for it we decided it was the right level of return and accepted the offer. There comes a point in every market where the prices get a bit silly, and that's when you should sell and take your profits.

There's one more thing I should say about Avanta. When David came to see me, he had already pitched to twenty other investors and no one had seen the opportunity. They had looked at external aspects – like the fact that commercial property was in the doldrums and that the serviced office sector was so weak after the dotcom fallout that Regus's share price had plummeted. They got so distracted by the clutter that they failed to see the opportunity. But the real opportunity here was David: he was bright, eager, well connected, and he'd done his research. I had looked at him and asked myself: do I think this guy can do it? As always, what I had really invested in was the person.

Chapter 31

You Win Some, You Lose Some (2005–2007)

'*They say in business that your best loss is your first loss.*'

I N THE WORLD OF private equity Hamilton Bradshaw is a boutique. Typically, we invest less than £10 million in each deal and we look to make two or three investments a year. We get hundreds of approaches – since I've been on *Dragons' Den* the number has skyrocketed – and of those I reckon we take about twenty seriously. Of the twenty, we reject half because the deal doesn't stack up, and the rest we spend a lot of time on.

I find that the £1 million to £10 million market is a very exciting place for us to be because, in the past five years or so, private equity has been about bigger and bigger deals. Firms were able to raise money from institutional investors so easily that they had to buy bigger and bigger companies to spend the money, hence the EMI and Sainsbury's takeovers. The bigger firms get consumed with one big deal at a time, whereas we have several eggs in our basket. I would say the average private equity firm has £250 million under management – maybe even closer to £500 million – and when you've got that much money it's not economically viable to spend your time on a £5 million deal. Hamilton Bradshaw has done so well because other private equity firms have migrated away from our turf.

One of the key things I've learned since starting the company is how to structure a deal. Typically, I look to take a 60 per cent stake in a target company, leaving the rest to the founders and management team who will drive the venture forward. It's important that they still have a meaningful stake so that they are motivated to build the company: as ever, I'm only interested in investments where we all win. As I can't make money unless they do, their stake has to be sizeable. Getting the equity split right is a delicate business: it has to be big enough to make it worth Hamilton Bradshaw's investment in time and money, but it has to be small enough to leave the management team with a meaningful stake in the company's success. I'm rarely interested in buying 100 per cent of a company, because I believe you stand a better chance of creating wealth as an investor if you do it in partnership with the management teams you invest in.

One way of creating wealth is by motivating the management teams to produce bigger profits, and so I usually look to stagger my investment over time. So let's say I take a 60 per cent stake in a company that's worth £10 million that has three founders. It actually makes no sense for me to hand over £6 million upfront because I want to make sure that the management team delivers on its growth targets. So I may give each of the founders a million each – £1 million is a good number, and people can really feel as if they are being rewarded for their efforts thus far – and pay them another million each if they reach their targets. This shares the risk between us: I may only have handed over £3 million upfront, but if the company fails I will have lost my money while they will still have a million quid in their pockets.

The targets I usually give management teams will be something along the lines of doubling the profits, and, if they do that, I can often take the extra million I'm going to pay each of them out of my share of the profits. So, although Hamilton Bradshaw has taken a 60 per cent stake for an initial outlay of £3 million, we sacrifice future income from profits to do this. The reason I like to structure my deals this way is because it incentivises the founders and managers, which in turn makes success far more likely. If the team stand to earn phenomenal bonuses for delivering on agreed targets, how often do you think they reach their targets? Pretty much every time.

As a small company with no investors to please, Hamilton Bradshaw can make decisions few other private equity firms can. Not only can we be quick – we share an open-plan office and talk constantly, so there's no need to wait for board meetings – but we have so much expertise that what we bring to a deal is worth so much more than money. Whatever problems a company has – sales, cash flow, legal structure, premises, anything – I have someone on my team who can find a brilliant solution. In fact, the most important thing I look for when I make an investment is our ability to add value. I'm not interested in anything that doesn't give me a 100 per cent return on my investment within three years, and finding a way that our skills can exploit the opportunity is the best way of getting that return. Unsurprisingly, then, one of our recent investments took me back into the world of recruitment.

Eden Brown is a high-street recruitment agency that had been going for fifteen years when we started looking at it. Its founder and chief executive is a guy called Ian Wolter, and, as is often the case when an established company is still run by the founder, the business had become a little complacent, and the board had lost the focus that we as outsiders were able to give. The company wasn't being challenged on the shop floor or in the boardroom, and I could see that it was essentially a very good company that just had a few structural problems. That made it a great investment.

I took on the role of chairman and, as a recruitment specialist, I could instantly tell from reading Eden Brown's board pack that they were measuring the wrong things. I'm sure most investors look at a board pack and think, 'I'm sure someone here understands this,' and don't say anything, but I have no qualms about questioning every little thing. It's just the way we are as human beings; we don't want to appear stupid and say things like, 'I don't understand the board pack.' But I'm not like that.

'I'm going to put my hand up straight away. Ian, forgive me, but I don't understand this. Can you explain it to me?'

It might sound really weird, but nobody ever says that.

'I just want to know the basic stuff. I want to see how many people you employ, what they do, if they make money. I want to know how much money you've got in the bank and if anyone owes you any money.'

It was all simple stuff, and, because I'm not an investment banker, I was speaking a language that the board could understand. They'd been tying themselves up in so many knots with graphs and pie charts and spreadsheets that they'd overlooked the basics. Once we started talking the same language, not only did I start to understand their business but they did, too. By my third board meeting I felt I had drilled down far enough into the company to start suggesting changes. I'd been looking at the figures and had identified a branch that wasn't performing, so I questioned its strategic value.

They told me that one of their key customers was based near the branch, and that they'd been operating in that location for ten years, but none of that explained why they were keeping it open when it was losing money. My questioning gave the kind of perspective they'd all been too close to the business to offer. Sometimes management teams just can't see the wood for the trees.

'I've put you on the spot. Tell you what, for the next board meeting just give me three reasons why we should continue to invest in that location,' I said.

Of course, at the next board meeting the first item on the agenda was the branch in question, and no one had been able to come up with any commercial reasons to continue in that location.

'Does anyone know a reason why we should keep it open?'

I went to each member of the board, and none of them had a reason.

'So what do we do with it?' I asked the financial director.

'Close it?'

'You tell me.' It was important that whatever happened was their decision and not mine. 'You've been running this business for a long time. What are the issues of closing a branch?'

There was the lease to be negotiated out of, customers to be taken care of by other branches, staff to be relocated – the board knew exactly what needed to be done without me having to tell them anything: all I had needed to do was ask the right questions.

'And how long will it take to find out about the lease? How long should the consultation be with the staff? What's the deadline for speaking to the key clients? And let's put a conference call in the diary for each of these events and make sure we're all on track.'

I knew that by gently asking relevant questions the team could deliver the return I was looking for – after all, nobody knew the company's strengths and flaws better than them. We went through every aspect of the company and introduced share option schemes to incentivise the workforce, more efficient management structures, and changed the payment terms to improve cash flow. All these changes were in response to me asking a question and the team coming up with the answers. I didn't have to do very much; it was down to them.

The observations my team and I were able to make identified huge opportunities for Eden Brown that increased profits and enhanced the value of the business. You might think that Ian would have felt undermined by me becoming his chairman, but he has said to me that he has really enjoyed working with me. Hamilton Bradshaw's input has given his company new vigour, new purpose and a clearer sense of direction, and it has been great to see him and his team respond to the challenge. Within a year of our investment, the profits had doubled and they look set to keep on doubling in the future.

I'd love to be able to say that the way to double your profits each year is x, but the truth is it's not that straightforward. Hamilton Bradshaw looks to find efficiencies in a business that will ultimately deliver better returns, and we do that by looking at an organisation from the ground up and assessing how every piece of the company performs – the changes we suggest could come from anywhere within the business, so that there isn't a one-size-fits-all formula.

Hamilton Bradshaw's investments now extend from health clubs to nursing homes to retailers and financial services. The firm's reputation within the industry has grown and, having developed a successful model, we have now extended the model to Pakistan – I have even advised the government there on its private equity strategy – to provide expertise in a developing country that could make a real difference to companies in Pakistan. I have a real sense that, with private equity, I am doing exactly what I ought to be doing: this business suits me perfectly and I thoroughly enjoy what I do, especially now that technology means I'm no longer tied to the office quite so much.

A few months ago I was on my yacht several miles out of Cannes when I took a call on my BlackBerry. I was able to patch through four other people for a conference call to hammer out a deal. Then the legal document was sent to me, I amended it and sent it back. And you know what? No one even knew I was on the yacht. Advances in technology have made my working life so much more efficient, and, although I can still work up to eighteen hours a day, I can do so much from home or wherever else I happen to be. And that means when I'm in the office the important thing is spending time with the team, maintaining the rapport and the spirit of the place so that we continue to excel. Paperwork and meetings can be done remotely, and that means I get to enjoy being in the Hamilton Bradshaw offices and hanging out with the team.

So far, only one of our investments has lost money, and that was a pretty high-profile flop. We got a phone call from a firm of accountants that was handling the administration of Benjy's, a high-street sandwich retailer. If Pret A Manger and Eat cater for the sandwich connoisseur, Benjy's was for the bloke who wants a cheap sandwich at lunchtime and doesn't want his taste buds educated – cheese and pickle, ham and tomato, BLT. It had originally been set up by the Benjamin family and they had sold up to another private equity firm three years earlier for £25 million. At the time of the sale it had annual profits of £2.8 million; three years later it was making an annual loss of £4 million.

'They're going to run out of cash on Friday,' the accountants told us. It was now Monday. If they couldn't find an investor, the company would be wound up and its entire workforce laid off. 'Would you be interested in buying it?'

It sounded like an interesting investment. It was a well-known brand, it had good locations, and, because I knew there wouldn't be many other people who could raise the cash in a week, I could also get it for a good price. So I went to meet the management team that the private equity firm had installed, and within ten minutes I thought I had spotted the problem. The MD wore an Armani suit and looked as if he'd had an expensive education. He gave me a very polished presentation on the business and, as I was sitting there, I couldn't help but notice the divide between the management's style and the brand. The two didn't marry. He should have been running Pret, because ideally there should be some sort of synergy between the product and the team at the top. This guy didn't understand his brand and didn't know his customers: he had the wrong approach. I imagined that the family which had set up the company in the first place must have had a passion for no-nonsense, sensibly priced lunchtime food, but this guy didn't have a passion for what he had been asked to do, and it showed. In successful businesses there is usually a correlation between the company's brand and the personal image of the person in charge, but with him there was an obvious disconnect.

Spotting the problem made me confident that the solutions couldn't be too far away, and that made it a decent investment opportunity. On the Tuesday I went into a branch of Benjy's – there was one on Oxford Street just a couple of minutes from my office in Hanover Square – and had a look round. Again, I thought I had spotted problems that could easily be solved. For starters, they had too many types of sandwich. I spent hours in there – God knows what the staff thought I was doing, and it was telling that no one offered me assistance – and it was clear that they were making most of their money from just a handful of lines. It was the classic 80:20 ratio where 80 per cent of their profit came from 20 per cent of their products. I thought we could change the range and make savings on ingredients and production. Benjy's had also moved into the healthy-eating market with salads and reduced-salt options and in doing so they'd moved away from their core market. We could change that, too. As long as I knew what was wrong, I was confident we'd be able to put it right.

Potentially, it was a very lucrative market to be in: McDonald's had bought a 33 per cent stake in Pret for £50 million back in 2001, Eat was valued at around £100 million, Café Rouge had sold for a lot in the past, so I knew if I could get the formula right there was a very big prize to be had.

On the Wednesday we met with the financial team to try to understand their balance sheet – this was a business with 600 employees, sixty-five prime retail sites, as well as 150 franchised units plus a factory. It was a big business and there was a lot to get our heads round. Thursday was spent with the lawyers and, on the Friday, Hamilton Bradshaw acquired the business, and 600 employees were spared the anxiety of losing their jobs.

We'd made enough investments by this point to know that it wouldn't be quite as straightforward as I'd made out: I knew there would be problems, but I didn't anticipate too many difficulties changing the range of sandwiches. I was wrong.

First of all, you have to source the ingredients and get out of supply agreements for the ingredients you no longer need. Different sandwiches need different machinery in the factory, and then there was the labelling that listed the ingredients: there were so many things that I hadn't anticipated and it took ten weeks to change a single sandwich! Meanwhile, the company was losing £100k a week. That was an additional million quid gone before we'd even started to turn things around on the retail side of things.

Once we'd looked at the business more closely, we reluctantly decided that we had to close some of the poorest performing branches. Making people redundant is never nice, but we hoped that by sacrificing a handful of branches we could save the rest. However, some of the branches we wanted to close still had several years left on their leases, and there were clauses that meant the landlord could force you to stay until new tenants were found. And if our rent was £100k a year and the landlord could only get £80k a year from the new tenant, then we would have to make up the difference – even though we were no longer trading there!

And it wasn't just the leases that cost us. We were making staff redundant, so we had redundancy packages to fund, often running to several months' salary in one hit. Within two months of buying the company, I was really tearing my hair out. We then had a rent review for the branch in Oxford Street, one of the best locations we operated. The landlord was putting the rent up from £200k to

£240k a year, so I asked to look at the accounts for that branch. Guess what? It was only making £40k a year and the review would wipe out the profit.

We needed to find a way we could either cut costs or increase profit, so I walked over to the branch to take a look. I went at breakfast time: it was packed. I went at lunchtime: you couldn't have got more people in and the staff were working their socks off. This gave us a really big problem: we couldn't get any more customers if we tried and we couldn't lose any staff. So I asked myself if we could put the prices up, but the only thing Benjy's had going for it in the crowded lunchtime market was price. If we put a cheese sandwich up from £1.25 to £1.50 we'd be at the same level as M&S, so customers might as well go there as they could pick up something else in their lunch hour at the same time.

I really couldn't see a way forward, so I called together the most senior people at Benjy's – the product specialist, the chief exec, the finance director, ten people in all – and asked them what we were going to do about the Oxford Street branch.

'You guys have been here longer than me; you know the business inside out. What are our options?'

Two hours later we had come up with nothing. I think it was then that I finally admitted what I'd suspected for some time: we weren't going to be able to turn it around. It was just too hard, but it was still losing £100k a week so we had to do *something*.

When Hamilton Bradshaw bought the company from the administrators what we had actually bought was a licence to trade for six months. That meant there was a six-month window in which to ratify the deal. At this point we had owned the business for five months and after serious discussion we decided we should simply accept a failure and take the loss on the chin. I couldn't see a way of turning it around: even if we worked on it full time for two years, I didn't see how it was going to stop losing money. So I called the administrators and told them to look for another buyer.

They say in business that your best loss is your first loss. What they mean is that, when you look at the books and you see a loss, you have a chance to get out before the next set of accounts arrive with an even bigger loss marked out in red. That first loss gives you an opportunity to get out, and that's what we did. You also hear the expression, 'Don't catch a falling knife'; with Benjy's we came close to losing our fingers.

Looking back, returning Benjy's to the administrators was the smartest thing we could have done in the circumstances. I am so glad that I put my hand up and said, *This isn't working.* Sometimes, out of pride people in business carry on just to prove a point or not to lose face. That's not me: we failed, we recognised it, and that meant we were able to limit our losses to the cash we'd already spent. If we had dithered over the decision to hand it back and breached that six-month deadline, Hamilton Bradshaw would have been saddled with the losses for a lot longer and we could have lost three times as much money.

On the one hand I was relieved that it was over, on the other hand I was absolutely gutted. Failure hit me hard, and I was so annoyed at myself for buying into a business that I didn't understand. And we'd bought it in a week! *What had I been thinking? That I could walk on water?* It was time to stop believing my own publicity!

Chapter 32

Kashmir (2005–2006)

'Close your eyes for a moment and imagine the end of the world.'

O N 8 OCTOBER 2005 a massive earthquake hit Kashmir. Initial estimates reckoned it had killed 20,000 people and made a million homeless. We now know it killed more than 80,000 people and left more than three million without shelter.

I saw the news that night and, as I watched the first images come through, I was devastated. I had been visiting Lahore every six weeks, and knowing that the disaster had occurred only a few hundred miles away made it feel peculiarly personal. I had some sense of how chaotic life is away from the cities, and instantly knew how difficult it would be for aid to reach the affected areas. But it was more than that; I felt angry because the people of Kashmir had endured a civil war for fifty years: hadn't they suffered enough?

In the days that followed it became increasingly clear how hard it was going to be to mount a relief effort: the area affected was vast, roads and telecommunications had been destroyed, and many of the people in the earthquake zone lived in mountain villages that would take months for the emergency services to reach. What made it even worse was the onset of the Himalayan winter: if people didn't get shelter within weeks, hundreds of thousands more lives would be at risk.

I couldn't get the images out of my head. How can you have three million people homeless? What will happen to them? How do you cope with that? Who's capable of burying the dead? All week I was restless. I felt I wanted to do something and on the Saturday, a week after the earthquake, I decided I had to go to Kashmir. I told Aisha what I was about to do, and from the look on her face it was clear she thought I'd lost it again.

Apart from Aisha, I didn't tell anyone in London what I was doing because I knew they would all tell me not to go. Either they'd tell me I'd get in the way or that the Foreign Office was telling people not to travel there because it wasn't safe. I didn't need to hear those things so I packed a bag with a few of my warmest clothes, and Stephen, my butler, drove me out to Heathrow. While I was in the car I booked a flight, then I called my cousin, a couple of ministers I had got to know quite well and someone from the army I had met at an official function. In a country run by generals, getting to know the politicians automatically introduces you to the military. I told them that I wanted to see what had happened first-hand and find out how I could help. I knew I needed to understand the issues before I could understand possible solutions.

I flew to Islamabad, where I was met by a contact at the Human Development Organization. As ever, I didn't have a plan, but I'm not the kind of person who needs to know too much in advance: whatever I found on the ground I knew I would deal with. It's just about going back to my favourite question: what's the worst that could happen? Would I need to hire a car? I didn't know, but I knew that if I needed to buy a car it wouldn't have been a problem that I couldn't have solved.

As we travelled from the airport to my hotel, the guy from the HDO tried to persuade me not to go. 'It's really terrible there. You will see terrible things. You can help from here.' At the hotel we met up with two friends of mine who worked in finance in Islamabad: when I'd called them from the car and told them I wanted to go to Kashmir they said they would come with me. One of them had a 4 × 4.

I knew Kashmir was fairly close on the map, but I had no idea how long it would take to get there: was it twenty minutes or two hours or two days? We drove to the town of Muzaffarabad, which is just over the border from Islamabad. The road took us through some of the most beautiful mountain scenery I have ever seen, and it was difficult to comprehend that we were about to enter a disaster zone.

After a couple of hours, we reached the end of the road. Literally. It had been destroyed in the quake and the road just stopped. A queue of cars had built up and so we left the 4 × 4 and continued on foot.

The first thing that hit me when I got out of the car was the smell. Corpses had been lying on the ground for a week and the stench was sickening. Close your eyes for a moment and imagine the end of the world. Imagine every building crumbled into rubble; imagine everything in sight destroyed; imagine bodies lying stiff in the street and blood smeared down the side of concrete slabs as people have tried to pull survivors out of the wreckage; imagine those who can still walk encrusted in blood they've not been able to wash off for a week; imagine people dying slowly of horrific wounds that no one has any supplies to treat: I really felt as if I was witnessing the end of the world. It was like a bomb had gone off and destroyed everything.

Nothing I had seen on TV had prepared me for how I would feel. No one can describe to you the smell of death. We walked among the ruins in silence as we took in what we were witnessing. A few people stared at us as we had clearly just arrived, but mostly the survivors were so focused on finding their loved ones that we were left alone. And it was cold, really cold, and the knowledge that the temperature would drop as much as twenty degrees overnight told me the death toll from exposure and hypothermia would rise if aid wasn't delivered quickly.

We carried on walking and came to huge crack in the road. At the bottom of the crevasse was a car. We passed a tower block that was now only one storey high. I've since learned that the quake was so intense it did what geologists term 'liquefy' the foundations. Bricks and mortar became dust in seconds and buildings fell in on themselves. It is horrific to try to imagine what must have happened in that building.

As we walked, we came across bits of road where cars and lorries had survived but then had nowhere to go. With no roads, there was no easy way of bringing aid in. The ground was too steep for planes to land: helicopters would be the only way. My friend with the HDO had arranged for us to be taken in one of the military's helicopters to see the scale of the disaster. The destruction we had witnessed in Muzaffarabad did not stop, and the further we got from the towns the harder it would be to reach survivors. We flew over the remains of countless isolated villages perched on the sides of mountains. Even in good conditions it would be hard to get more than a mule up there.

The scale of need overwhelmed me. There were no schools, no hospitals, no shops, no town halls left from which to organise relief. No water supply, no sewage: everything had gone, including the stores of harvested food that were now rotting in the ruins. We passed a valley that appeared to be full of nothing but dust. It was cold, grey and unbearably sad. I couldn't believe the things I was seeing, and I still can't really express the effect seeing those things has had on me. I feel as if I have seen something I shouldn't have, that no one should have to see, and on that trip I was actually learning what it means to be alive. I was profoundly moved by what I saw. I still am.

Where do you start? I'm a pretty resourceful guy, but I couldn't find any solutions. People had no means of earning money to pay for any of the materials they needed to rebuild their homes. With the local economy and the infrastructure wiped out, it just wasn't straightforward to work out how I could help. You couldn't get aid in and you couldn't get the people out.

We had taken some water with us but no food, but I didn't really have an appetite anyway. Remarkably, we found a shack of a hotel that was still standing and, because no one had any money to pay for accommodation, there were still rooms available and we checked in. I barely slept that night, in part because of the images I couldn't get out of my head, but also because of the cold.

In the morning I decided to try to find out how I could help. The army had arrived in Muzaffarabad and were handing out tents and taking a register of the survivors. I went to talk to the commander.

'What are you doing here?' he asked.

'I live in London, but when I saw the news on TV I just had to come here and see if I could help.'

'We need more tents,' he said.

At last! Something I could do! But where could I get tents from? I called London on my mobile that – incredibly – still worked and spoke to someone from my office.

'Do me a favour, will you? Go on the internet and find me a company that sells tents. They've got to be ones for winter, for serious cold.'

They called back with a number and I was able to buy the company's entire stock. I then met a local MP and told him that I was going to be sending 1000 tents and I needed someone on the ground to collect and distribute them.

'I'm going to ship 1000 tents over in your name,' I told him. 'Is that OK? Will you collect them from the airport and make sure they are distributed?' Pakistan's national airline, PIA, had said it would put on a special flight from the UK taking aid from the

British Pakistani community, and I was able to arrange to get the tents on the aid flight. I had done something, but it was the proverbial drop in the ocean.

The more I talked to officials and the army, the more I understood just how chaotic things were, and the immensity of the task ahead. It was becoming clear that they just didn't have the resources to reach everyone by winter and so they developed a strategy that would concentrate on the towns in the low-lying areas. At least there they could get aid in and help the greatest number of people. I understood why they would do that, but I couldn't stop thinking about the people in the isolated villages we had flown over the day before.

Muzaffarabad is surrounded by mountains, and from where we stood we could see villages that we now knew wouldn't be helped. I had to do something. We – that's me and my two banker friends – drove as far as we could and then got out and walked. I needed to get into the villages so that we could assess what needed to be done. We walked for about an hour before we reached the first village. Buildings either side of the path we were following had collapsed, and it was evident that the damage in the villages was much worse: the steep terrain meant the ground had simply slipped down the mountainside, taking everything with it. The villages had been densely populated – up to fifteen people lived in each house – but now the only ones left were those who couldn't move – the elderly, those with young children, or in many cases the young children who now found themselves alone and utterly lost in the world.

I spoke to the villagers and heard heartbreaking stories. The Punjabi and Urdu I had learned as a child had become much more fluent since I'd been making regular trips to Pakistan, and I was able to make myself understood. I met one man who had lost his wife and three children, another woman who had six kids to look after and no food to offer them; in one village the children had gone off to school in the morning and not come back: everyone we spoke to was grieving. I talked to one man who described the moment when the earthquake struck. His house started to tremble, so he made his way to the room where he knew his wife and children were. Then the shaking became more violent and although he could see them at the other end of the room he couldn't move to reach them. Then a crack appeared in the floor and he was left standing in one half of the room as his entire family slipped away as the other half their house fell down the mountain-side.

'All I can hear is my daughter screaming,' he told me.

I looked at him and wondered what could be done for him. He had his pride, he didn't want handouts, but with no job, no food and no shelter he had no way of supporting himself. I looked across at the valley and saw other ruined villages in the distance and knew that the stories I had just heard would be repeated in every place we went to. It was too much to bear, and I just had to leave. I was struggling to take it all in and I was exhausted and I was angry: *Why do these disasters always happen to the poor?* Why are the people most affected by natural disasters always the most helpless? Leaving was a luxury few people had, but I knew I would be back. I just had to work out how on earth I could help.

On the plane back to the UK, I wasn't myself. I wasn't positive and confident that there was anything I could do: I was really quite bruised by everything I had seen and for the first days back at my desk I didn't have any enthusiasm for work. All I could think about was Kashmir.

I rang my friend Seema Aziz who had been so helpful when I had been setting up my school. 'What can we do?' I asked.

'I don't know, but we have to do something.'

I told her about what I had seen and together we came up with a plan that would see us build 100 homes in the valley where I had seen so much devastation. We didn't know what it would entail, but it was a target, an objective, something to aim for, something to drive us forward.

A couple of weeks later I got back on a plane and together Seema and I talked to everyone who we thought could help. We talked to a number of architects, but the concept of building something quickly and cheaply in a disaster region was beyond them. They made suggestions, but they were things that would only work if you could drive an articulated lorry to the building site. No one seemed to be able to comprehend the complexity of the task, and once again I returned to the UK feeling quite demoralised.

I was telling friends in London about my frustrations, and one of them suggested I contact a friend who ran a structural engineering consultancy called Buro Happold that had just done lots of rebuilding work after the Indian Ocean tsunami. So I called up the chief exec and within minutes I knew I had found someone who understood the complexities and limitations of working in a disaster zone.

'When can I come and see you?'

'Can you get here this afternoon?'

Their office was just five minutes from mine. I couldn't quite believe that the solution I had been looking for was so close at hand. I arrived there a couple of hours after my initial phone call, and they had already downloaded aerial images of the area and come up with some suggestions of what kind of construction would be possible. At the end of the meeting I had a list of questions for which they needed answers in order to proceed, such as what resources were available on the ground: there was no point in them designing buildings to be made of wood if there were no trees to cut down. To get those answers, we needed someone on the ground, so Seema put us in touch with a local guy who could assess the availability of materials and manpower locally.

The buildings that were needed had to fulfil so many criteria. They had to be quick to construct because people were homeless. The best design was a modular one: a basic two-room structure that could be built quickly, with bathrooms and kitchens to be added in the months to come. The architects thought of everything: obviously the buildings had to be earthquake-proof, but the angle of the roof also had to be just right so that it could hold several feet of snow (too shallow and it would collapse with the weight); they even calculated how many human beings it would take to get the interior to a survivable temperature. There was no heating in the basic modules, but the body heat of four humans would get the internal temperature of each room to five degrees. It would still feel like freezing to anyone in Britain, but it would mean they would survive.

The houses had to be constructed with materials that were readily available. The best way to get over the lack of manpower was to prefabricate most of the components so that, once delivered, they could be assembled by the villagers. Our man on the ground was finding it hard to find a factory where the pieces could be constructed. The only place that said they could take on the work was in Lahore, which was 300 miles away. How were we going to transport 100 houses 300 miles? We'd have to find out about that later.

Within a few weeks it was clear that the factory was having difficulty following the designs and it was all taking longer than it ought to. Someone who understood the designs had to go out there and oversee construction. A woman from Buro Happold called Julia had just come back from one of her tsunami rebuilding projects. She had five days before she had to be in New York, and she offered to spend those five days in Lahore, so I bought her a ticket and arranged everything for her on the ground.

With the construction now under control, Seema got back to me about the transportation costs. They were more than we had bargained for, but it was a problem that could at least be solved with money. With one solution found, we were faced with another problem. I went back to Kashmir just before Christmas and spoke to an army brigadier who was distributing tents: it was so cold I couldn't believe that anyone could survive without a proper roof over their heads – this was the Himalayas in winter, after all. I told him about the prefab houses that were being made and where we intended to build them. By this point, they had completed their register of survivors and told me there was a problem with my plan.

'You have to be careful who you give a house to.'

'Why is that?'

'You can't build a house on a piece of land that doesn't belong to you.'

It made perfect sense, but it was something we hadn't considered.

'Leave it with me. I will go through our records and see who is still alive and who is also on our land register.'

It would take him a day or two to do it, so I decided to go back to the valley to see what had been done. Mercifully, the corpses had been removed, but I couldn't see any evidence of rebuilding. I had hoped we might have been able to do something by now, but everything had been more complex than I could ever have imagined. People were living communally in the buildings which still stood, and their living conditions were verging on the inhumane. We had to step up the pace. These people were in desperate need.

The land registry revealed there were 700 families in the valley that could prove they owned some land. We were only having 100 houses built: how were we to allocate them? I went through the list of survivors. There was a seventy-six-year-old who was looking after six grandchildren: he would get a house. A woman who had had a leg amputated and had lost her husband and still had four kids to look after: she got a house. We chose the people in the greatest need with the fewest number of able-bodied relations.

Eventually, the factory told us that the manufacturing was complete and the houses were ready for delivery. Seema arranged transportation, and it was absolutely fantastic to know that within a couple of weeks people would be able to see out the rest of winter in their own homes.

Back in London, I got into the swing of things again: now that something was happening and I felt we had made progress, I could concentrate on work, the deals we were considering. I was giving a presentation to a bank when my phone rang. Thank God for caller ID, because 90 per cent of the time when my phone rings I don't answer it, but it was Seema and I knew it had to be something to do with the houses.

The lorry driver had called: the roads hadn't been built yet and he couldn't go any further.

'I don't know what to do, James.'

Neither did I, but I knew a man who would. I called the brigadier I had dealt with about the allocations.

'Where are your trucks at the moment?'

I wasn't sure, so I gave him the mobile number of one of the drivers.

'I'll call him and get some guys in 4 × 4s to him and deliver the houses piece by piece.'

I couldn't have asked for more, but then we got word that the 4 × 4s couldn't go any further either. The only vehicle that could make it to the villages was in fact a mule. I called the brigadier again.

'I'll send some mules.'

I've said it before but it's worth repeating: in Pakistan it really is about who you know, and being able to get the right person on the end of the phone was the only thing that was going to get the villagers their houses.

I eventually got the call that the houses had reached the village, but there was one last problem: there wasn't enough labour. The houses had been designed for the landowners to build themselves as much as possible, but so many of them were injured or old that they just weren't strong enough to dig the foundations. So I called the brigadier one last time.

'You couldn't let me have eight soldiers for a couple of weeks, could you?'

It took far longer than we had anticipated – organising such a complex task remotely was a logistical nightmare – but after three months of conference calls and miles of fax paper the houses were built. It was a remarkable achievement, and when I told my YPO forum members about it they wanted to go and see what we had done. So I called my friend the minister and told him I wanted to bring a team in, and asked if he could organise some security for us. Some of the guys were Jewish and fairly high-profile, so going into a Muslim country where extremism is an issue was a concern for them. The minister arranged for us to get special clearance and for a UN helicopter to take us to the valley where the houses were now standing.

We met several people who were living in the houses we'd had built, and one woman invited us in. One of the YPO guys told her that I was the person responsible for her house and immediately her eyes filled with tears and she put her arms around me.

'Thank you,' she kept on saying, 'thank you.'

As we flew back to Islamabad, we saw several of the new houses and it is hoped that several more will be built. The prototype was donated to the government with a set of plans so that anyone could copy the design. Three years on, there is still so much to be done, and I sometimes wonder if the best aid that can be given after a disaster is entrepreneurs' time. We are often so much more effective at taking decisions and making progress that we will always be able to get quicker results than bureaucratic agencies and governments. There's something about the character of an entrepreneur that gets things done, and sometimes I struggle to think of a better use for our skills.

Chapter 33

Into the Den

(2007–present)

'*The first thing I did was check out the pile of money on the table in front of me. Well, wouldn't you?*'

I N EARLY 2007 my office took a call from a woman who works as a talent scout for TV companies. She'd been asked to find someone to take part in a new format for a business show the BBC was developing and wondered if I'd be interested. She told me I'd been recommended to her by a mutual friend and, although I'd never thought of going on TV before, I was curious to find out more.

We had a really positive first meeting, and she asked if she could come back again to film an interview with me so she could see how I came across on camera. We got on so well that I completely forgot about the camera and our interview was over in a flash. After she'd left, I became so busy with other things that when she called back a few weeks later I'd almost forgotten she'd ever been in touch.

She told me that she'd shown the tape to the producers of the new format, one of whom also worked on *Dragons' Den*.

'Do you ever watch it?' she asked.

'I've seen it a couple of times, but I don't get a lot of time to watch TV.'

'Well, when they looked at the footage I filmed they thought you might have something that could work in the Den and they'd like to meet you.'

I'd always enjoyed the *Dragons' Den* format when I got to see it, as watching budding entrepreneurs pitch their business idea to established entrepreneurs for investment is a very condensed version of what I do for a living. If I was at home when it was on I would usually watch it.

I went to BBC Television Centre where one of the show's producers had arranged for me to hear the pitches of three entrepreneurs while they filmed me. They wanted to see how I interacted with the pitchers and how I assessed the investment opportunities as a kind of screen test. As I spend every day assessing investment opportunities, I found asking questions very straightforward, even though there were several cameras in the room.

The producer called me up a couple of weeks later and asked if I'd like to view the tape with him. Well, of course I was curious, so I went to meet him again. By this time, several people in the BBC had seen the tape and apparently they were all quite excited about it.

'They can't believe you haven't done this before. You're a natural!'

When he showed it to me, I was quite surprised myself: I seemed reasonably relaxed, and I thought I'd asked some pretty good questions. All of a sudden the idea of going on TV wasn't just plausible, it was actually quite appealing.

'Would you be interested in joining the show?' he asked.

'I'm not sure. I think so. Do you think I would fit it in?'

'Well, I think the next step would be to get you and a couple of the Dragons together. You can ask them what it's really like and we can see how you interact.'

They arranged for me to do a similar session with Deborah Meaden, who's been on the panel since the third series. I'd sometimes thought she could come across as quite hard on TV, so I was a little surprised when she was so friendly and chatty, really warm. And as soon as we started rehearsing, I realised just how good she was at assessing opportunities and the way she was asking questions – really getting to the nub of the issue very quickly – which reminded me that at the end of the process I really could be parting with a lot of money. *My own money*. Working with her certainly helped me focus.

We went for a coffee afterwards and I asked her for advice. The thing she was keen for me to understand was just what an impact being on TV would have on my life. I was doubtful it could really make that much difference.

'Trust me,' she said, 'your life will not be the same.'

The BBC then arranged a second session, this time with Deborah and Duncan Bannatyne, who again comes across as quite dour on TV, but with whom I got on straight away. Duncan's got a great sense of humour and is a very open and direct person. He's been in the Den since the start and told me that being on the show had been great for his profile. He'd gone from being just another successful businessman to a household name, and that had helped his business – a chain of health clubs – to become a brand.

'Don't underestimate the public's interest in a new Dragon,' he told me, but I couldn't really believe it would make that much difference. As someone who only watched it occasionally, I didn't really believe that viewers could be *that* interested in the Dragons.

At this point, however, I hadn't actually been asked to join the show. I wasn't thinking that I wanted to do it or not do it: that's not how I make decisions. Generally, I just go on a journey and 99 per cent of the time the decision is a consequence of that journey. My journey was about meeting everyone and talking to Aisha and the girls about it, but I never thought, 'I really want to do this and if I don't get it I'll be gutted.' The decision about whether I joined the panel or not would be made by the journey, not me.

Of course, there was one thing that no one was mentioning: were they considering me as an addition to the panel, or were they thinking of replacing a Dragon? When they told me they would be making a substitution, the obvious question was 'Who's leaving?'

'We can't tell you that.'

I was then introduced to the series producer, and she talked me through the filming schedule and commitments, and eventually they asked me if I wanted to join. I had enjoyed meeting everyone on the show so much that I said yes. Ever since my gap year I had been interested in projects that created change, and I saw joining the show as a huge opportunity for change: who knows what will come of it, I thought. They then made the announcement to the press, which confirmed that I would be replacing Richard Farleigh, the very popular Australian financier.

Duncan and Deborah were right: the attention was instant and, it turned out, unstoppable. I hadn't even started filming and already journalists were calling the office every day. Suddenly I was being asked for my opinion on interest rates and the economy and invited on to news programmes as a pundit. I was stunned. Then the Asian press picked up on the story, and suddenly every Asian magazine and newspaper wanted to profile me: an Asian Dragon was big news.

It was also news to Richard Farleigh. I read an interview with him in the *Evening Standard* saying he was disappointed to have been asked to leave. He had relocated from Monaco to England to be part of the show and had made more investments than some of the other Dragons. I don't know why they chose to replace Richard – I thought he came across very well on TV and brought something different to the panel – but the fact that he was so popular inevitably meant there was some hostility towards me at first.

The first challenge of making the series was finding the time. All five Dragons are incredibly busy, and coordinating our diaries to find days when we were all available was a nightmare for our PAs and the production team, but eventually the dates were agreed and off I went to the studios where they were making the fifth series. There's something about being in a film studio – it felt incredibly glamorous. Much more glamorous, I'm told, than the first few series which they filmed in a real warehouse.

I had met the other two Dragons – Peter Jones and Theo Paphitis – at a dinner the production team had arranged for us all. Apart from the fact that I got neck ache talking to Peter – he's so tall we call him Pylon Pete – I found both of them easygoing and a good laugh. It was clear that the two of them were genuinely good friends, and the conversation never stopped.

One morning I drove to the studios in my convertible Aston Martin. It's the most beautiful sky-blue car with a cream interior and, when I parked up, Peter and Theo – who were having a chat in the car park – started teasing me about it: they thought it was a bit flamboyant. When we broke for lunch, I realised that Peter had tipped a bag of rubbish into it. I couldn't believe he'd done something like that: he is such a kid! What really amazed me was that a couple of days later the story appeared in the papers! *Could the press really be that interested in what went on the Den?*

The next day I took my Rolls-Royce Phantom, and Theo and Peter both arrived in their Maybachs. It was a real case of boys and their toys, as then Theo drove up in something that looked like the Batmobile with tinted windows and fluffy dice – it was like a disco on wheels. Peter obviously couldn't be left out, so he turned up in a Ferrari while I gave my new Maybach an outing. We were often outside between pitches, and on one of those breaks I noticed something funny about Peter's Ferrari. It was the number plate. Theo must have got his driver to change the plates while we were filming: it read W411 KER with a well-placed screw in the middle of the 11. I thought it was hilarious.

The filming itself was harder work than I had expected, and on my first few days in the Den I was exhausted. The warehouse set was inside a box inside a huge aircraft hangar of a studio and walking into it was strange – it looks different with all the cameras and the lights and the crew in it. With all the other chairs allocated, I took the one on the end, and, of course, the first thing I did was check out the pile of money on the table in front of me. Well, wouldn't you? I was just relieved they weren't expecting me to go the cashpoint every morning.

Then the hair and make-up people popped in to check we were still as beautiful as we were when we'd left their department a few minutes earlier, and I was quite pleased to find that I wasn't nervous, just really excited.

The next thing I knew, the director had said 'Action' and the first entrepreneur was walking up the stairs.

'Hang on. Stop!'

'What is it, James?' he asked.

'I haven't had my pack.'

'What pack's that?'

'The one with all the details on the people who are coming to pitch. I haven't been shown anything.'

Theo turned to me. 'What makes you think you're so special?'

'You mean we don't get told anything in advance?

'Welcome to the club.'

I felt hugely embarrassed as the director said 'Action' again and we started for the second time. I had always thought that assessing an investment in less than an hour – which is the most people usually get in the Den – was pretty tough (in the real world, you get weeks if not months to tie up a deal), but I hadn't realised that we wouldn't even be given a business plan for each of the entrepreneurs. How on earth was I going to assess the financials? Or their CVs? Or their sales figures? I picked up my pen: I was going to have to make a lot of notes. And I was really going to have to pay attention.

For the first couple of days' filming I was on a really steep learning curve. Things that take up ten minutes on screen can take a whole hour to film, and with about 250 people coming into the Den each series I soon realised that not all of the people we film would make it on to TV. For the first couple of pitches I don't think I said much, in part because most people were pitching to other Dragons. They didn't know who I was, and I was realising that many people come into the Den hoping to get the interest of one particular Dragon – tech people clearly court Peter, retail people are after Theo's cash – but no one was after my money because none of them had heard of me. I was going to have to be a bit more assertive to compete with the other Dragons for the good investments.

I was also discovering that what I thought would be my strength in the Den – the fact that, unlike the other Dragons who operate companies in specific sectors, I am a full-time investor – was potentially my weakness. I was used to taking my time to reach a decision about an investment, but in the Den not only is there never enough time, but you are also in competition with four other people for the good opportunities.

I was surprised just how competitive things got between members of the panel. If we sense a chance to make money, then we really want to keep that chance to ourselves, so there's often a bit of brinkmanship going on. I also hadn't realised that the editors of the programme do a terrific job making some of the pitches intelligible, because some of the visitors to the Den aren't very skilful at presentations and it can take quite a few questions just to understand what someone's business does and how that makes money. Eventually, though, one of us will ask the question that unlocks the opportunity.

'So, how many of them have you sold?'

'Twenty thousand.'

'That's interesting.' It's the kind of answer that gets us sitting a little more upright. Or sometimes people will say 'zero', in which case one of us will be pretty quick to say 'I'm out'. Each of the Dragons has their own style. I think Peter's pretty laid-back and is quite happy for the rest of us to make the running and then jump in at the end. Duncan seems either to like things or not and rarely changes his mind. Deborah's great at finding flaws and she's very aware of where Theo is heading as I think the two of them like to invest together.

It was a lot to take in, and after five days' filming I still hadn't made an investment. I was finding it so difficult to assess the opportunities in the time available – did I like the person? Did I believe their figures? What equity stake did I want? What was my exit strategy? – that I could see me going an entire series without getting my chequebook out. I discussed my concerns with the producers and they were very understanding. 'It's your money, James, you've got to be completely comfortable with it. There's certainly no pressure from us.'

Maybe I sensed a little pressure from the other Dragons, I'm not sure, but it was starting to bother me. When Aisha asked me how it was going I had to confess that I was still a Den virgin. She knew I was a fairly prolific investor and wanted to know if anything was wrong.

'I'm just finding it tougher than I expected, that's all.'

I spoke to Deborah about what it's like to be the new Dragon and she remembered how she had also found it difficult to make an investment in her first series. 'Everybody's come to pitch to their favourite Dragon,' she said.

But this is a show where the whole premise is that Dragons invest, so one morning when I woke up I just told myself that this had to be the day that I was going to make an investment. I had a feeling that the time had come. On the car into the studio, I even decided that I was going to invest in the first thing that came into the Den that day. It was time to do my first deal.

As I went through the increasingly familiar routine of wardrobe and make-up I was getting quite excited: I knew that today I was finally going to get to say 'I'm in'. We took our seats, the director said 'Action' and then a Labrador came up the stairs. The first business in the Den that morning was a dog treadmill! Well, that wasn't what I'd been expecting!

Fit Fur Life is run by Sammy French, a single mum who had modified the kind of treadmill you find at the gym to be used for animal training and rehabilitation after accidents and operations. My initial response was that it was a bit of a challenge to make a business out of the product, but as Sam made a great presentation I realised I would be able to come good on my pact with myself to invest in the first deal of the day. As she talked, I realised that she was somebody I could work with: I liked her *and* I liked her business, so I just had to pay close enough attention to make sure there wasn't a really good reason why I *shouldn't* get my chequebook out.

As ever, I was looking to invest in the person rather than the business, and Sammy seemed down to earth and very professional, and she was handling the Den brilliantly: so many people fall apart, but she was taking the pressure. Not only did Sammy stack up, but her business did, too. I started to think of all the professions that train dogs – the police, customs, RNIB, obedience schools – and I could see that there was a market. And then I thought of all those dogs kept in apartments in New York and I could even see that a dog treadmill could become a designer accessory. I could see Theo was thinking it was a joke, but I was starting to see the opportunity.

One of the things that impressed me was the margin she was making on each machine: it was over £1000. This was a business with hardly any overheads – Sammy was running everything on the phone from her council flat – so that £1000 was virtually all profit. And she had already sold 147 of them. I sat there looking at Sammy and admiring her: she was single mum in a council flat but she was determined to do something with her life.

She needed investment to place more orders, but the panel suggested she could either do that by getting some customers to pay upfront in exchange for a discount – which was perfectly plausible with her profit margin – or from a loan. And that's when her pitch crumbled: she revealed she'd been turned down for a loan and at that point Deborah, who was the only other Dragon showing any interest, pulled out. But I wasn't going to do that: I was in.

'Sam, I'm going to make you an offer.'

As I said those words there was a huge smile on my face, because I knew what they were all thinking: *He's mad*. Everybody just stopped and looked at me. Peter was shaking his head. Theo was trying not to laugh.

'Sam, I'm going to offer you the full £100,000 you're after, but I want 50 per cent of the company.' She had only been offering 25 per cent.

Everyone was silent. Then Duncan spoke.

'You should rip his arm off!'

So Sam said yes and we all shook hands. As we walked out for a smoke, Peter said he would eat a packet of dog biscuits if I made any money on the deal and Theo asked which planet I was orbiting.

'Seriously guys, I think she's a great investment.'

And you know what? It *has* been a great investment. The first thing me and the team at Hamilton Bradshaw did was update Sammy's website with a video demonstration on it so she no longer had to take the treadmill to potential customers to demonstrate it. We looked at her pricing, at her manufacturing deal, we made modifications to the design, and within six weeks Sam was on a plane to Taiwan to check on an order of 200 new machines. It was a huge shift for Sam, so it was important that she knew she could call me if it ever got to be too much: whatever problem she was having me or someone else at Hamilton Bradshaw would be able to help.

My target is for Sam to sell 350 treadmills a year, which will make Fit Fur Life very profitable and give Sam a great lifestyle. For me, that's what *Dragons' Den* is all about – the ability to get into a business and create change. I'm not sure what my exit strategy is for Fit Fur Life. I doubt it will make me a million but I will at least double my investment. Right now, my vision for the company involves Sam feeling secure enough and successful enough to go out and buy herself a house and maybe a Mercedes to park outside it. In the meantime, Peter Jones can eat his dog biscuits.

All the investments I have made in the Den have followed exactly the same philosophy as when I started Humana and all the Alexander Mann joint ventures: find the right person, give them what they need and back them to the hilt. When a young guy called Laban Roomes came into the Den looking for £60k to franchise his gold-plating business, all the other Dragons rejected him because the franchising model didn't make sense. I looked at it differently: I saw a young, bright, charming and determined young man who had already achieved a lot. I could see that he knew his business could go places but he was working so hard that he was struggling to find the right way forward. Franchising was the wrong option, but I could still see a big future for him. Observe the masses: do the opposite. I invested.

I had a brief chat with him after the cameras were turned off.

'Laban, before you leave, I want to know where you want to go in your life.'

'Right now I work in a shed in Enfield. If I could work on this for another seven years and turn it into a proper brand, with a proper product range and I could sell them in Harrods, then I will think I have arrived.'

It took seven weeks, not seven years. We approached Harrods pretty much straight away and there's now a whole section selling GoldGenie products. Laban's gold-plated roses sold out on Valentine's Day and Mother's Day, but that was just the start. We've also helped Laban get GoldGenie into Selfridges, we've signed a contract with Apple to gold-plate iPods and we've also done a deal with Carphone Warehouse. There's a GoldGenie poster in their shops, and if people want to upgrade to a gold-plated model, Laban will take care of it.

When people walk away from a deal in the Den because they think the Dragon is asking for too much equity, they're not thinking about what a Dragon can really do for them: we offer so much more than cash, and Peter Moule was the one entrepreneur who came in to see us who really understood what we can offer. He wasn't really looking for our cash, he wanted our expertise.

Peter had invented a device called the ChocBox that makes connecting electrical cables a doddle. He had been running his business for ten years and he was doing really well, so well in fact that he was selling a million units a year and making a £300k a year profit. No wonder we were all confused as to why he had come into the Den and was asking for £150k for 10 per cent of the business. Peter Jones thought he was only there to get some publicity, but he had watched the show enough to know that Dragons can make a difference.

He told us he'd taken this business as far as he knew how to and he needed one of us to help him grow the business. He knew there was potentially a lot of growth as fourteen million connectors are sold each year to join cables: that meant there were another thirteen million chances to sell a ChocBox.

Peter Moule confused the panel so much that their questions

started veering off at strange angles: how much money have you got in the bank, do you have any loans, what do you need our money for? They had all missed the point. Peter didn't need the money, he needed some introductions. So I made him an offer, and he was so confident of his projections that I offered to return a per cent of equity for each year he hit his targets. The only catch was that I wanted 40 per cent to start with, falling back to 36 per cent if he delivered the growth. I could see Theo sitting there thinking: *Clever*. Duncan was looking at me thinking: *I'm in with James*. He matched my offer and we did a deal. The cash already in the ChocBox coffers meant we could have actually paid ourselves a dividend straight away and got our investment back, so there was actually no risk.

Afterwards, Peter and Theo were quite convinced the deal would fall through because we had asked for so much more equity than Peter Moule had wanted to give away. 'He'll think about it, he'll call you in the morning and tell you he's changed his mind. I promise you,' Theo said.

I went to have a quick word with Peter Moule before he left the studio. 'Are you happy with the deal, Peter?'

'Yes, James.'

'You've been in business long enough to know how you work. When you agree to a deal, are you the kind of guy who follows it through?'

'When I've made a decision I stick to it.'

In the car park afterwards the others still weren't convinced, but Duncan and I compared notes and we drew up a draft Heads of Terms agreement, the piece of paper that outlines how a deal will work. I called my lawyer at Hamilton Bradshaw and got him to write it up and e-mail it to someone on the production team who then printed it out. Thirty minutes later I showed the Heads of Terms to Peter Moule. The other Dragons were stunned that I could get things moving so quickly.

'Is this what we have agreed, Peter?'

He looked at it. 'Yes, it is.'

'Take it away and tomorrow morning, when you've given it some thought, sign it and send it back to me so we can move it forward.'

By the time I got to the studio the next day, Peter Moule had faxed it to the production company's office. Peter and Theo were, frankly, gobsmacked.

A couple of weeks later I was in the South of France and trying to work out who I knew who could help ChocBox. In twenty-five years in business I've come across people in all sorts of industries, and I remembered that an old YPO contact of mine, Richard Rose, used to be in the electrical business. I called him up and told him about the product.

'Can we meet up about this?' I asked.

'Well, I'm in the South of France at the moment so . . .'

'Whereabouts?'

'Monte Carlo.'

'I'm in Cannes. What are you doing this morning?'

'Having coffee with you!'

Richard knew exactly who we needed to talk to. GET are the largest distributors of electrical components in the UK, and he set up a meeting for us.

The chief exec of GET took one look at the ChocBox and said that Wickes and B&Q would be selling them all day long and he offered to distribute them exclusively.

'What do I get for letting you have it exclusively?'

'I'll guarantee you a million units a year.'

'We're already selling a million units a year. Give me something I haven't got.'

'How about two million units a year?'

I thought about it. 'For an exclusive deal I need five million.'

By the time we left the meeting we had a deal for five million units for the next five years at a projected retail price of £1. That's a £25 million contract.

As we walked out together, Peter looked at me and I could tell what he was thinking: *That's exactly why I needed a Dragon.*

Chapter 34

Getting the Most out of the Den
(2007–present)

'We're not just looking to put money into new businesses; in a few years' time we also want to be taking our money out again – with profits.'

I HAVE A LOT OF admiration for Peter Moule. He had watched *Dragons' Den* and knew what we would need to see to take him seriously. He did his research. He also recognised that a Dragon doesn't just offer money, and that's really why we are worth giving meaningful equity stakes to. If you are prepared to give away 25 per cent for our money, I think you should be willing to give away another 25 per cent for our contacts and know-how, but so many people come into the Den and walk away from a deal because they want to hold on to their equity. Without investment in the Den, many businesses fold, and what many entrepreneurs fail to realise is that owning 100 per cent of nothing is still nothing.

Coming into the Den must have been about the best day's work of Peter's career. These days, his job basically involves placing orders. GET tell him how many units they need, and Peter forwards their request on to the factory, which then ships the ChocBoxes directly to GET. Not exactly a tough day at the office. And not really the best use of his skills. So I've made Peter my personal technology Dragon. When I get an approach about an electrical invention – and via my website I get an awful lot of approaches – I pass them on to Peter to assess. Not only is the guy a technical genius but he's been working in the field for twenty-five years, so he's a far better judge of what would work than me or my team.

'Duncan and I gave you the £150k because we wanted to invest in *you*. We don't need it in dividends, so if you like one of these ideas', I told Peter, 'call up the people involved and say you're ringing on behalf of James Caan. If you think they're worth investing in, then ChocBox Ltd makes the investment.'

Peter has now invested in two new ventures, taking a 50 per cent stake in each of them. It's a great way to grow his business and it means my 20 per cent (which will drop to 18 per cent on the claw-back deal we agreed in the Den) is increasing in value and I'm getting a share of businesses I wouldn't otherwise invest in because I don't understand them. I would say that Duncan Bannatyne's done very nicely out of his investment, too.

Peter did well in the Den because he'd realised that what the Dragons ultimately want is profit. We're not just looking to put money into new businesses; in a few years' time we also want to be taking our money out again – with profits. I get a lot of people these days asking me what the secret to being successful in the Den is, and the best thing I tell them to do is to watch the show. I think it's clear from looking at old clips on the BBC's website what marks a presentation out for success. Generally, the people who get investment are the people who have done their research.

Dragons' Den is not a fashion show, but you only have a short period of time to make an impression, and I am genuinely surprised at how little effort some people put into their appearance. We're all smartly dressed: I think that means there's a message in that. If you turn up and you've not made an effort, what impression does that give?

The next thing to do to get the most out of your trip to the Den is to learn and rehearse your presentation thoroughly. Normally if you're fundraising you talk to one investor at a time. In the Den, you're facing five of us, so really a visit to the Den is worth rehearsing five times more than you would for any other pitch. And, of course, it's actually not just us you want to impress; it's the viewers, too, because even if you don't get investment you might reach potential customers. So rehearse, rehearse, rehearse: it's the best way to deal with your nerves.

I reckon only about 15 per cent of people who come into the Den give a good account of themselves. We sit through a lot of pitches that are unfocused and can occasionally feel like a waste of our time: if you come in and are professional and pleasant, then you've got our attention and you've actually gone quite a long way to being taken seriously.

The next piece of advice is probably the most important: know your numbers. And if you don't know your numbers, don't be shy about bringing someone with you who does. Rather than waiting until you're stumped and having to ask your numbers expert to join you, I think you're better off coming into the Den together and showing us that you're a team. Make sure you rehearse together, too: if you've seen the show, then you'll know you're going to be grilled about your figures. Ask each other to go through them backwards and sideways – you should know your year two projections as well as your month two figures.

I've been surprised how often someone will finish their presentation and I still won't understand what their product or service does! With new inventions, it can be particularly difficult for us to work out who it's for, what it achieves and why it's useful, so a key part of any presentation is explaining the most fundamental thing: why someone would pay money for it. And of course, saying 'My mum thinks it's great' is not enough! We want to see sales figures, or proof that customers have placed orders. If you've gone out to your target customers and got them to agree to buy your product, then the chances are much greater that you'll get our money to go into production with it. When it comes to risk, I'm the kind of guy who's pretty comfortable turning right when the road signs tell me I'm not supposed to, but I'm never going to be Evel Knievel. Business isn't about taking risks, it's about minimising them, and by showing us orders or sales figures you reduce our risk and maximise your chances of investment.

The next thing I would advise people coming into the Den to do is to make their business plausible: if you oversell something then it's difficult for us to make the leap. The business you show us has to be logical. Let's say you've invented a gadget that's a phone with a built-in satellite TV receiver. It would clearly be the best phone in the world, but if you come in and tell us that you're going to make it a mass-market product with a retail price of £2500 we probably won't believe you. Either you've got to find a way of retailing it for £199, or you've got to recognise you've got a luxury business with customers who would probably pay £10,000 for one. If your pricing is wrong, your product won't sell, and we won't be able to believe in your business.

I also want you to give me an overview of your market. The chances are that I'm not familiar with your industry, so you need to explain why you're different, how you fit into the marketplace and who your nearest competitors are. If you tell me your product sells at £199, one of my first thoughts is *I wonder what else is available in that price range?* First-time entrepreneurs – especially inventors, I've noticed – can be so focused on their product that they somehow forget about the market. Products don't sell themselves, markets do, and you've got to know – and we've got to understand – where your business fits into the market. Your presentation should always tell us who your competitors are and why customers would choose you over them.

The Dragons also need to understand the logistics of your business, things like how you are going to get your product to the market or who's going to manufacture it. Sadly, the cost of manufacturing in Britain means that if your answer is that you'll be making your product close to home, then you need to be able to reassure us that your product is not going to be more expensive than a replica that could be made in somewhere like China. And once you've got your product to market, we then want to understand how your potential customers will know about it: don't forget to tell us about your customer acquisition and marketing strategies.

It's really important that we get a clear sense of where your business is headed. Ultimately, we're doing this to make a return on our investment, so you've got to tell us how you're going to grow your business and, in turn, your profits. However, you've also got to be sure that your ambitions are realistic. So many people come into the Den and say something like: 'The global market's worth £17 billion, and we're just looking to take 1 per cent of that,' thinking that makes it seem like they've got really modest and achievable ambitions. But the truth is that it's actually a meaningless target and it's one that is likely to see you leave the Den with nothing. That's because you may as well be telling us that you're going to get 10 or 20 per cent of the global market – it's just as meaningless because predicting the eventual size of your business isn't related to abstract percentages.

Projections for growth are notoriously difficult to get accurate, but the way to do it is to base them on achievable actions. Tell us something like you can sell ten a week, but with investment you could sell fifty a week because you can mechanise production or increase marketing, and we will understand how you will grow the business and the profits. Working out the potential size of your business starts by working out the potential of your team. For instance, if your top sales guy can only make 100 calls a week because there aren't any more hours in the day, and he can only turn 10 per cent of those calls into sales, then the size of your market is the number of people on your sales team times ten. So the real question is, how big can your sales team get? The more realistic you are, the more we will believe you, and if we believe in you we are far more likely to back you.

The next thing I want to understand from any pitch I see in the Den is the margin, and to do that I need to believe that your costs are realistic and your selling price is achievable. If the gap between your income and your costs is too small, then you're a risky proposition for us. The wider your margin, the thicker the insulation you've got before you start making a loss and the better an investment your business is likely to be. Be warned, though: one of the things that can really eat into your margin is your salary, and if you've watched the show enough times you'll know that one of the things Dragons don't like their investment being spent on is the founder's salary. If you were to say 'I need £50k so that I can pay myself a salary for the next two years and get this off the ground,' the chances are that you won't get our money. It's not that we don't want you to earn a living; it's that we *do* want you to earn it. If we just give it to you, where would your incentive be? And when you do start taking a salary, it should always be in proportion to your profits. If your business makes £50k a year and you take £45k of it as a salary, it won't leave much for your investor. The key to what you tell the Dragons is that everything you say should be plausible, proportional and profitable.

I love it when people come into the Den with preposterous valuations for their businesses because it makes for great telly when the Dragons burst out laughing. A successful pitch involves getting your valuation right. Businesses are usually valued on their assets and their income, so if your business doesn't make a profit yet then it's unlikely to be worth very much. Ideas – even really great ones – aren't worth all that much, so when people come to us at the very early stage of a business, when it's not much more than an idea, and say they want £100k for 10 per cent of business, not only are they valuing their business at £1 million but they're actually saying that their idea is worth £900k. No wonder we laugh. If you want to be taken seriously, then my advice is to think seriously about what your business is really worth at the time of your visit to the Den.

I've already said this, but it's worth repeating: there's no point in being greedy with the equity you're prepared to offer in exchange for our investment. As Peter Moule's story proves, Dragons can transform businesses, and our experience and knowledge is often just as valuable – if not more so – as our money. Take Levi Roots and his Reggae Reggae Sauce: it was probably one of the most memorable Den presentations ever, and Peter Jones and Richard Farleigh have now got him selling his sauce in Sainsbury's and Asda. Had Levi Roots heard of Sainsbury's before he went in the Den? Of course he had. Could he have picked up the phone and called Sainsbury's to get an appointment? I think he probably could have done, but the key question is this: would Sainsbury's have placed an order without Peter and Richard's involvement? Possibly not. The Dragons were able to turn his sauce into a business.

In the fifth series I wanted to invest in a baby towel called CuddleDry, but the founder wouldn't give me the 40 per cent I asked for. She would only go to 30 per cent and for the sake of 10 per cent she walked away. I sometimes wonder how much bigger her business would be now if I had been able to get her products into every baby shop in the country and if she's ever had second thoughts about that 10 per cent.

There's no time limit on presentations in the Den and occasionally they go on for over an hour (sometimes, though, they're over in five minutes). That's a lot of scrutiny to withstand from five experienced questioners, so being prepared for that level of examination can increase your chances of success. In the fifth series, Theo invested £200k in an online poker company; now I don't know much about online gambling, but it was such an impressive presentation that I was tempted to invest, too. I remember asking something fairly obscure about the margin – if they'd miscalculated the speed of uptake. This was about half an hour into the pitch and the woman making the presentation – who had already taken quite a grilling – came up with the figure I was looking for!

'How did you know that?' I asked.

'I was expecting you to ask it so I memorised it.'

Now that was impressive. Was she just naturally that brilliant? Probably not. In all likelihood she had just rehearsed more than anyone else and had gone over her presentation in front of lots of friends all asking her questions they thought she'd come up against. Consequently, she had every angle covered. It was clear that she had watched past series and was very well prepared. And with that level of preparation I'm not surprised she got £200k, which I'm pretty sure is the biggest individual investment of the series to date.

Before I went into the Den, I too watched past series to understand what I was letting myself in for, and I think anyone wanting to get investment should do the same thing. With constant repeats on cable and satellite and highlights available online, it's easy to see the kinds of questions we all ask, the stumbling blocks that other presentations can't get over, and to pick up tips on what works and what doesn't. Whether you're raising finance for your business in the Den or elsewhere, the first thing to get right is your research. Just ask yourself what an investor needs to hear, and then tell them that as simply and concisely as possible.

Chapter 35

My Life as a Dragon (2007–present)

'*Money's great, but it's what you do with it that counts.*'

WE HAD PLANNED that we would watch my first episode of *Dragons' Den* as a family. Normally when I get in from work I change into comfortable clothes, but Aisha said I should keep my suit on because it would be nice to go out for a celebratory ice cream afterwards. I went upstairs to freshen up, and at 8.55 p.m., five minutes before *Dragons' Den* came on, she suggested we watch it downstairs in my office where there's a big screen.

'I'll be down in a sec,' I said.

I suppose I was a bit nervous, but mostly I just really curious to find out how it had all been edited together. I opened the door to my office and where I expected to see Aisha, the girls and a bowl of popcorn, I found fifty of our friends and family!

'Surprise!'

I was really surprised, so surprised in fact that I was quite confused. How had they all got in without me hearing the doorbell? For a few seconds my head was all over the place, and although it was lovely to see so many friends, it made watching myself on TV an even stranger experience. What was odder still was that as soon as the show started broadcasting my BlackBerry started ringing. I had to put it on silent so that we could actually hear the TV. By the end of the show I had 100 e-mails, and that night my phone did not stop ringing. Literally every second it would bleep with a text, an e-mail or a call. People I had gone to school with had Googled me, found my website and sent me a message. People I had worked with twenty years earlier were getting in touch. People I'd placed in a job. People I'd never met! It was extraordinary.

The next day, as soon as offices were open, journalists started calling. Could I give them five minutes, could I talk about the current investment climate, could I give them a quote on the Chancellor? The attention was unbelievable. When Deborah and Duncan had told me to prepare for some coverage, I had anticipated a bit in the *Radio Times*, not constant visibility!

In the weeks that followed, I started to appear on the cover of magazines – a new Dragon was very exciting in the business community – and every day my name appeared in the papers. Before *Dragons' Den* I had just been a guy running a business. Now it seemed I was a celebrity.

If the reaction of friends and the media was one thing, the response of the public was another phenomenon all together. I came out of the office one day, on my way to an appointment, and there was a guy standing there with an envelope.

'Excuse me, James.'

I looked at him and thought: *Do I know you?*

'My name is Darren and I've just walked all the way from Bradford . . .'

Really? But then I looked at him: he actually did look as if he'd just walked all the way from Yorkshire.

'I've tried to contact you but I've not been able to get through. I've seen you on TV and I believe you're the only person who can make a difference to my business.'

I was stunned. For starters, I wasn't used to being recognised in the street, and I certainly wasn't used to people walking hundreds of miles to see me as if I was some kind of historical monument! So I had a chat with him and took his business plan off him. I actually understood why he had done it. It's pretty difficult to get my attention – I get hundreds of business plans a week – but by waiting for me in person he made sure I looked at his plan. I was impressed, but his business wasn't for me and I didn't invest.

It's actually not just me who gets attention. I have a personalised number plate and when my car's parked outside my office it's not hard to guess who the car belongs to. People tap on the window and ask my driver to pass on their business plan to me! I have been amazed at the lengths fans of the show will go to to get my attention. I was asked to take part in a charity auction for the *Evening Standard*'s campaign to raise money to fight HIV in Africa. Only for the first time they weren't asking me to bid on anything: they wanted me to be the prize! They thought offering lunch with me would raise funds, so I said yes.

The auction started on a Monday and finished the following Wednesday at noon. Of course I was curious to see what the bidding was doing: I wanted to know what the public thought I was worth. The opening bid was £500. I didn't think that was too shabby. Then my PA called to say someone had bid £1200. That made me feel pretty good. On the Tuesday the bidding went to £1800 and I couldn't believe it. Who would want to have lunch with me that much? By the Wednesday morning, it was over four grand. Then it crept up to £5k. When the auction finished, someone had paid £5800 to have lunch with me. I found that quite scary: how could I possibly live up to their expectations?

I arranged to meet the winner at Cipriani's. Carina Sacher was in her late twenties and had set up her own recruitment agency specialising in reception staff. She had been a receptionist herself and knew the difference between good and bad temps. Her staff were better trained, better mannered and she had no trouble finding clients, but she had one problem – she wasn't making money. She had researched my career and was convinced I was the one person who could help her turn her recruitment business around.

'How have you been able to afford this lunch if your business is in trouble?'

'My old boss has been very supportive and he's paid for it. I told him you were the guy I needed.'

What a story! 'How can I help you then?'

'Just tell me where I'm going wrong.'

As we talked, I thought I'd identified the problem: she knew an awful lot about being a receptionist but not all that much about recruitment. For instance, she knew what an agency paid the temp because she had been one, but not what the temp agency billed the client. When I asked her what her margin was, she had to confess she wasn't really sure. The more she talked the more I thought the best thing she could do was to put her agency on hold while she got a job in recruitment and learned the ropes.

I was able to introduce her to people I knew in the industry and helped her get a job in recruitment. I heard from her a couple of months after she started her new job and she told me she could already see where she had been going wrong and what she would do differently in the future. After paying that much to get my attention, I was glad she felt I had helped.

Dragons' Den has had a big impact in the UK, but I was nevertheless surprised when the producers told us that we would be making a Christmas Day special. It was their biggest show of the night on the biggest TV-watching day of the year. We were also asked to film a special show for Children In Need where kids would pitch their business ideas to us. Most of the children who came to see us were fourteen or fifteen, but this nine-year-old called James Buckley tap-danced in and told us about his Look for Loneliness campaign in schools. Lots of kids felt left out, he said, and he wanted £5000 to print posters and badges for schools to distribute that encouraged kids to include less popular kids in their games.

I was very impressed by him, and really quite touched by his selflessness, so I offered him the £5k he asked for. Then Duncan also offered him £5k and this poor kid had to decide which Dragon he wanted to take the money from, or if he wanted £2500 from each of us. Let me tell you, my heart was pounding as if I'd run ten miles: there was no way I wanted this little boy to choose Duncan over me!

'I think,' said little James, 'I think I'd like to take the money from James.'

Oh! The relief! We all shook hands, but as James was leaving the Den Duncan had to ask him why he had taken my money and not his. James thought about it for a second and then said: 'Because James is the new Dragon and I didn't want him to be lonely.'

My heart melted, and when Christmas came round, I really wanted to do something for him. I called his mum and asked what James would like for Christmas. She said she'd give it some thought and get back to me. I thought it might be a go-kart or a Wii, but when she called she said that James had thought about it and what he really wanted was to meet Ed Balls, the Secretary of State for Children, Families and Schools!

How on earth was I supposed to get him that? Out came my Rolodex, and I found a friend who knew that there's a children's party at the Houses of Parliament every Christmas, and this year the man in the Santa suit was going to be Ed Balls. *Perfect.* I arranged for security passes for us all and I booked a minibus to collect James and his friends from their home in Halifax for a day out in London. After we'd been to Westminster and James had had his Christmas wish granted, I took them all to Harrods and headed straight for the toy department where there was a grotto. So the kids met two Santas in one day and seemed to be having the time of their lives. Afterwards we went to the ice-cream parlour in Harrods, where they have more than 100 varieties of ice cream, and between us I think we tried them all. Before they got back on the minibus I had one last surprise for them – gold-plated iPods from GoldGenie. I don't think it's a day any of us will ever forget.

Appearing on *Dragons' Den* has had an impact on my business as well as my personal life. I now get many more invitations to many more events, parties and charity fundraisers, as well as requests to offer my opinion on things like *Newsnight*, *Sky News* and Bloomberg. I'm asked to talk about the economy or comment on changes to the trading environment, but sometimes I get asked my opinion on whatever is in the headlines. During one interview I was even asked what impact I though the Indonesian elections would have on the economy. I had to stop myself from saying live on air: *What Indonesian elections?*

My diary is now so full that my PA has had to hire an assistant just to cope with the calls and requests I get each day. But that's not the real impact on Hamilton Bradshaw; it's the number of deals that are now brought to us. Whether it's the chance to acquire a freehold building in the West End or the opportunity to invest in a business before the market gets wind of it, the offers are non-stop. That means more staff to filter the deals and more work. Although eventually, of course, it should also lead to more profit, in the meantime I still find myself working the kinds of hours I did at Alexander Mann. That makes it all the more important that I find time to be with my family, and, whether it's a quick weekend away skiing or Sunday brunch out at a café in St John's Wood, we spend as much time together as possible. In the past couple of years Aisha has become just as big a fan of Chelsea – probably bigger, in fact – than me, and now that we have season tickets those couple of hours we spend at Stamford Bridge for home matches have become really important to me. Watching the team I love next to the woman I love is a great way to forget about work for a while.

It's been a pretty crazy time and I am so proud of the way Aisha, Jemma and Hanah have handled it (although Hanah finds it slightly alarming that I get suggestive fan mail from women of a certain age). I have been blessed in business, but it's my family that makes me truly thankful, and in 2007 we decided that it was the right time to make the pilgrimage to Mecca, the hajj, that Muslims are expected to make at least once in their lifetime, so that we could thank God for all that we have.

It was one of the most extraordinary experiences of my life. When you have two and half million people in one place for the purpose of worship it is immensely moving. Jet lag meant I miscalculated the timing for one of the prayers and I found myself at my hotel window looking out at millions of people – there were people as far as the eye could see – and they were all bowing in unison. It was, in the very literal sense of the word, awesome.

I couldn't have gone to a better place to reflect and to look back on my life. It also helped me appreciate my success and allowed me to thank God for all that has happened. I still have the fear that I could lose everything I have been given and I felt it was important to acknowledge that before God. I was reminded of the teaching in the Koran that you are not in control of your wealth. In the West we are led to believe that we create our own wealth, that it is a consequence of hard work or being really smart, but the book says this is not the case, and I know this must be true just by looking at my family.

I grew up as one of seven. We had the same father, same mother, same education, same upbringing, same everything, so why should one be so much more successful than the others? I know my brother Adam is just as hard-working; in fact, I would say he's harder-working than me. Academically he's brighter than me, he's been to university and he's incredibly astute, yet he hasn't had my level of success in business. The more I thought about what the Koran says about wealth, the more I understood its meaning. I have come to the conclusion that we can only be partly responsible for our success, but there is so much more that we are not in control of.

When two and a half million people descend on Mecca at one time, the accommodation and food available can only ever be basic. Part of the ritual is to live in the desert for three days of the pilgrimage, as the Prophet did, and so we camped in conditions where there was perhaps one toilet for fifty people, and if the toilet broke it just wasn't possible to get a plumber. People started complaining about the conditions, but it just made me grateful for everything I have. In Kosovo and Kashmir I have seen how people survive with nothing, and when I think about their lives I am really quite humble: recognising how blessed we are is one of the reasons to go on the pilgrimage.

The year 2007 was the right one for us to make the journey to Mecca. Jemma had just moved to Paris to complete her degree, Hanah had started at the London School of Economics, Aisha was nearing the completion of a Master's degree in design and, with *Dragons' Den* and Hamilton Bradshaw, my career had never been so fulfilling.

The four of us are incredibly close, and when we are together we have the best time. If I'm honest, I can't wait until there are more of us: of all the things the future holds I am most excited at the prospect of having grandchildren. I joke with the girls that if they happen to give me a grandson I may never let him leave my sight! Now the girls are in their twenties, they're such good company and our conversation never stops. There was a night recently when the four of us were in Cannes and we walked out of our front door and strolled along the beach until we found a restaurant for dinner. We were laughing our heads off about something and I looked at the three of them around the table and wondered: *Does it get any better than this?* I really don't see how.

There are people who spend their lives looking for happiness, but happiness is only temporary. There are others who drive themselves forward in search of satisfaction, but the truth is you're never satisfied for long. What I have with Aisha and the girls is contentment, and contentment lasts. It's sustaining, rewarding, comforting. I've been happy, and I've been satisfied, but I'll take contentment over both of them. I'm sure it helps that we have everything we could possibly want, but I think the four of us would still have been laughing our heads off that night even without money.

I don't know what the future holds, but I've never been much of a planner so that doesn't bother me. I imagine there'll be a few more series of *Dragons' Den* and who knows what will come of that? I'm certainly enjoying work far too much to think of retiring any time soon, although I don't see myself doing it for ever. Long term, I think my future probably lies in philanthropy. In the years to come I certainly see the money Hamilton Bradshaw makes as creating a fund that I will donate to causes I believe in. I've learned it's not just my money that can make a difference, but my skills and ability to make things happen, and that's why I feel philanthropic ventures will tempt me more and more as the years pass. Money's great, but I've learned that it's what you do with it that counts.

Index